Advance Praise

"From campus days as a student manager, to stints at all levels of pro sports, to founding a sports-based nonprofit, Brandon Tosti has dreamed and lived the sporting life since he was a kid growing up in eastern Kentucky. In *Bright Lights & Long Nights*, he shares hard-won lessons from that career in the sports business and lays out what can happen when you lead with the heart while keeping your head. Anyone interested in making a life in sports, or simply curious about how teams and fans fill up arenas and stadiums, will find inspiration, fascinating stories, and valuable lessons in these pages."

—Alexander Wolff, former *Sports Illustrated* writer and author of *Big Game, Small World*

"I have known Brandon Tosti for over 25 years. He was a vital part of one of our companies at one time. I have never had anyone who I worked with who was a BETTER person than Brandon. His faith and belief in finding the best in people was unequaled in others who I have worked with over the years; his work, for example, with the youth of Denver. His work in moving his full effort to help restore Louisiana after Hurricane Katrina is stuff that movies are made of--yet no one can point you to someone who did it. Brandon not only did it, but also lives the kind of life that very few people do—but many talk a good game. Brandon has!! His first book was about how he got his impetus for life. This one will be even better. I can't wait to read it."

—Jim Host, sports marketing industry innovator and legend

"Brandon Tosti is one of the people who, when you meet him once, you feel like you have known him all your life. Or, in my case, you wish you had. His humble approach can mask his interest in fellow humans, but I can assure you that his insights are anything but low-key when he shares them with you. I am excited to read Brandon's second book, as the past few years have made it even more vital that we find sources of inspiration and motivation to fuel our lives."

—Mark Harrison, Founder, T1

"The sports industry is ever-changing, and relationships are vital to having any success working in the sports business. I often tell students and those just starting out that although getting a college degree is vital, the reality is it is a people business: 10% what you know and 90% who you know and how you work with and treat people. Brandon is an amazing storyteller with tremendous real-world sports business experience who knows the importance of establishing and maintaining relationships for success. From internship to entry level to management to owner, the guidance he provides is well-experienced. As someone who has worked in the sports business for over 30 years, I am excited to learn more from Brandon's experience via this book."

—Dan Butterly, Commissioner, the Big West Conference

"I have had the pleasure of knowing Brandon since his collegiate days at the University of Kentucky. From our first meeting in my office through his days of event management working with the Denver Sports Commission and still today, Brandon has always looked for the message, 'How can I give back?' His stories and his ability and willingness to engage with anyone are true testaments to his writings and books. I always look forward to chatting with Brandon, learning about his new encounters, and hearing him say, 'Hatch, you got a minute?'"

—Rick Hatcher, President /CEO, Treasure Coast Sports Commission

"I've known Brandon Tosti for over 15 years and am grateful to have met such a genuine, caring, and authentic individual. In his latest book, Brandon provides a thoughtful account of his journey through the sports and events industry and lends valuable perspective to anyone looking for a career in the field. He centers his storytelling around the value of relationships and how they helped define his experiences throughout his career.

I spent four years working with Brandon at Dick's Sporting Goods Park when I worked in ticket sales for the Colorado Rapids, and I interacted with some of the wonderful people he features in the book. Brandon truly cares about people. He is always focused on doing the right thing rather than the easy one. His unique pathway, coupled with his humble and inclusive reflection on his life's work, makes for an easy read, leaving the audience with some invaluable takeaways."

—Graham Wincott, Senior Director of Marketing, Phoenix Suns, Phoenix Mercury and Footprint Center

"My first internship was with the Colorado Rapids and Dick's Sporting Goods Park. Thankfully, I had the privilege of working under the guidance of both Brandon Tosti and Jeff Mathews (who has an extensive cameo in this book), and their wisdom left an indelible mark on my 10+ year career in this industry, with values and insights that I continually return to as a guide for success. This book is not only a treasure trove of those insights and valuable lessons learned in the sports industry, but also a valuable resource that can be applied to any business that revolves around relationships (hint: that's all of them)."

—Justin Anderson, Director Content Marketing, National Football League

"Although many of us that end up in the sports and entertainment business share a passion for the industry since our youth, everyone's journey is unique. I enjoyed Brandon's account of his journey in *Bright Lights & Long Nights*. It should be on the reading list for any aspiring student looking to get into the business."

—Nate VanderWal, Senior Account Executive, Sponsorship Sales, Colorado Rockies Baseball Club

"Tosti breaks down the sports industry through firsthand experiences, funny stories, and a genuine approach. These stories provide an excellent behind-the-scenes peek into the sports industry for individuals hoping to make the cut, while simultaneously generating laughs and relatability for those who've been in the industry for years."

—Adam Boettgger, Senior Director of Corporate Partnerships, San Diego Seals

"While securing an internship as a senior at the University of Colorado in the professional sports field was a dream come true for me, the cherry on top of the experience was the opportunity to work with Brandon Tosti and the team he had assembled at Dick's Sporting Goods Park. Through that experience, I came away with two takeaways that I still utilize in my career to this day. The first is to treat all employees, patrons, and customers with respect and as you would like to be treated. Now this may seem like a no-brainer, however Tosti and Nate Stahlecker treated interns the same way they treated their co-workers or higher-up executives. This was reflected in how the complex ran its business both internally and externally. Tosti told me on day one at our introduction lunch, 'J.P., I wouldn't treat you, our new intern, or Fred in maintenance, any differently than the CEO of our organization.'

The second takeaway is that networking and relationships are key! Tosti showed me what he described as his 'networking binder' towards the end of my internship. *What is a networking binder?* you may ask ... Well, in this case, it was an old, grimy three-ring binder that was thicker than the Denver Broncos playbook, filled with business cards from Tosti's career in the field. This was before the time of major social media, but the point was the same: you never know who you may run into, and you never know who you may work for, or with, in the future.

This book is a must read for anyone interested in working in the sports and entertainment industry!"

—J.P. Lefever, Park and Recreation Manager

"Growing up as a competitive athlete, it made all the sense in the world to me to pursue a career in the sports industry. My career in sport has provided me with the same pride, camaraderie, and passion that I had once had on the field, and now get to continue into my professional life. If you are considering starting a journey into the sports industry, I would highly recommend reading this book. Brandon Tosti was one of my career mentors, and his career reflections provide a great representation of the incredible experiences that come with working in sports."

—Brandy Medran, General Manager, Commercial and Events at USA Rugby

Bright Lights & Long Nights

Brandon Tosti

Melissa

Thanks for your support!
I hope you enjoy the book.

Brandon Tosti

1/23/25

Printed in the United States of America

Hardcover ISBN: 978-1-7365815-3-7

Paperback ISBN: 978-1-7365815-4-4

Ebook ISBN: 978-1-7365815-5-1

B2 Ventures, LLC

Dedication

This book is dedicated to one of my best friends, Marisa Colaiano. We worked at the same company together for five and a half seasons. She was a fiery leader and played an integral role in the success of the company's Community Relations department. She managed the Colorado Rapids soccer team's foundation, summer camps, and major events.

Sometimes in life, it is easy to play it safe and go with what has worked in the past. Every team and nonprofit hosts a charity golf tournament. Marisa helped manage the Colorado Rapids' golf tournament, but she wanted more for the team, the fans, and the kids whom she dedicated her life to in the metro Denver area. She pushed for change and was vocal about her desire to create bold programs and take chances, such as the wildly successful World Cup of Wine & Beer tasting event. This was just one of her creative ideas, and it started with wine. Her story is meaningful, and that is why I am including it here, even though you will not read about her in a sports business textbook.

Marisa taught me that it is okay to raise your voice, and even yell sometimes, at work when you are passionate about a project. This was something she reserved for limited occasions when someone was being disrespectful to her or someone else. She was not an imposing figure, physically speaking, but her passion and enthusiasm were clear to anyone lucky enough to call her a friend or teammate. We crammed a number of wonderful memories into a short period. She was more like family to me than a coworker.

We played together in a coed softball league. If you didn't sprint to first on every ground ball, you heard one or two choice words upon your return to the dugout. I am lucky to have some wonderful friends, but I am also lucky to have had someone who was more than a friend. She was my lunch buddy, my sarcastic little sister, and the unofficial spark plug in our office. We both have Italian heritage, and coworkers would hear us yelling at each other. They wondered if we were mad at each other. No, we were just two close friends passionately expressing an opinion—or arguing occasionally.

During our time working together, I created a sports-related nonprofit. Unfortunately, the timing of our volunteer trips never worked out for her to join us. Without prompting, she donated $50 to the cause, and she never asked for recognition nor a tax receipt, because those things didn't matter to her. She was helping a friend, and that was what mattered most.

Marisa passed away on July 17, 2012, from complications of multiple sclerosis. She is dearly missed by family, friends, and coworkers. We still talk about her and share heartfelt stories. I know she would be mad at us for praising her name and celebrating her accomplishments, but that is what good friends are for, especially a wonderful teammate like Marisa Colaiano.

Contents

Contents

Foreword

Growing up in the 1980s, before my family embarked on a significant summer vacation, Mom or Dad would pick up a Triptik from the local AAA office. If you are over the age of forty, perhaps you remember these things. Beginning with your home location, they would create a customized booklet of your upcoming trip, where each page would contain a small, manageable portion of the map leading to your ultimate destination. As you completed each segment of your journey, you would simply flip the page and begin the next segment. It would include interesting places to stop, recommendations on where to refuel or where to grab a bite to eat, and the highest-rated places to lay our collective heads down at night.

I had a love/hate relationship with the AAA Triptik. What effectively broke the trip into small, bite-sized pieces for my parents seemed like page upon page of pure torture to a child like myself, anxious and ready for the fun that surely awaited us at our vacation destination. Yet at the end of every vacation, I always asked to keep the Triptik. When the fun ended, these booklets became mementos to be cherished...page-by-page memoirs of the journeys we went on and the memorable things we saw and experienced along the way. Not to be overly nostalgic, but maps today just are not the same. Turn-by-turn instructions from Google Maps on your smartphone just don't yield the same satisfaction of flipping to the next page, nor do online maps lend themselves well to reminiscing about the details and memorable moments of vacations past. It makes me a little sad that our current generation might never know the subtle joys of the Triptik.

It is an odd analogy, but the attraction of a career in the sports and event industry is like that childhood vacation destination. Whether we are tempted by the perceived glamor and glitz of working in sports or lured by the appeal of taking a hobby we enjoy and turning it into our profession, the attraction and anticipatory excitement of sports as a career choice is easy to understand. The work itself can be incredibly rewarding. In this line of work, you are directly responsible for bringing joy to people's lives, and it is a rare career choice where you get to see, touch, and experience the eventual fruits of your labors and see the joy on the faces of the people you serve. Yet, despite its inherent attraction and appeal, the eventual realization is that a successful career in sports or sports management is a lesson in hard, difficult work: a long slog, a winding journey full of starts, stops, detours, engine trouble, and burnout. "Work in sports," they said. "It will be fun..."

Viewing the journey in its entirety can be overwhelming and deflating at first glance. Having been a professional in the industry for over twenty years myself, I am no stranger to those feelings, and neither is my friend Brandon. In the pages ahead, you will get a unique opportunity to experience Brandon's personal journey through the ups and downs of the sports industry by flipping through his own personal "Triptik"—from the long hours and underappreciation as a lowly intern navigating the challenges of demanding bosses to the highs of five-star award recognition and the fulfillment of building out a deep and meaningful professional network. Each bite-sized portion of his trip will yield insights, takeaways, and lessons learned while providing encouragement and advice for "where to lay your head" during your journey.

This trip is long, but an exciting, fulfilling destination awaits those who embark on it. I hope that as you flip through the following pages, you reflect on Brandon's experiences with joy, sadness, anger, laughter, and reflection, and, in turn, find your *own* appreciation for the stops along the way that enrich our journeys and make them memorable.

—Nate Baldwin, Associate Executive Director, Emerald Kidsports

Author's Note

This book is a retrospective view of my career path in the sports industry, told with an honest approach. It provides a genuine look behind the scenes of how things work, ranging from a halftime promotion to managing a twenty-four-field youth soccer tournament. The book is primarily a memoir, with a touch of career advice for those aspiring to work in the sports industry. My writing style is inspirational by nature, but I did not shy away from writing about difficult situations. I have told friends this is the career book I needed when I was twenty-two, and I hope it helps others chase and achieve their dreams.

For close to eighteen years, I was fortunate to work in practically every level of the industry: grassroots event management, high school, college, and side by side with a pro team. The one area I wanted to work in the most, and have not yet, is the Olympic sector. I have a small number of friends who work for different national governing bodies. There is still time to pursue it, but my runway to retirement is getting shorter with each passing year.

For most of my career, I lived in Denver, Colorado. I had chances to accept a promotion and move to another city, but I remained in the Mile High City for the benefit of our family. I love it here and believe it is one of the best cities in the country. San Diego and Portland are in my unofficial top three rankings, as well. Other road warriors I worked with made multiple stops, from Boston to Kansas City to Miami and back to Phoenix. My wife often reminds me that people in this industry move across the country for higher salaries, professional development, or experience in a different market. I do not fault them for chasing career advancement or more lucrative job titles, but that was not the best path for me, and that is okay. I had a blast, and I have wonderful memories.

My longtime dream job was to work as an athletic director at a Division I institution. I love the college campus atmosphere, especially the lore, the game day pageantry, and the jubilant energy of the students. Give me a college football game, regardless of the conference or national rankings, and I am a happy sports fan. The traditions, rivalries, mascots, and historic trophies all make the game-day environment special and memorable. Due to my high energy level and ADD, I do not watch movies or much TV because I cannot sit still for more than thirty minutes. However, before we had our children, I might have watched college football from 10 a.m. to 10 p.m. once or twice with little issue.

My career path has been a wild ride filled with surprises, hard-to-believe stories, and a closet full of golf shirts, running shoes, and Nike jackets. I would love to tell you how it all turned out, but what fun would that be? Did I swing and miss? You bet. Did I succeed? Sure. Did I fail? Sometimes. Did I learn, have fun, and make memories for a lifetime? Absolutely!

Why I Love Sports

My love for sports began at an early age, most likely when I was six or seven years old. My best friend, Marty Preston, excelled at sports and won every game we played. I jokingly blame him for my love of everything sports related. Whenever we weren't in school, we lived outside, always doing something together—throwing a baseball, shooting hoops, or talking about sports teams. It helped that he lived less than a block from the city's tennis courts and our high school baseball field. Marty had a sports-themed room complete with University of Kentucky Wildcats wallpaper and framed *Sports Illustrated* covers, such as the famous 1983 "College Basketball Preview" issue that featured University of North Carolina Tar Heels Michael Jordan and Sam Perkins. My friend rooted for the Pittsburgh Steelers. I naturally gravitated to cheer for their rival, the Dallas Cowboys.

My first experience playing organized sports was T-ball in Paintsville. Basketball is king in the Bluegrass State, but I would not discover my love for hoops until three years later. Soccer was nonexistent in eastern Kentucky, but everyone played T-ball in first grade. I played pitcher's mound because pitchers often field slow rollers, and I was the fastest kid on our team. The felt letters on the front of my T-shirt made me proud.

That first season I played T-ball, yours truly fielded the first hit of the game. I calmly pulled the ball out of my glove and fired a rocket toward first base. Unfortunately, I could not throw straight, and there was a small creek just beyond first with no fence line or dugout to stop an overthrown ball. I watched in horror as the ball went past the first baseman and rolled down to the creek, and the runner made it to first before the ball could be retrieved.

After that, I was terrified at the thought of making another bad throw. So I didn't. For the rest of that season, instead of throwing to first, I chased runners down and tagged them out. My parents have a newspaper clipping somewhere with a photo of me running toward first base. I still cannot throw straight.

My summer days were spent riding my bike to the local mom-and-pop grocery store, Pic-Pac, and buying as many packs of baseball cards as I could carry with one hand for the ride home. As I got older and started earning money, I opted to wait until I had $12 to buy a full box of cards instead of three or four packs. I can still see the white dust and taste the bitter, chalky gum that lost its flavor in four seconds. The sound and feeling of glue separating at the seams as I ripped open a new pack of cards remains a core memory.

The following season, I moved up to our small town's youth league, the county's version of Little League. My jersey number was 9, and our team was called the Phillies. I was an outfielder. Brian Hardison was my best neighborhood buddy, and his dad, Gary, coached our team. We played every sport in his front yard. Gary often volunteered to be our all-time quarterback or pitcher, depending on the day and the game.

One routine grounder during a youth league game impacted my outlook on baseball. I hit a slow roller to the pitcher and took off running to first base. The pitcher ran to his left and must have not realized how close he was to the first baseman. He fired way too fast, and the ball tipped the top of the glove and cut the first baseman's eyebrow open. I say cut . . . it was more like a perfect slice of skin divided by a paring knife. I rounded first and trotted back to the base, and I heard the gasp from the stands. Blood was gushing from the first baseman's eyebrow, and it did not appear to be slowing down. I can still see my dad sprinting across the diamond with a white handkerchief and applying it to the young player's forehead, trying to stop the bleeding. The red blood on the pristine white cloth made it worse. I knew two things for certain that day: (1) I would never play first base, and (2) my baseball days were numbered.

After two years of baseball, I gravitated to basketball and fell in love with the game. I played in the Johnson County Buddy Basketball League for four years. During my third season, our tiny Catholic school team upset the #1 seed to win the championship. My final year, which I think was seventh grade, I made the All-Star Team as the tenth player out of ten roster spots. It was a proud accomplishment and meant everything to me. I could not wait to make the drive to play our games, because for two years, I had listened intently to my friend tell me all about his experience, and now it was my turn. Normally, the team traveled two hours to West Virginia to play in a tournament, but it was canceled my final year. I was crushed but cannot remember why the event was not held.

Keep in mind, there were no professional sport leagues in the state of Kentucky other than minor league baseball teams sprinkled throughout small towns such as Paintsville and Pikeville. The University of Kentucky's men's basketball team filled this void. These guys were heroes and legends to every middle schooler in the state. The Cats, as the team is affectionately called, were the minor and major league teams of the state.

I vividly remember that when the season ended, the seniors would go on a summer barnstorming tour across the state and play exhibition games in small to midsize towns. The post-game autograph sessions were the best part. The chance to watch the UK seniors play a game in your town or the next town over, along with a free autograph session, was simply too much to take in. To a young boy, it was like meeting a movie star. These tours just ingrained the fandom even more. We lauded these athletes for their athletic accomplishments. Some of the UK players were wise to turn their basketball fame into business opportunities within the Bluegrass State and beyond.

It was during this time I developed a deep passion for the game of basketball. Every friend had a hoop in their driveway or backyard. My cousin Richard nailed a rim and a wooden backboard into a massive oak tree, and his court consisted of dirt and tree roots. It was more of a shooting contest than a traditional pickup game, but we still played on it. Our driveway was slanted downhill. Anytime you drove the lane for a layup, you adjusted your speed to ensure you didn't trip on the asphalt curb. Each hoop was different, and we came to appreciate the quirks and varied landscapes, like professional golfers and their affinity for the characteristics of different course layouts.

My neighborhood buddies and I hooped in any weather, often playing until our fingers bled. The smack talk was nonstop, and we all knew when the others were going to shoot or use their favorite post-move to win the game. We often called it out before the shot left their hand. These neighborhood games are some of my favorite childhood memories.

In the early '80s, bicycles were kids' primary mode of transportation. We viewed Saturday mornings as special treasures with unlimited possibilities. After polishing off a bowl of sugar-laden cereal and an hour of our favorite cartoons, we left the house for a day of freedom. Each week, someone different led the group and was the first one to ride around the neighborhood, knocking on doors and recruiting friends, one house at a time. Then we played outside—dodgeball, Wiffle ball, basketball, you name it.

Fueled by cherry Kool-Aid, Otter Pops popsicles, and Doritos, we played until the inevitable point in the day when someone's mom yelled for them to come home. It was all downhill then, and we knew it, especially in baseball. It meant our crew began dwindling slowly, one by one. After all, you can't play baseball with only five players.

It was a true blessing to grow up in a safe neighborhood where we left the house on our bicycles at 8 a.m. and did not return home for dinner until the streetlights came on. As I reflect on my childhood, I realize how much fun we had and how the hours of a long summer day seemed endless.

These games taught us how to mediate disputes. We kept score, played all day, and settled our arguments on the baseball diamond by talking through our disagreement and agreeing to alternate the right or wrong call, depending on which team you were on. I learned how to present my case and argue the right way. The crew ranged in age from eight to eighteen years old, and the older boys looked out for us and were more like big brothers than adversaries. Sure, occasionally the older guys picked on us, but not as much as one would think. The other fun memory is all our goofy nicknames, which included Oatmeal and Toasty. The grassy lots and makeshift basketball courts taught us all valuable life lessons in the southern humidity of a small eastern Kentucky town most people have never heard of.

Enough of the pep talk and pregame jitters. It is time to lace up your shoes because the equipment manager has a jersey with your name on it. Consider this book your All Access Pass to go behind the scenes and see what it feels like to work in one of the most exciting and unpredictable industries—the world of sports!

Johnson County Youth League Baseball. Me at 8 years old.

Me with my Chuck Taylor basketball shoes. Age 9.

One of the basketball posters in my childhood bedroom.

Me and my Kentucky Dunks Nike basketball shoes. Age 11.

Chapter 1
The Grind

Pre-game: What do you do for a living? This is often the initial question asked when meeting someone for the first time. It is the gold standard icebreaker and provides a glimpse into the person you are talking to, and sometimes even more. Based on the answer, the human brain makes some type of assumption regarding the job title, industry, and common facts or stereotypes one knows about the job. For example, if someone replies with a sales job, you might think the person is outgoing and has tons of energy. If the reply is an engineer, you might assume one is good with numbers and enjoys anything math related.

On some level, the work you do defines you. That should not be the case, but society has led us to believe that work matters more than it should. For example, we perceive certain jobs as higher in status based on the salaries they command.

When meeting new people, we sometimes stereotype them and make assumptions as to why they chose their career path. We've probably all made or overheard small talk along these lines: "You don't look like a teacher. I assumed you were a banker." If one party decides the other party has a cool job, more in-depth questions may follow. What's it like? Is it exciting? Do you wake up energized to go to work every day? Tell me a good story.

People choose career paths for a multitude of reasons. Most people would say their job is a passion or one of their favorite things to do. Others might have followed in the footsteps of their mother or father, perhaps inheriting a family business. Some people change jobs every three years to find something new and challenging because they get bored.

The occupation you choose is a major decision you will make in life. Take time to think about the choice and where the first job might lead you. Remember that if the original plan does not work out, it is perfectly fine to change gears and start an alternative career path. In the sports industry, this happens more often than you think. In fact, it is a common occurrence because of the high pressure and cutthroat nature of the business. Sports is also a highly competitive industry, and sometimes people lose energy and patience waiting for the next opportunity that never comes to fruition.

To the avid sports fan in the bleachers, with his face painted and proudly sporting his favorite team's tattered jersey, the idea of working for a professional sports team sounds like a fantasy job. The same fan arrives at the game thirty minutes before tipoff, then rushes to exit the arena at the final buzzer to beat the inevitable traffic jam on the highway.

However, the front office personnel do not share the same schedule--not even close. The game entertainment director, the sponsorship sales vice-president, and the assistant event manager arrived at 8 a.m. to prepare for that night's third home game of the week. They do not sleep in and avoid rush-hour traffic. Do not forget, those same employees worked until 11 p.m. the night before because last night's game went into two overtimes.

Game days mean long hours and an emotional roller coaster, depending on the opponent and the outcome of the contest. There is a misconception that working in the sports industry is nonstop fun. Most of the time it is exciting, and it is always unpredictable. You will face some slow-paced and tough days, especially when a star player suffers an injury and is out for the remainder of the season or when a fan favorite is traded. Team employees who work behind the scenes are the first ones to arrive at the arena and the last ones to leave. Parking nightmares rarely occur at midnight, but a sport's season runs anywhere from three to nine months, and the early-morning start time plus late-night games and special events take a toll after a while. For those students aspiring to work in the sports industry, the crucial fact to know is that you will be working when other people are having fun, especially nights and weekends. It is a well-known tradeoff and one that is non-negotiable. Be prepared for this sacrifice because it is not for everyone.

Another misconception is the idea that front office staff spends time with the players. A professional athlete is there to collect a paycheck and is not interested in engaging in small talk or hearing about the sponsor who is upset that their promotion did not go as planned. During my career, I met fewer than ten athletes from the teams I worked with.

Most teams have strict rules regarding socializing with players, too, whether you are a sales executive, a cheerleader, or a marketing intern. Countless things can go wrong in this situation. It still happens, but it is best to avoid it as much as possible. Be smart, play it safe, and keep all interactions professional.

The sports industry is different for several reasons. First, you can ask fifty sports executives how and where they began their career, and you would receive fifty wide-ranging stories of hard work, determination, good and bad luck, and being at the right spot at the right time. It is rare that two people share the same story, especially in this field. That said, one characteristic the sports executives all share is a strong work ethic. Lazy people do not last long in sports. There is work to be done, and always more to be accomplished. If you do not want to put in the effort, managers know there are at least a hundred people waiting at the door for their shot to take your job.

What drew me to my career choice is that I relished the excitement, passion, and unpredictable endings inherent in athletic contests. For comparison's sake, a music concert is scripted and planned to the final song and minute. A loyal fan knows the artist or band will open with a crowd-pleasing, upbeat melody, then mix in a ballad, and end on a high note with their biggest hits and a cool encore. A game, on the other hand, can go down to the wire, an underdog can pull the upset over the heavily favored team, or the contest might go to overtime. You honestly never know when you are witnessing history or watching a remarkable play that will be replayed over and over on ESPN's *SportsCenter*. It is as exciting for staff as it is for fans to be able to relive and reminisce about a great play for decades, and to be able to say they were there as it unfolded.

Remember I said the job market in the sports industry is highly competitive? Here is why: Every large metro area, and even midsize town, has hundreds of accountants, engineers, nurses, real estate agents, lawyers, and bank employees. For example, there are over one hundred engineering firms in Denver, Colorado, with an estimated average of five hundred employees each. The same cannot be said for sports teams and jobs. The average professional sports team has approximately sixty jobs, and some are specialized and narrowly focused.

Even though I knew the challenge and adversity I faced choosing to pursue this path, I could not resist the lure of the passion, energy, and excitement of working in the sports industry. It was a long-time dream, and I was determined to chase it with everything I had.

For the Love of the Job

What attracts people to certain industries? Is it status, clout, public perception, money, or even fame? Personality and how a person is hardwired play a pivotal role. High-risk, high-reward jobs typically attract risk-takers. The base salary might be lower than normal, but the potential upside is much greater. Sometimes the world depends on the company and products, which is appealing to jobseekers who appreciate the adrenaline rush associated with building a new company or researching a groundbreaking product. The opportunity to travel within a certain region, or the entire country, makes a job look cool, and rightfully so. However, traveling across the country or around the globe means time spent away from home, family, and friends. The road can be a dark and lonely place and sleeping in a hotel bed five nights a week and eating meals at all hours is far from ideal or glorious. These jobs are a perfect fit for young, single individuals.

Perks of the Job

Job perks fascinate me; I love learning about the different benefits companies offer their employees. The primary perk in sports is free tickets. It doesn't happen every week or even every month, because chances are you are working during home games, but it is a common benefit. Plus, you meet other team employees in your city and you help one another out once or twice a year with complimentary tickets to a game. Even though you might not be close friends with them, you share a bond and an unspoken level of mutual respect because you know how hard you all work and the time you invest in your respective teams and seasons.

The perk of free athletic apparel and shoes is a close second. Athletic brands invest large sums in marketing and licensing agreements with individual players, leagues, and conferences. They are proud of their product, and the more team employees there are walking around town sporting a Nike, Adidas, or Under Armour logo, the better. Passionate college alumni might purchase a T-shirt, golf shirt, sweatshirt and running shoes featuring their alma mater's logo or mascot. Depending on their level of fandom, the passion can even extend to housewares, luggage, and yard games.

Most teams I worked with had a standard apparel kit for most, if not all, employees. It usually included two golf shirts, a lightweight jacket, and a T-shirt. Sometimes running shoes, my favorite item, were included in the mix. It also depended on the league and the months of the year. In outdoor sports, waterproof pants and jackets were great additions that came in handy, not to mention oversized down-filled jackets. A team-branded winter coat retailed for $200 or more, and a golf shirt probably was $75 or more. Everything was high quality, and it was a nice perk to get them for free as part of the job.

Friends, the Best Perk of All

Salary is essential, and perks and benefits lure you or pique your interest, but the friends you meet at the office keep you sane and happy and make the long hours worth it.

A bond and a deep friendship form because you spend forty to fifty hours per week with a particular group of coworkers or teammates. Multiply that by ten years or more, and one quickly comprehends why certain coworkers stay close friends for life.

Through this experience and time spent with one another, you develop and earn trust from your close work friends. A healthy combination of humor, sarcastic rants, and playful griping pull you through the muck and dark days, early mornings, and late nights. You earn badges of courage together, side by side, enduring slumps, winning streaks, injuries, and cash-saving trades.

As the days turn into months and sometimes a decade, the same work friend stands by your side through promotions, missed opportunities, lay-offs, and other work-related letdowns and disappointments. They know and understand what level of effort you invested in the season, the franchise, and your job.

At the core, work is a dynamic environment flush with personalities, egos, dreams, and disappointment. Some days we love our jobs, and other days, the clock on the wall crawls by, second by excruciating second. Most people in the industry are competitive by nature and would like to be promoted and accept additional responsibility, not to mention make more money and improve their job title.

Work is an essential part of life. Everyone travels a different career path. Sometimes our choices are driven by passion and happiness; other times they are fueled by lifestyle preferences and salary; and yet other choices are focused on helping others or making a true impact on the world we live in.

To put a life of work into perspective, let's do some quick math. If a person enters the workforce at 22 years old and works 45 hours per week until they retire at age 65, he or she will spend about 96,000 hours of life working in some capacity.

It is a good idea to find something you enjoy. That advice is repeated often, but not heeded by everyone. Money is essential, but it should not be the number one reason you take a job. We all struggle at times with finding the right balance of satisfaction, fulfillment, and income, but after a strategic career choice, what makes us happy guides our next landing spot.

Your Office is Located Where?

Most workplaces consist of a brick building with offices, cubicles, and conference rooms overlooking a city's skyline or other natural landscape. Sports teams' workspaces are a little different, because the offices are housed in basements, underneath a stadium, or even above it sometimes.

A walk down the hallway at an insurance firm versus an arena offers contrasting styles. Insurance firm employees pass one another in the hall talking about industry trends, major storms, and troublesome customers. Sports employees discuss trades, injuries, and postseason hopes while dodging a forklift moving synthetic turf on the arena floor. Better yet, sometimes they swap stories watching a Zamboni clean the ice for the hockey game scheduled later that evening.

The other vast difference is how the type of clientele varies for the sports team. A traditional company's daily interaction is predictable, as clients arrive dressed in casual attire or suits, depending on the size and nature of the company. A stadium, however, takes on the personality of each event, which changes weekly and sometimes daily, depending on the versatility of the venue.

Thursday morning starts with a basketball game, Friday is a hockey game, but Saturday afternoon welcomes the #1 country artist's world tour or a monster truck event the following week. This continues for over 250 nights of the year.

During my career, my office has looked and felt differently than the offices of my counterparts in other jobs. My desks have been in a tiny office in an 18,000-seat NBA arena and one of the largest youth sports complexes in the world. I currently work out of the upscale and architecturally beautiful Ellie Caulkins Opera House at the Denver Performing Arts Complex in the heart of the city.

I believe one of the inspirational aspects of working in the sports industry is the constant need and push for creative programs. How can we sell more tickets to a Monday night game featuring a basement-dwelling opponent? How do we garner additional media coverage and become more relevant in our city? What type of new charity event can we bring to life this season?

People tend to fear change, but I thrived on the unpredictable nature of the business. Boredom at work rarely happened. Plus, I never knew what issue was lurking around the corner. Every day you walked into the office wondering what client, new project, or wildfire would unfold before lunchtime.

Leagues and teams often share best practices and other relevant data. If the Detroit Lions conduct a highly successful ticket promotion, chances are the Dallas Cowboys will hear about it and might try to replicate it in their home market. Creativity is encouraged at most levels, specifically with ticket sales, in-game promotions, or sponsorships that integrate corporate partners.

Dollars and Sense

Low entry-level salaries are well known, but that does change with experience and the sales commissions associated with ticket and sponsorship sales. These two areas are popular, yet high-risk and high-reward, opportunities.

A six-figure executive salary looks desirable on paper, but it comes with lofty expectations and increased pressure to perform at a high level. We all should remember that each one of us can be replaced. The term *success* is viewed differently when referring to the number of team wins and new revenue streams.

Moving with Momentum

Another characteristic of this industry is the difficulty of finding advancement opportunities. It is never easy to get promoted with the team or company. Often, you must make the decision to move across the country time and again because you cannot wait for an internal opening that may never happen to occur. It is a competitive industry and once someone reaches the higher level, chances are they will not leave soon.

The advantage of working for different teams in various parts of the country is it provides you with experience and perspective. It is also a powerful reminder that not every in-game or ticket sales promotion will be popular everywhere. This experience becomes a distinguishing factor in your interviews because you can reference what you learned in four jobs, versus just one.

In summary, you might spend a season with the Amarillo Sod Poodles and the Altoona Curve to switch gears and leagues to work for the Atlanta Braves. This is commonly referred to as "paying your dues" or "earning your stripes." Do not be afraid to switch jobs or cities, because it is an opportunity to gain experience from the culture and the people and gain helpful skills that transfer seamlessly to your next job. The chase is not for everyone and that is ok, too, if you decide to stay put. It is not required to zigzag across the country three times in a U-Haul truck, but it does help sometimes.

The Truth about Job Security

Job security is a popular term in the workforce. It is a nice term, in theory, but to discover what it truly means, you must take a deeper look. A championship-contending team is just a broken leg or offensive slump away from lofty postseason plans crumbling right before the fans' eyes.

Thursday night you are planning a postseason trip, and Friday morning, you might start looking for a new job.

It can occur for a multitude of reasons, but even when you suspect it might happen, it still burns. It impacts your finances and self-esteem. Occasionally, the team rebuilds and fires everyone, or the new owner replaces the executives when ownership is officially transferred. The term "cleaning house" is what it is sometimes called, and the owner often brings in his or her "people." It will most likely happen and comes with the territory of the job. It is a challenging experience, but it builds resilience, character, and determination. Trust me on this one, I know it all too well.

On a personal level, my experiences in this area helped forge my confidence and the ability to not fear anything job related, particularly a terrible boss. I am sometimes stubborn, but I tried my best not to sacrifice my character, regardless of my drive to advance in my career or earn a promotion.

The one exception to this rule is a proven track record of ticket sales. If you can sell tickets in sports, I promise you will not be unemployed for very long. There will always be a need to fill the stadium seats each season, especially when the team is having a down year. I hold anyone who sells tickets in high regard, but it is a tough job to spend eight hours a day on the phone, repeatedly hearing, "No thanks."

The ABCs of the Venue
Access, Badges, and Credentials

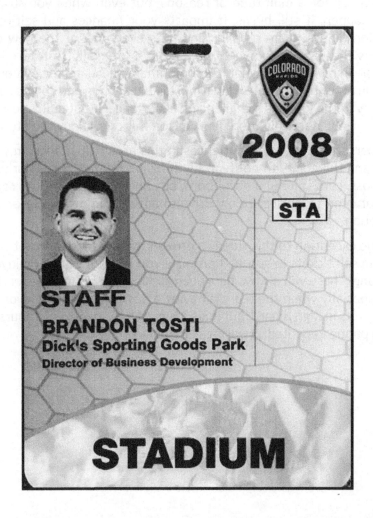

Sports stadiums are massive structures. They are filled with seating, lights, and lots of tunnels and secret hallways that fans never see. The priority for any team is safety for the fans, players, and team staff. Second is accessibility for heavy equipment, players, and mascots to move quickly from one side of the arena to the other.

On game day, team staff members must navigate both the inside and out-side of the arena. To ensure safety, every employee must wear a company-issued credential or badge. It will include a color photo of the employee, their name, department, and which areas they can access. Credentials are vital in the sports industry, because they help venue security monitor private areas, such as the locker rooms, and the court, pitch, or press box.

The credential also serves as a beacon for fans or patrons who might be confused, lost, or just curious. When a patron stops you to ask a question, take a moment and listen to them. You might save them fifteen valuable minutes by redirecting them to their seats. Otherwise, they stumble unnecessarily around the concourse while missing the opening song of their favorite band or the pre-game theatrics.

What the badge is *not* is a free pass to blow by the security guard. This is rude and you wouldn't do it in a normal office setting. Please refrain from operating this way when you find yourself in this situation. If it is not a serious emergency, just pause for a second, show your badge with a smile and ask for the guard's name, then thank him or her for doing their job. When something goes wrong, they are often the first in line to blame, and security is a thankless job. After all, they are constantly dealing with people trying to sneak into the locker room or simply take advantage of them. Establish rapport with them. There will be a time in the future when you need to rush by. If they know and trust you, they will smile, nod, and wave you through. It might seem like simple advice, but I promise you, it comes down to treating others with respect.

Changes in the Industry

First, I need to backtrack a bit and tell you about how the college sports landscape has evolved over time. Sports marketing grew in popularity once teams realized the massive potential for corporate sponsorships and naming rights for stadiums and athletic training facilities. For years, cor-porate sponsorships were primarily locally based companies with small to moderate investments. Friends close to the athletic program called the athletic director to arrange a lunch meeting or golf outing to discuss busi-ness opportunities. It is possible that some of them were handshake deals without detailed legal documents.

Collegiate sports and corporate sponsorships grew together over time. Before this happened, Smith University might have had a $15,000 agreement with a family-owned auto dealership. National corporations and brands with larger advertising budgets began to negotiate conference-wide contracts, not just with individual schools. The result was revenue sharing for all twelve member universities of the conference. The contractual elements and expectations of the sponsorship drastically changed, and the level of work involved in managing these contracts increased, as well.

As sponsorship revenue increased, legal issues, contracts, and multimedia broadcasting rights came into the picture, the Health and Physical Education degree of the former football coach serving as the new athletic director was not adequate to qualify him to manage the new business components of the athletics department. As the dollars increased exponentially, the need to negotiate contracts and the ability to navigate delicate legal matters became a top priority. There is a major difference between raising five thousand dollars and five million dollars.

The business of athletics was no longer simple math, but a complicated web of finances, pressure, and passionate and petulant alumni. The never-ending arms race to build a bigger stadium or a practice facility to compete with your in-state rival and the athletic conference itself escalated. The fundraising model drastically changed, requiring a multi-faceted leader steeped in raising capital funds and with proven success managing major projects—in other words, a professional businessperson.

I am not sure which university was the first to make the switch, but someone realized the importance of employing someone with a legal or business background. Suddenly, CEOs were making the leap from pizza chains and Fortune 500 companies to home football games, tailgate parties, and fundraising dinners with alumni chapters across the country. They traded in their Wall Street suit for a Nike golf shirt and hoodie of their alma mater. The financials might have been smaller in scale, but the passion for college sports could not be matched.

Financing, bonds, and the ability to understand these convoluted topics were a prerequisite to being a prominent fundraiser in the evolving role of athletic director.

My career goal was to be an athletic director at a Division I institution. I viewed my career path as a Trivial Pursuit game piece, with the different colored pie pieces representing the building blocks, or skills sets, of the role. Here is a simple list of jobs in a sport's front office:

- Ticket sales
- Sponsorship sales
- Sponsorship activation or fulfillment
- Social media management
- Community relations
- Media relations
- Sports information
- Coaching
- Athletic trainer
- Human resources
- Legal
- Finance
- Facility management
- Venue operations
- Marketing and public relations
- Creative department (graphic artists, sound, video)
- Travel
- Team personnel (executives, scouting director, player personnel)

To open the door, I had to find it — or a friend to set me on the right path. How did I get started in the field? What changed my career path, this time hopefully for good? Well, that is a good story. I have kept you in suspense long enough. Grab some popcorn, your favorite ice-cold beverage, and sit back in your courtside seat.

Taking My Shot: My Path Before Sports

Jobs sometimes find us, and opportunities arise from unexpected sources. Then there is me, who changed my college major five times and took close to five years to complete an undergraduate degree.

I started in pre-optometry, but the idea quickly died after one semester of Chemistry 105 at the University of Kentucky. Next on the spinning career wheel was sports journalism. I took one journalism class and met with the campus student newspaper, but it didn't last long. The thought of beating a deadline and having no control over what I wrote about did not appeal to me. I have a creative mind and can be stubborn when it relates to brainstorming and believing in a concept. Deep down, I knew I would struggle to write an article about a news item no one cared about. I don't say that from an ego perspective, but more from my deeply rooted passion to write inspiring pieces.

I went back to Paintsville for the summer, and my neighbor, who wrote a popular lifestyle column, asked me about writing for the local newspaper, *The Paintsville Herald*. I would have worked for free. I covered high school sports, and the first question I asked the editor was whether he would let me write a weekly column about the lighter side of sports. He agreed, and "The Inside Pitch by Brandon Tosti" came to life.

Next was health care administration. I remained in this lane for almost two years and considered transferring to Eastern Kentucky University to pursue this career opportunity. That campus was located approximately thirty minutes south of Lexington, and I knew the area fairly well. I even had a roommate from my hometown lined up. Healthcare policies, and how the world viewed them differently than the United States does, was both a fascinating and terrifying topic. Health insurance is a significant revenue generator for private companies and equipment manufacturing corporations and, of course, the pharmaceutical industry.

After I volunteered to observe two surgeries at a local hospital, fate intervened by way of a fainting spell. Once the ammonia in the operating room reached my nose, I became lightheaded and collapsed into a chair. I knew I would spend most of my time in the job behind a desk, but the restlessness and uncertainty in my gut told me there was something else out there for me; I just had to find it. My weak stomach proved to be my downfall, but it led me to something else I enjoyed even more.

My Unofficial Career Coach

It is often said that the college years are a time of personal growth, maturity, and establishing lifelong friendships. I started my collegiate career at a local community college in Prestonsburg, Kentucky, located fifteen minutes from my house. It was affordable, but I also earned a scholarship, which sounds more impressive than it was, but it saved my parents $2,000 per semester. All my credits were transferable to the University of Kentucky, which was a bonus.

I was excited to leave my hometown and join my other high school friends who had gone away to college immediately after senior year. I felt like I had to make up for lost time, and I wasted no time getting involved with student leadership programs after transferring to the University of Kentucky. The first group was the Residence Hall Association (RHA). Each residence hall had its own student officers, and all twenty-two halls met once a month. These meetings were managed by four elected student officers. I lived on South Campus in the Kirwan-Blanding complex, which consisted of eight low-rise halls with three floors and two towers of twenty-three floors each.

The purpose of the organization was to improve residential life through social, educational, and cultural programs focused on student health and needs. I was never a fan of politics, but this was different. I felt as if we could make our fellow students enjoy "dorm life" and improve morale inside our building. My roommate and I ran for hall president and vice-president, respectively, and we won. RHA is where I met Brad Eggert. He was a neatly dressed kid (think L.L. Bean), and his leadership skills were on display from our first campus-wide meeting. We saw each other a week later at a campus recreation softball game; after talking with him for mere minutes, you knew he was highly intelligent, well-spoken, and could get along with anyone. Brad engaged in a wide variety of campus activities. This guy was everywhere and seemed to know a bit about everything, similar to the wise senior, except he was just a sophomore, whose maturity stood out to me immediately.

One night, we were talking about our majors and career plans. I told Brad about my failed optometry plan and my uncertain future.

Brad then told me his major: Sport Management.

I did a double take and asked him to repeat his statement. "Are you being serious? How is that possible?"

My initial response could be described as utter disbelief. I was think-ing: Do you mean I can get paid to watch a university basketball game? Someone's job is to organize baseball and golf tournaments in exotic loca-tions? Please stop joking around with me. I was weary from the career roller coaster I had been on up to this point, and it seemed too good to be true.

I held Brad in high regard because he balanced school, leadership activ-ities and his social life, and invariably made it look easy. He had a sharp business mind, was funny, and everyone loved him. Brad was a leader in other student organizations outside of RHA and knew people across cam-pus. He carried himself with a combination of low-key demeanor, seren-ity, and quiet confidence. One of his admirable attributes is how he fits in with all kinds of people. "Polished" would be an understatement, because Brad can talk about world politics, the latest sports news, and also fill you in on a popular restaurant off campus without a long pause.

He is on my shortlist of friends I would choose to be my partner on the hit TV show, *The Amazing Race*. Brad is typically in a good mood, stays calm in pressure situations, and I want him on my side if I am ever in a foreign country and cannot speak the native language. I guarantee he would fig-ure out a way to negotiate a result that would satisfy all parties. Plus, he keeps life in perspective, even when we were immature and irresponsible twenty-one-year-olds.

*Brad Eggert and me at a Residence
Hall Association Conference.*

Brad and me joking around at the Grand Canyon.

Moving Ahead

I had finally found my home in the Sport Management Department at University of Kentucky. I was thrilled to have landed on something I loved. The next step was to select my concentration—the aspect of sport management where I would focus my attention to prepare for a career. I wanted to chase a dream, but I did not want to waste energy chasing the wrong one. Fortunately, I knew my weaknesses and strengths. I immediately eliminated any type of media jobs because they did not seem right for me. I also knew I wasn't interested in statistics. I am not a numbers guy. Though I appreciate an interesting player or team stat here and there, the topic did not move the needle for me. I needed something more.

I loved working with people and hosting events of any size. The planning elements made sense to me, and it was one area where I rarely felt nervous. Event management appealed to me for a wide variety of reasons, but now I had to figure out which sport or lane I wanted to explore to find the right future job for me.

The class load included the standard courses on venue management, marketing, and multiple athletic classes, such as fundamentals of dance, gymnastics, swimming, tennis, and principles of conditioning. Every university's sports management program was slightly different. Some programs were designated as business school options, while other degrees lived in colleges of education under the umbrella of kinesiology and health promotion.

I often had athletes as classmates, primarily football players. It was fun to hear their stories and they appreciated having friends that did not view them from a fan's perspective. As a nice bonus, the majority of my core classes were located less than 250 yards from my residence hall, Blanding 2, or B-2, as it was better known back then. B-2 is also the name of my author LLC company that I share with my college roommate, Chad Randall.

I gravitated to live sports and the event management side of the industry. The in-game promotions were fascinating and intriguing to me. Entertaining people and relishing a hard-fought, closely contested game were both passions of mine. My competitive streak is intense despite my lack of athletic ability. I am not a sore loser, but I hate losing, and despite the fun we had razzing each other as kids, I have become a muted competitor. I do not need to talk trash on the court or field. I leave that nonsense up to my opponents. My focus is helping my team win, whether by cheering for my teammates or passing the ball to an open guard for the game-winning shot.

Since I was playing catch-up, academically, I faced an uphill battle in terms of time versus the number of credit hours required for graduation. Normally, you try to save an easy class or two for your senior year. I did not have the luxury of picking a friendly senior schedule—you know, the kind where you have only midmorning classes and none on Fridays. To graduate on time, which was now five and a half years, I stacked my class load and took eighteen credit hours my final semester. Granted, some of these were one-hour electives, such as principles of dance, conditioning, weightlifting, and other physical fitness classes, but I still had class time and assignments.

I worked with my advisor to juggle everything. I realized I had to take a one-hour swimming class, but I had no time slot available, and of course, it was one of those classes offered only once per week. Immediately, I asked other classmates for advice and consulted with my advisor and learned that this class had caused others a similar dilemma. The final plan included a hybrid independent study and test-out option. I wasn't the best swimmer, but I leaned on my lifeguard and swimming tests from my Scouting years. I had completed a half-mile swim in open water, not to mention surviving all the scenario-based training. I knew I could handle an indoor pool test.

What I didn't know was that the professor despised anyone who tested out of the class. The written test was detailed and harder than it needed to be. At that point, I focused on finishing my academic requirements so that I could graduate in May. Besides, I had one goal: I just had to pass the class. It wasn't as if a future employer would ask me for my swimming class grade. I think I ended up with a C+. Stupid written exam.

As I mentioned, I lived on South Campus, a three-minute walk from the recreation center where most of the physical education classes took place. Of course, one of my classes was on the far side of campus, and it was offered only on Mondays and Wednesdays at 8 a.m. The class was titled something like Fundamentals of Dance 105, and was held in a historic building, the Buell Armory.

The instructor loved everything about dancing. She knew every intricate detail of all the famous dances. It was her passion. She smiled during every demo as we students looked on wearily, dreading our turn to embarrass ourselves.

I have little rhythm and would never make fun of another person's attempt to dance, but on one occasion, I was secretly glad that I got to go immediately after a strong offensive lineman. The tiptoe segment was the funniest part. After his performance, I knew I could stumble through the line, miss the beat, and still be okay. Everyone laughed a lot, and we all became closer by laughing at our awful performances.

The only class in our program I did not like was KHP 155, Principles of Conditioning. Dr. Taylor could have passed for an *American Gladiator* stunt double and was in incredible shape, well into his fifties. We learned about every form of exercise, dance, and cardio activity in the free world, or so it seemed. First, we explored different ways to burn calories and experience cardio options. Believe it or not, I held my own in gymnastics class on the floor routine and wisely went slowly on the pommel horse. Students took turns leading the class. Remember my lack of rhythm? It reared its ugly head once again. I had to lead a step aerobics class for one minute, and it was sixty seconds of pure hell. I crossed my feet, lost count, and just wanted it to end.

Learning on the Job—Internship Madness

One would think the 18 academic hours would be enough, but I still had to complete 180 internship hours to graduate. Looking back, it was the busiest year of my life. I am not sure how I balanced everything, or even had much of a social life my senior year.

As you start searching for an internship, my advice is to try to focus on the summer months when you don't have to balance academics as well. An internship is not a full-time job, but it can feel like one. You want to maximize the experience to learn and make a good impression.

One common characteristic in the sports industry is that we all spent months or years as an intern, hustling to find our next opportunity. Everyone works long days and nights and understands the next job might take four months, or four years, to come to fruition. Some individuals stick it out and others change careers.

Job Hunt

When I felt like I was heading down a dead-end road, I reminded myself I just needed a chance, a break from one team or one company. I invested hours and researched all facets of the job search process including interviewing skills, resume development, and cover letter essentials. I studied articles, printed documents with key learnings, and created a three-ring binder as a resource guide.

As I mentioned, my path was not a simple one. It was filled with disappointment, frustration, hope, and setbacks, but I refused to give up on my goal. Week after week, the routine was predictable. I would scour job boards on campus and on the internet, searching for an internship or entry-level position. I would spend a night or two customizing my cover letter and then make copies of my resume. A month would pass, and I would receive a stack of rejection letters from universities, sports marketing agencies, and minor league baseball teams.

I was doubting myself and needed to stay motivated. For a strange reason, I used my rejection letters as a positive influence. I kept them all in an oversized manila envelope, reminding myself I refused to lose this battle. I scribbled an inspirational quote on the outside: "Fall down seven times, stand up eight."

The Million Dollar Question—How do I Break into the Sports Industry?

The sports industry is massive in all facets, including team values, sponsorship revenue, global reach, team merchandise, and ticket sales. The mass appeal shows no signs of slowing down as billion-dollar stadiums continue to be built across the world and new leagues continue to develop at all levels.

During my career, I was often hiring full-time positions based on the high turnover that is common for entry-level positions. Finding quality candidates was the challenging part. When a pro sports team posts a job opening, one thing is for certain: the hiring manager is guaranteed to see hundreds of resumes. It is a mix of highly qualified candidates and individuals with zero experience in the field who feel compelled to take his or her shot.

Public speaking came easy to me, and I enjoyed the opportunity to share some wisdom and lighthearted stories to undergraduate Sport Marketing and Sport Management classes. It helped me from a professional development standpoint, but also served another purpose: giving back. I struggled for over two years trying to break into the sports industry and made a commitment to help other aspiring sport-industry students and peers once I secured my job.

Years later, I brought the tattered envelope with me to speaking engagements as a prop. I shared it with the students to remind them of the journey they would embark upon sooner rather than later. It was fun to look back and see how some NFL teams had changed both cities and mascot names. I also kept the envelope for another reason. I wanted to ensure I would not forget where I came from, and I never wanted to be cocky or content with my job.

The rejection letter envelope I kept for motivation.

My rejection letter from the Houston Oilers NFL team.

Fiesta Bowl rejection letter.

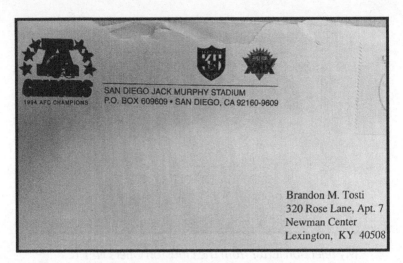

San Diego Chargers rejection letter.

I am dating myself, but when I was finishing my undergraduate degree, *Jerry Maguire* was a surprise blockbuster movie, and the field of sports marketing was still evolving and remained an enigma to the public. Anytime someone asked me what I was studying, I mentioned sports marketing, and the response was predictably the same every time: "Cool, you want to be a sports agent, like Jerry Maguire!" Not exactly. I tried to explain to my parents what I did for a living for years and it took a while, but I can empathize with my liberal arts major friends' struggle when describing their career goals.

> *Post-game recap: It is important to set goals and spend time thinking about your career path, but remember it rarely goes as planned, and that is ok. You will make mistakes and grow from those decisions as you move forward. Don't waste time worrying about a timeline and never judge your success against that of someone else in the field.*

Chapter 2

The Clubhouse:
Wild, Weird, and Wonderful Teammates

Pre-game: The one bond we all share regardless of profession—whether you are a police officer, a teacher, or an engineer—are certain stereotypes and personalities of coworkers. This is my honest but whimsical view on who you can expect to meet in your office. The environment might be a professional basketball arena, a high-rise, an open floor plan, or a performing arts center, but the types of people you encounter are often the same. I will use alternating pronouns, since both men and women can be any of these personality types. Please don't take this section too seriously. I wrote it with a touch of sarcasm, yet also with a realistic viewpoint. Besides, we all need a good laugh now and then.

Workplace Personalities

The Egomaniac

He wants credit for every success and avoids any controversial event or situation. Conversely, when an event doesn't go as planned, he is the first to point a finger or deflect blame from himself. Sometimes this is your boss, and that is never easy to stomach, but you must fight through the rough spots. If it is your boss, you must be patient and let others see it. It is not worth investing your time and energy in a fight, because things will work out eventually.

The Robot

This employee works forty hours a week—no more, no less—while displaying little or no passion. The robot clocks in, clocks out, and shows no emotion at the office. A friend worked for a city government agency for ten years, told me this profile fit multiple employees, and not just in the one department where you think you might find them. The Robot expends the same amount of energy every week of the year. The job is simply a means to an end.

Operations (OPS) Commander

This person has a one-track mind, and that track is narrow. I often refer to this mentality as "black or white." There is no middle ground and no gray area. He dislikes differing opinions, and he truly struggles when things change or do not go as planned. He sets his mind and plan in stone, with no room or time for debate or flexibility. Sometimes this outlook combines with cockiness, bull-headed opinions, and firm beliefs.

The Box Checker

This individual focuses on the empty boxes and must check each one before she can move on to the next project. This is not a poor system until her stress spills over to other teammates, which it always does. Simply put, she cannot sleep knowing a task has not been completed.

The Idea Guy/Girl

This individual is constantly generating new ideas and promotions. He has high energy and zero risk aversion to trying new concepts or changing procedures. He lives in the gray area, because that is the real world. He doesn't bend the rules, but he is willing to make adjustments as needed.

The Devil's Advocate

A highly opinionated and outspoken critic, she plays a valuable role on any team, because you need to consider what could go wrong and how the event might be perceived or misconstrued from the public's standpoint.

The downsides: She is never positive about anything and likes to let everyone know the worst thing that could happen. It is a serious challenge for her to see possibilities.

The Smartest Person in the Room

This one is predictable. She believes she has the correct answer every time. Think The Devil's Advocate on steroids. She constantly offers her opinion, even before you ask.

You could make the comment, "The sky is such a beautiful dark blue today." Her response? "No, it's more a shade of Carolina blue." She has to be right, undoubtedly believes she is correct, and cannot comprehend why anyone would disagree with her.

The Controller

Every conversation, project, and upward communication must go through him. He is overprotective of processes, procedures, and equipment. He finds it difficult to trust others or delegate tasks to teammates or other departments.

The Numbers Person

Trust the numbers! Numbers are king in this coworker's mind and world. She is conservative by nature, yet she is brilliant and a quick thinker with budgets, risk analyses, and financial projections. She constantly saves the company a ton of money by catching mistakes and tempering aggressive decision-making. If you are in sales or marketing, she is an excellent ally to keep close. Learn from her how to present risk factors and to supplement your presentations with well-researched, realistic numbers, not outlandish, self-serving projections.

The Event Guy/Girl

Some people on this earth love the rush of planning and orchestrating an event. It can be a classy dinner, a national tournament, or a going-away party. The Event Guy loves entertaining people, the mad rush leading up to the event, and all that comes with it. This employee can see shades of gray. He is flexible, smart, and an excellent problem solver, but most of all, he thoroughly enjoys planning events and entertaining people. I often joke about my current job and claim that I play multiple roles: firefighter, politician, negotiator, DJ, and party planner.

The Sales Guru

This employee has energy and a voice that can overpower anyone within an eight-foot radius. She does not lack confidence and is usually a driven, Type A personality. She is competitive and hates to lose.

She is eager to learn and fascinated by trivial facts that are crucial to a brand's success and longevity. A great Sales Guru listens to what the customer needs, then calmly inserts her brainstorms, feedback, and suggestions into the conversation without being obnoxious.

The Long-winded Emailer

Send this colleague a project update, and he will reply with a document as dense as a White House security briefing. Every possible scenario, from routine to outlandish, will be analyzed, with detailed contingency plans for each. When possible, keep your questions short and to the point, and sometimes it is okay to include a line or two of text to anticipate his concerns.

The Meeting Lover

She is a staunch believer that meetings are essential and productive. She sets up pre-meetings to discuss the agenda for the actual meeting. She will gladly arrange another meeting to discuss what you might have missed in the last meeting. It is maddening, and at some point, it is okay to respectfully question the need for multiple meetings.

The Meeting Hater

This person despises meetings, especially lunchtime ones. His nemesis is The Long-winded Email Person, who speaks at every meeting and asks ten far-fetched questions. Meeting Haters dislike the social aspect of having to talk in front of a large group, while others see all meetings as a drag on their time and productivity.

The Martyr

She is a hard worker and dedicated, which is valuable for companies of all sizes. The martyr is the first one to volunteer to pick up the proverbial slack. She possesses pride in herself and never wants the company to be viewed in a negative light. The problem arises when she works too much, then gripes about the high volume of days or hours she has invested when it wasn't required by her supervisor.

Bosses: The Good, Bad, and Awful

Bosses are part of every job. If you are an entrepreneur, your boss is your bank or venture capital fund. The boss sets the tone and the vibe of the office to a certain extent. In theory, a good boss is a positive, encouraging leader who is patient, kind, and a team player. This is the ideal situation, but it is not guaranteed.

Most companies put bosses, especially new ones, through a leadership training program. Job performance is evaluated in an annual review. Strengths and weaknesses are identified, progress plans are made, and everything is quantified and documented.

One tough part about being a boss is knowing you cannot be friends with everyone. Ultimately, you make tough and unpopular decisions. You maintain a professional distance by keeping emotions and friendships separate. This is often difficult because you might get along well with members of your team.

A good boss routinely checks in with employees for no reason at all. They coach you through mistakes and avoid belittling anyone in front of the team. That does not mean a boss never raises his or her voice or expresses displeasure, but there is a time and place for these things.

I keep in touch with a good boss, sometimes for years after I've moved on from the job. If you are lucky, you'll be able to count your best bosses as mentors, as I do. To this day, I still call two or three of them before I make any major career-related decision. I share my gratitude with them and tell them how they helped me in my career.

Good bosses genuinely care about your career success, but they also care about you as a human being. Their emphasis is not solely on generating more revenue for the company. They have sincere concern for your mental and emotional health, too. They take time to listen if you need to discuss something that might not be work-related.

There is nothing worse than an awful boss. A bad boss usually lacks experience in managing others. With a bit of training and effort, he can improve if he wants to, but it must be a point of emphasis, and effort is required. Expensive leadership programs and coaching classes go only so far in terms of developing managerial skills.

You will meet a fair share of egotistical and hyper-competitive bosses, but you will also meet some of the most amazing people in the world. I promise the latter will outnumber the egomaniacs. Just chalk up troublesome people to another valuable life experience. You will quickly decide that under no circumstances will you ever treat an employee the way you were treated. The myriad of unpredictable professional experiences should not scare you, but rather shape and define you as you move forward.

I believe it is beneficial to experience a terrible boss so one can truly appreciate the good ones. It can be emotionally draining and discomforting for your mental health if you wake up every day dreading going to work. I have experienced this only once, and it was while my wife was battling breast cancer.

I share this section with you to show that you can overcome a bad boss. Things will get better, even if you must leave and take another job. Two times in my career, I stood up and fought for myself. Ultimately it cost me my job, but I do not regret it, and in both cases I moved on to new and better opportunities.

The Different Types of Bosses

Entitled

The entitled boss seems to have forgotten the hard work and dedication that got him to this level. Please do not be this kind of boss. A title is just words; it isn't an excuse not to do a menial task or work an early weekend shift. Step up to help your team, and I promise you good things will happen. Your staff will remember your unselfish behavior and take away an emotional boost from it. When you inspire their pride and enthusiasm, your team will rally to support you.

Nonconfrontational

This boss doesn't want to upset anyone. Rather than dealing with issues head-on, she lets issues fester. Everyone on the team gets upset, and someone finally shares their frustration, either in a team meeting or one-on-one.

Rookie

This is tough, and I hate to be critical, but I had to endure a rookie boss once, and it was brutal. Every manager must learn how to manage, which means mistakes will be made, poor choices will occur occasionally, and the rookie boss must deal with the blowback that occurs. It can be a roller coaster ride for employees as a new boss finds his footing. Try to be patient, because we all make mistakes as we learn.

Sink or Swim

This one is challenging. She does not want to invest time and effort in coaching and properly developing her staff. Instead, she watches as employees sink or swim, saying things like "Learn from your mistakes" or "You'll figure it out." Maybe it is how she was coached, but, frankly, it is a lazy and selfish approach. No one wins in this situation, and it is beyond frustrating to me. Not all managers are great leaders, but every manager should at least try to lead. It is necessary for the team's success, as well as the sanity of each employee.

Step up While Standing on the Sideline

This boss lets his ego get in the way and decides he does not have to be a leader. Instead, he questions the team and loves to ask one of them to step up, every time, while remaining quiet and sitting on the sideline. If the boss stepped up himself, the team would run through a brick wall for him. But because he doesn't, they build one to protect themselves.

> *Post-game recap: Bosses are part of work life. They present challenges and learning opportunities, some good, some bad. It is okay and common to professionally disagree with someone.*
>
> *Try to learn what you would do differently, then apply it when you reach a leadership position.*
>
> *That said, don't let anyone walk over you. Sometimes the only solution is to leave for a new opportunity. The sports world is a small community where everyone knows each other. Try your best not to burn a bridge, because you never know when you might need something from someone down the road. Always try to leave on good terms.*

Chapter 3

Hardwood Heaven & Ice Time: Internships, 1995–1996

Pre-game: The common thread of the sports industry is the importance and necessity of completing not just one, but multiple, internships. The aspiring professional learns specialized skills, such as marketing, game entertainment, community relations, media relations, and ticket sales. The goal is to be well-rounded because it's a small industry and a job opportunity might present itself in any number of areas of the business. If you focus all your energy on marketing and decline a ticket sales internship, you might regret it later when you are applying for jobs and there are no marketing jobs to be found.

The good news is, every team, regardless of the level of the league, offers internships. The bad news is, if there are ten spots, it can feel as if a thousand people are vying for them. Sometimes that is not far from the truth. This is where the industry naturally sorts the determined candidates from the pretenders. I attended a sports career fair in Columbus, Ohio, where a team executive told us: "One in ten aspiring sports marketing students will make it. What number are you?" His words stuck with me for a long time.

1995-96 UNIVERSITY OF KENTUCKY WOMEN'S BASKETBALL SCHEDULE		
Nov. 16	HUNGARY (SOPRONIA)	7 p.m.
Nov. 24	KY. INVIT. (VS. UNC-ASHEVILLE)	7 p.m.
	Toledo vs. West Virginia	5 p.m.
Nov. 25	Consolation/Championship	
Nov. 29	OHIO STATE	7 p.m.
Dec. 1-2	Loyola (Md.)--Northwestern Tnmt.	6 p.m.
	Northwestern vs. Penn	8 p.m.
Dec. 5	at Western Kentucky	8 p.m.
Dec. 8	Indiana (W. Lafayette)	7 p.m.
Dec. 16	at Florida (Orlando)	4:30 p.m.
Dec. 21	SYRACUSE	7 p.m.
Dec. 23	at Miami University	2 p.m.
Dec. 29	Duke (Greensboro, N.C.)	9 p.m.
Dec. 30	N. C. State (Greensboro, N.C.)	7 p.m.
Jan. 3	MISSISSIPPPI	7 p.m.
Jan. 7	LSU	2 p.m.
Jan. 11	at Vanderbilt	8 p.m.
Jan. 14	TENNESSEE	2 p.m.
Jan. 20	Alabama (Birmingham, Ala.)	8 p.m.
Jan. 24	S. CAROLINA	7 p.m.
Jan. 28	ARKANSAS	2 p.m.
Feb. 7	at Marshall	7 p.m.
Feb. 10	at Auburn	1 p.m.
Feb. 13	at Georgia	7:30 p.m
Feb. 17	MISSISSIPPI STATE	7 p.m.
Feb. 19	LOUISVILLE	7 p.m.
Feb. 24	at S. Carolina	7 p.m.
Feb. 27	EASTERN KENTUCKY	7 p.m.
Mar. 1-4	SEC Tournament (Chattanooga)	TBA

Home games in caps • All times Eastern and subject to change

*My copy of the 1995-96 UK Women's
Basketball Pocket Schedule.*

University of Kentucky Women's Basketball

My first internship was with the University of Kentucky women's basketball team. One of my friends from the Kinesiology and Health Promotion discipline, Kim (Locke) McFadden, worked as a manager for the team. After one of our classes, I asked her about internships and the possibility of my working as a student manager. I expected her to tell me the team had enough managers on the roster and a wait list, too, but instead, she smiled and asked if I was serious because they needed an extra one.

The following week, I interviewed with head coach Bernadette Locke-Mattox. She was well-known in basketball circles, having been a talented guard for the University of Georgia. A quick peek at the University of Georgia's basketball website, and one can see her talent and athleticism on display. Not to mention, she made history by becoming the first female assistant coach in NCAA history. She was one of Rick Pitino's assistant coaches for several seasons.

Two minutes into the interview, Coach Locke-Mattox put me at ease with her smile and down to earth personality. She was driven and competitive, but kind when needed. I was impressed by her knowledge of the game and the way she shared it with her team. Her enthusiasm was contagious. She made everyone feel welcome, regardless of job title.

The team of managers were in charge of preparation for practices, as well as home and road games. For home games, we prepped both home and visitor locker rooms with towels, stocked each team's Powerade coolers, and took care of minor details including chair placement and dry erase markers for the coaches. The away games were the challenging part. For those, we were responsible for packing and loading the gear bags, which contained extra shoes and uniforms and close to fifteen basketballs. Depending on the day, we were sometimes first or last on the bus. If someone forgot an item or access to the locker room was delayed, we patiently waited to gather the team's equipment bags.

Kim's outgoing personality and ability to make me laugh at any moment were welcome reprieves from the season's grind. As our leader, she knew how to balance work and fun. She understood mistakes were going to happen, but impressed upon us how you respond to adversity matters.

During practice, we chased down errant passes and refilled the ball racks, similar to the ball boys and girls you see running through the scene at Wimbledon. To maximize time and effort, we had three managers. Our friendship was solidified by helping the coaches and players, and we supported each other when school or life became too stressful.

The best part was when Coach was trying to make a point and she called for the ball. She often referred to me as "Brando." I knew that when she called my name, followed by "Ball!", I needed to deliver a sharp pass, because she wanted to show the point guard how to start the offense. Often, she jumped in and ran the play, then smiled at the player and encouraged her to do the same.

Coach genuinely loved the game of basketball. It was apparent in her energy and excitement for teaching players how to properly execute an offensive set. I rooted for her and the program to take the next step to

SEC prominence. It meant something to be part of a rebuilding program as we battled for wins, consistent improvement, and, ultimately, respect.

Preseason practice began, and we quickly got into a routine. Keep in mind, I am 5' 11" if my vertebrae line up perfectly. One of my duties was to play defense against the entire team—not just the lightning-quick guards, but also the muscular and much taller power forwards and centers. I preferred role-playing as the opponent's point guard in order for our team to prepare for their offensive sets, but my job called for both tasks, depending on the focus of each practice.

The assistant coach gave me a jumbo football blocking pad to use in the individual drills, which helped some, but not really. The ladies were stronger than me, not to mention much better athletes. Regardless of being overpowered, I hung in there and battled at every practice. One day, a power forward beat me on a post move three times in a row. I was playing solid defense and pushing her elbow and ribs as hard as I could. I felt like an overmatched superhero in a comic book movie, swinging with all my might as the muscular villain mocked me, swatting me away like a small fly. The player patted me on the back and encouraged me to shake it off and play through it.

The assistant coach immediately yelled at me with his southern twang: "Brandon, you need to play defense and stop her!" I had had enough and retorted with a sly grin and angst in my voice, "Coach, make me four inches taller and forty pounds heavier, and then we can talk." (For the record, I do not recommend this approach!) He turned his head, momentarily fighting back laughter, then encouraged me to keep working on it.

We student managers spent hours at a time with the players on and off the court. Naturally we supported one another because we saw firsthand the rigors of the season and the toll they took on the players, both mentally and physically. The experience provided a realistic insight into what it means to be a college athlete. I was amazed at how well the players balanced everything.

I am normally a reserved and level-headed person, but after that incident, I had one more ill-advised outburst. We rode a charter bus to West Lafayette, Indiana, to play in the Big 10/SEC Challenge. The games were held at Purdue University's Mackey Arena, which was a cozy gym. It was a long ride and my first exposure to what a student-athlete deals with when they travel for a road game or multi-day tournament. Some of them were reading textbooks, while others were reviewing class notes. Keep in mind, we left on Wednesday morning, which meant the players missed three consecutive days of classes. Road trips for student athletes are not about sightseeing. After practice, we had meals and study hours at the hotel. We even did walk-throughs at the hotel by putting tape on the carpet in one of the hotel ballrooms to represent key spots on the court based on our opponent's offensive schemes. The focus was on the game and trying to return home with a win, while also keeping up with academics.

During the game, Kim and I quietly commented on two of the referee calls. At least I thought my comments were not being heard by anyone else. It was mostly me joking around. Apparently one sarcastic comment crossed the line, however, and was not appreciated by one of the referees. His next time down the court, he ran by our bench, angrily pointed in our direction, and said, "That's enough. Next time, I will assess the bench with a technical foul!" I didn't murmur a word the entire second half. Thankfully, Coach was occupied by the action on the court and didn't hear about our shenanigan until we left on the bus. She took it better than we expected and told us to be careful in the future.

From this internship, I also learned about collegiate recruiting. I witnessed the recruiting experience from the initial planning stage to the wooing process that occurs during the athlete's actual campus visit. There is a significant amount of creativity and work that goes into every recruiting visit. It was standard for any program to print a jersey with the player's last name on it and stage a locker to depict what it would feel like to be a Wildcat basketball player.

We customized a pre-game hype video on the Jumbotron to simulate what it would feel like running out of the tunnel for a home game. Crowd noise is easy to replicate and blast through the speakers. Although it was just the recruit and her parents, a current player, and the coaching staff standing alone at half-court, staring at the rafters, it made a profound difference. The rest of us patiently waited and hoped the young athlete would accept the scholarship offer and commit soon after the visit to campus.

The recruiting process is a highly competitive environment, and high school kids have egos. Coaches try to include little things that might stand out to a prospect. Sure, playing time is the hot topic, but parents are smart to ask other questions about the program, especially the academic portion and the long-term benefits associated with being a UK Wildcat.

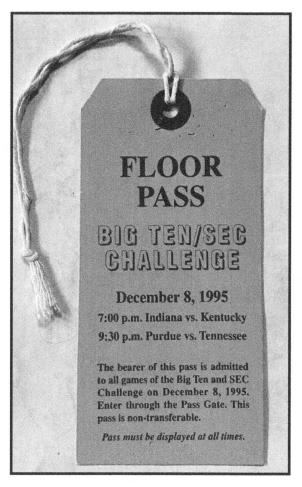

My game day credential and floor pass for the
Big 10 & SEC Challenge Tournament.

Me and a young hoopster at camp.

A Player's Perspective—Vonda (Jackson) Young #51

Now that you've heard my story, I thought you should hear from a player on the team also. In preparation for this book, I interviewed one of the power forwards who played on the team during my season as a student manager. Vonda Young grew up in eastern Kentucky, like me. She excelled at Clay County High School, in the coal mining town of Manchester. The school has a long-standing and successful boys' basketball program.

Vonda was the fifth child in a family of ten. Money was tight, yet her parents made sure every child played a sport. Initially, she wanted to be a cheerleader. Her dad told her she could not join the cheering squad, but she could play basketball or softball. Vonda's older sister, Lynn, was a talented hoopster and played on the eighth-grade team. Vonda followed in her footsteps and began playing basketball in the fourth grade.

From there, Vonda excelled and had an illustrious career. She played varsity for six seasons, helping her squad reach the Sweet 16 State Tournament in each of those seasons. She was named to the Sweet 16 All-Tourney Team in '92, '93, and '94. In 1992, her team finished as the State Runner-Up. During her high school career, she was one of two players to score 1,000 points and 1,000 rebounds. She finished with 1,956 points and 1,196 rebounds.

I asked Vonda when she first thought she might have a future in the game, and she referenced her junior year of high school. The recruitment letters from coaches began arriving daily. In fact, Vonda received hundreds of recruitment letters, if not more. Vonda realized she must be pretty good if colleges were reaching out to her and communicating so often with her high school coach. However, she kept a level head and dedicated time to more skill development. She despised losing more than anything, and she assumed every other basketball player shared her sentiment. Vonda was a fervent believer in doing whatever you could to win the game.

Her accomplishments caught the eye of major basketball programs, including the legendary University of Tennessee program. Head coach Pat Summitt paid Vonda an in-house recruiting visit, which was a highlight for the standout player. Vonda regretted not taking a photo with Coach Summitt. In the 1990s, the recruiting process differed greatly from what it is today. Coaches had to travel to see players in action. Now, every regular-season game and major summer tournament is available to watch online. Technology has improved access, but it has also made the process impersonal and less about building a relationship with each player.

The time, effort, and energy that go into being a collegiate athlete is something the public struggles to understand, yet pundits often voice their opinion on things students should do differently or better. Sports at the college level put a combination of mental and physical stress on the players. Vonda mentioned the importance of time management and self-motivation. If you lack these two traits, then you might not last long at any school, regardless of the division, academic rigors, and high expectations.

Vonda shared a glimpse of her personal struggle to adapt early in her college playing career. The preseason portion of the year was the most difficult. Lots of tears were shed daily for three weeks, but it did get easier for her. The biggest change from high school to college, she said, is that everything you do gets tougher. The conditioning, practices, academics, and general pressure are a powerful combination that quickly separates the pretenders from the ones who truly want to be there.

She mentioned how players typically have a positive experience playing on a team at any level benefit from lifelong friendships and a true sense of belonging. You run endless wind sprints with your teammates; you win and lose close games; and, when your legs are heavy, someone is there to pick you up and cheer for you. On a different day, it might be your turn to encourage a teammate or help them deal with a bad exam grade.

Vonda spoke highly of her high school and college teammates. It is a true sisterhood, and she said it is something everyone should experience because the team becomes your family away from home. She is grateful for modern technology because it allows her to keep in touch with her former teammates, as well as her high school coaches and one of her college coaches.

It was not all serious business, at least, not for Vonda, who had a penchant for speaking her mind and a bit of sarcastic humor to go along with it. One morning during her freshman year of college, she made an audacious comment she may or may not have wanted to take back. During preseason, the team focused on intense fitness and conditioning programs, which were held at 5:00 a.m. For whatever reason, Vonda was tired of the drill and brazenly asked if the team could do something different. The senior point guard started yelling at Vonda and repeatedly told her to *Shut up!* Seconds later, the entire team started running the concrete bleachers of the historic Memorial Coliseum. The trainer let them know the running would continue until he instructed them to stop. Unfortunately for Vonda, the screaming and frustration from her teammates did not cease.

Initially, Vonda chuckled, but after the third lap, pain set in. It was the last time she questioned the trainer during a conditioning session. She can laugh about it now, but as I listened to the story, my shins hurt just thinking about my experience of running concrete steps as a cross-country and track athlete in high school.

Toughest Player

During her freshman year at University of Kentucky, Vonda emphatically recalled the feeling that enveloped her body the first time she watched an opponent, the powerhouse Tennessee Volunteers, jog onto the floor. It was as if they were floating, and each player entered the arena in perfect step with the player in front of her. At this point in the season, Vonda had made the starting five for the Wildcats, which meant she lined up against one or two of the top ten players in the country. The first possession was predictable: three passes and a missed jump shot. When she turned around, her opponent came down with the rebound and looked like she was seven feet tall with sculpted arms like a bodybuilder. Vonda remembers seeing her face filled with fury and intensity. The opponent's bright orange mouthguard seemed to burn a hole through the gym floor. At that moment, Vonda knew it was more than just a game at this level. The long hours of conditioning, weight room sessions, and practice had prepared her body, but now her mind had to match the intensity of her prolific competitor. She was a long way from tiny Clay County High School, but she remembered it was still the game she loved, and she never backed down from a tough challenge.

I was proud to represent the program as a student manager intern that season, and I appreciated the friends I made. Often the student managers would be the first ones to arrive at practice, which meant we had the historic Memorial Coliseum to ourselves. We played countless rounds of H-O-R-S-E, launched half-court shots, and played every other basketball game that came to mind. Even as an adult, it never gets old pretending you hit the game-winning shot, especially when you grow up a UK fan. The players are the stars of the show, but interns are essential, and internships are a crucial part of preparing for a career in sports.

My Thoroughblades staff credential.

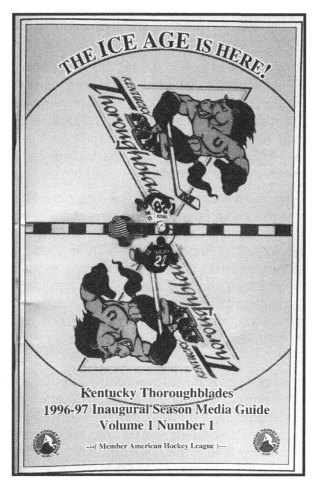

Kentucky Thoroughblades Media Guide.

I mentioned earlier that I changed majors. When my second senior year finally arrived, I still had to complete an internship to earn my degree. Lexington, Kentucky, is known for two sports: thoroughbred horse racing and college basketball. It is a mid-size city with limited sports jobs. I did not have the option to be picky. The city happened to be hosting a lower-level PGA charity tournament at the time. I met with a friend who handled their marketing and promotions. Unfortunately, nothing worked out, but he helped me revamp my résumé and cover letter.

Kentucky is a basketball-crazed state and always will be. In the fall of 1995, a New England businessman, Ron DeGregorio, announced that a minor league hockey team would call Rupp Arena home. The owner conducted a "Name the Team" contest. "The Kentucky Thoroughblades" came out on top. The Thoroughblades were the triple A affiliate for the AHL (American Hockey League) San Jose Sharks, triple-A being the highest level in the minor leagues of hockey.

Someone told me about internship opportunities in the Thoroughblades' game entertainment and promotions department. I thought it would be a perfect fit for my personality. Later in the week, I called the gameday entertainment director to hopefully set up an interview. Smartphones were still years away. Each day for a week, I ran home to check my answering machine to see if she had called. I anxiously awaited her response while wondering if I should call her again or not. I left her five or six voicemails. I was almost ready to quit trying and change direction when she finally called me back to schedule an interview. Both patience and persistence were rewarded!

The following week, I raced downtown for my interview. The gameday entertainment director acknowledged my determination and apologized for her delay in responding, explaining that the office schedule had been chaotic. The fact that I kept calling proved I was not giving up. The lesson stuck with me for a long time. If I had given up after two or three calls, who knows how my career would have turned out?

Me and the official Kentucky Thoroughblades Dodge-sponsored truck at a team promotional event.

Walle Adams-Gerdts

The person I called was named Walle. Her passion, creative mind, and high energy level made her perfectly suited to her job. Walle exuded a positive attitude and incessant energy every day, and it was impossible to be in a bad mood when you were working with her. Her background in radio promotions had prepared her for her role in more ways than one. She had conducted popular contests in the Lexington area, and a number of them had taken place in front of the largest shopping mall in town, which would pay dividends in an unlikely way later on.

The owner of the Thoroughblades, being an outsider to Lexington, knew that a top priority was to identify a local businessman who could quickly establish a rapport with both community leaders and corporate executives. Such people are vital for ticket sales, as well as sponsorship dollars. The general manager of the local Sears department store was chosen to lead the team. When Walle interviewed, he said to her, "I am familiar with your work and know what you are capable of."

I initially wrote this section based on my limited and vague memories of my internship with the Thoroughblades. But I knew it was missing significant pieces of the story. I had not kept in touch with Walle, and given that twenty-five years had passed, I thought I would not be able to find her. A month before I submitted this manuscript to my editor, a college buddy of mine who also worked for the team changed my mind. He told me I should try to track her down. On a whim, I headed to google. com, found her company, and left her a voicemail within the hour. We set up a Zoom interview and I was able to include Walle's perspective in the stories that follow.

When I asked her if she loved that job, her answer was a resounding yes. She recalled that she worked closely with ticket sales, media relations, and marketing, but when the puck stopped, it was her show! She praised her talented and professional team who brought the zany promotions to life forty nights each season—a number she said she will never forget.

The name of the team's mascot was Lucky, and his suit cost $5,000 to make. The employee who eventually stepped inside the costume spent hours on the phone interviewing other pro mascots to learn the nuances and best practices from some of the best in the business. He knew the team and its new mascot would be scrutinized by local media and fans, and he wanted to deliver a premium performance the first time he touched the ice, and every time thereafter.

Another vital element of the game entertainment plan is how the team enters the ice. It usually involves loud music, lasers, and a hype video. Walle wanted something both kids and adults would talk about long after the game ended. She refused to settle for something simple like every other team used. The staff worked with a promotional company in Florida to design a one-of-a-kind entrance piece for when the team skated onto the ice.

The team spent $25,000 on an intricate and well-designed archway. As sometimes happens with any type of construction project, the massive horse head and associated artwork fell behind schedule. Walle logged sleepless nights for weeks and started to doubt if the piece would make it to Lexington in time for opening night. The company promised her it would. To ensure a safe and timely delivery, they drove it to Lexington from Florida. It arrived hours before the puck dropped in Rupp Arena.

The anticipation, stress, and effort leading up to opening night culminated in an emotional outburst in the form of happy tears and a giant smile. Walle proudly watched the first player skate out from underneath the vibrantly colored, horseshoe-shaped arch. Walle told me she was responsible for the crucial signal to trigger the pyrotechnics, lights, and music. She had one job, and she missed her mark. Thankfully, the game entertainment team had rehearsed it multiple times. Another employee made the call, and the fireworks, lights and music were in sync at precisely the right moment.

It wouldn't be the only time Walle missed a special call. Her team produced a major fan contest on opening night: a $10,000 slap shot contest from center ice. These types of promotions are popular with sports teams at every level, but what the public does not realize is that someone has to negotiate the legal aspects, including rules, waiver forms, and the provision of video proof in case any ambiguity or discrepancy occurs. A local car dealership had agreed to sponsor the event and covered the $2,000 insurance policy. If the shot went in, the promotional company would be sending a $10,000 check to the winner.

Walle made sure everyone was ready for the big event. The contestant was escorted to the official line, and the PA announcer encouraged the crowd to get loud. Live entertainment is a beautiful thing to watch unfold, but sometimes the smallest detail is the key to success. Walle looked down at the ice and saw the contestant taking a warmup swing and thought she had a moment to check in with a staffer. As she turned away from the ice, the contestant fired his shot, and the PA announcer screamed, "Oh my God, he made it!" The arena erupted as the puck slid through the hole and into the net! Walle quickly turned around and was speechless. How had she missed it? She was frantic: not only had she missed seeing it with her own eyes, but what if the cameraman had missed it too? How would they prove it to the promotional company? This was one of her worst fears.

She regained her composure and slowly asked the question: "Uh, guys, please tell me someone got that on video. Please? Please?"

"Yes, we did, Walle. We're good!"

Her primary responsibility was to book performers for the intermissions. These individuals likely made good money traveling the country entertaining fans with their special skills and talents. Zigzagging the country entails long days and nights on the road, not to mention juggling the event-booking calendar. Think about the large number of games being played in the various professional leagues during seasons of anywhere from 82 to 162 games. Now, multiply that by five or six major leagues. And that doesn't even include minor league sports.

Needless to say, this part of the planning process requires a centralized spot to keep notes as the performers are confirmed for various promotions. Walle had a massive five-foot-wide Microsoft Excel-style programming calendar that spanned the entire season, which was over six months long. This allowed everyone on the team to stay on the same page and work seamlessly for what sometimes amounted to eighty promotions: forty home games per season times two intermissions per game.

We opened the season in early October and concluded our last regular-season game in mid-April. Like most teams, we had theme nights, such as *Star Wars*, '80s Night, Boy Scouts and Girl Scouts, and other common promotions every sports team hosts.

The critical part of a game day promotion is ensuring it will work as planned with no visible hiccups. There is nothing worse than a promotion that falls flat in a sports arena. It is embarrassing for the partner, the team, and the contestants. Thankfully, the game resumes after the timeout, but sometimes the damage is done and the blooper is shared repeatedly on local television broadcasts or across social media platforms.

The ice element of the rink surface added a challenge to every promotion. One afternoon, we experimented with industrial-sized inner tubes and dubbed it the "Human Slingshot." The plan was for the fan to sit in the tube, be pulled backwards by oversized elastic bands that, when released, propelled the inner tube and fan across the ice, and then see which contestant traveled the furthest distance.

One by one, each of us tried to slide across the ice, but one student's tube kept getting stuck after we released the tension on the resistance band. This simple promotion turned into a discussion of scientific and mathematical principles as we all tried to figure out what was going wrong.

We finally talked to the ice manager. It turned out that the student didn't weigh enough. The ice manager mentioned that one option was to use a small amount of ski wax, which would not affect the ice. The other option was to give a gentle push as the band was being released to ensure the tube would have some momentum. One attempt later, the extra push did the trick and our problem was solved.

Walle reminded me how crucial it was for her to maintain a close relationship with Rupp Arena's primary user, the University of Kentucky men's basketball team. After some home games, the conversion crew spent hours assembling the basketball court. Walle did not want to do anything that would jeopardize the court or cause a delay in the conversion process. She mentioned the owner of the Thoroughblades paid for the conversion crew and associated expenses.

It was great to reconnect with Walle because her stories helped round out the material for this chapter. We both enjoyed reminiscing and the opportunity to catch up after all these years. Best of all, I only had to call her once this time.

Walle Adams-Gerdts, May 2023.

Post-game recap: Internships and part-time jobs provide valuable opportunities to gain hands-on experience and develop lifelong job skills. The salary is disheartening, as you will work for free or three hundred dollars per month, but I promise, it is worth it. Try to listen and learn from the people in charge of the department where you work. Pay attention to their mannerisms, attitude, how they interact with others and ultimately manage their job duties. You are only there for a limited time, usually three to six months. Be sure to ask lots of questions and try to establish a connection with at least one employee to network with. It is your responsibility to leave a good impression, which will hopefully create a dialogue for future job opportunities.

Chapter 4
Selling My Sole
Lexington, Kentucky 1996–1998

My name tag while working at The Finish Line.

Pre-game: Two of the most stressful years in my life were my senior year of high school and my senior year of college. As a dreamer, I was enamored by the opportunities available to me in the wide-open world at my fingertips. I was frightened, too, but mostly excited about my future and where life might lead me.

Looking back, I wish I had taken a year off to travel, volunteer, or even work part-time in a foreign country. Society often pushes a life script in which everyone should go to college, get a degree, and start working right away. We all have forty years to work, but some life experiences are invaluable, and you cannot place a dollar amount on them.

I did all the right things and worked diligently at all my internships, yet for over a year I could not secure a sports-related job.

I politely declined a regional position with the Boy Scouts of America, even though I was an Eagle Scout. I knew I was not passionate about it and would always be looking for an opportunity in sports.

It disappointed me that I did not land a cool job in a new city right away, like my peers. Sometimes I felt left behind. It was frustrating because I had worked hard to find an entry-level sports job. One thing I did know is that my mind was set on moving to the western region of the country. Soon, an opportunity arose that would help me achieve that goal: an Assistant Manager position in Lexington, Kentucky, with a rapidly expanding athletic shoe company, The Finish Line.

It was a job with plenty of upside, but in my heart, I knew I was biding my time until I landed that elusive and highly coveted sports job. I was grateful and excited to escape the retail world and ready for the next challenge. Based on what I had read about the company, it seemed like an excellent place to learn more about corporate sponsorship, sports marketing, and sales in the college market. Plus, the position was a true sports job. I finally caught my break.

Introduction

As you approach your final year of college—or fifth year, in the author's case—you anxiously look forward to landing the coveted first job. It is a stressful time filled with uncertainty, guarded optimism, boundless questions, and fear of the unknown. Often, close friends compare interview notes, talk about lofty dreams, and promise to visit one another in whatever city or small town they land in. Seniors invest time and money for interviews near campus, around the state, and, of course, across the country. The uncertainty is difficult to tame, even though everyone is battling the same fear. It often feels as if you are the only one without a good job lead. Do your best not to compare yourself to everyone else. Be patient, because your time will come.

I worked for a retail department store during my high school years. It was a great experience for learning how to deal with the public. My time there taught me key lessons about problem-solving and treating everyone with respect.

I worked in menswear and shoes, primarily. From time to time, I helped assemble bikes in the toy section. Buying shoes is a personal choice, and consumers can be picky. Whenever you spend hard-earned money on a high-priced item you are passionate about, it is only natural to have high expectations for the product. When these expectations are not met, you want your money back, and you voice your frustration with the innocent cashier who is working that day.

During my final year of college, I needed a part-time job. Three of my friends worked at an athletic retail store, which is how I secured an interview, and a job, with The Finish Line in the Fayette Mall in Lexington. We called it "TFL" for short. At the time, The Finish Line was one of three athletic retail chains that focused on sneakers.

Every sales associate's daily sales performance was tracked for personal development and growth opportunities. We did not receive any type of sales commission, but anyone working on the sales floor was expected to sell a minimum of two items per transaction. The Finish Line's name for this was UPT (Units Per Transaction). It may sound petty, but every dollar counts in retail. Simply put, if every associate sold an additional item at $5, it would be great for the bottom line of the store and the company. If the store sold $500 in accessories each month, along with $10,000 in shoes, that extra $500 added up over a year's time.

The other accessories were the different colors and styles of shoelaces. The laces were priced at $1.99, an easy add-on when you are spending $120 on a pair of running shoes. It is a simple way to change the aesthetics of the shoe and allows you to show some of your personality.

The Shoe Wall

The first thing a customer saw when they entered our store was the massive shoe wall. By design, it stretched from the floor to the ceiling. The material consisted of bright, shiny oak that resembled a basketball court. It served as the focal point for the store and was eye-catching from the outside. It began at the store entrance and stretched the length of the store.

The newest shoe style was strategically featured on the first panel and often duplicated to highlight our inventory. There were also display stands featured in the store window for mall patrons casually passing by. Window shopping was a focal point for brands, and we wanted to let customers know when we had the latest color or shoe in stock.

The shoe wall was also where we stood patiently waiting for customers to browse the wall and then turn to ask if we had their size. Similar to the kitchen in a house, the shoe wall served as our unofficial meeting spot to congregate and catch up with our teammates on life and comical customer stories.

Pro forms

A pro form is a discount program for retail employees. Each shoe company labeled it something different. It is a tri-folding brochure that listed a short list of styles for 40 to 50 percent off the retail price. It provided us with an affordable way to try different brands of shoes. Then we could speak intelligently with customers about the comfort and other features of the shoes. After all, we were standing on our feet eight to ten hours a day, and we knew the importance of comfort. We sometimes brought a second pair of shoes to work with us to change if our feet got tired after a long day. Besides, how can you pass up a $40 pair of Nikes?

The best and worst part of the job was that being around sneakers for forty-five hours a week meant you talked about sneakers every day. We knew every brand, the price ranges, and what new color scheme was scheduled to be released next. Your coworkers sported new shoes and the employee discount meant you could buy two or three pairs for a reasonable amount of money. It did not feel like peer pressure, but we all owned different styles of shoes. One day you might wear Nike Air Max, and other days it was a pair of Vans or Airwalks, even if you did not own a skateboard. We halfheartedly justified purchasing multiple pairs to protect our feet and back.

Everyone on our team had different opinions on their favorite brands and style of shoe. One teammate raved about the Adidas Trail Response trail running shoes and bought a new pair every time a new color scheme was released. The one shoe we all agreed on was the Nike Air Max '95. This is a quintessential shoe when referencing culture and the cool factor. The other one would be Nike's all-leather, low-top Air Force 1s. Those will never go out of style.

Customer Stories

Anytime you work with the public and money is involved, one thing is guaranteed: you will encounter wacky stories and interesting personalities at every turn. The shoe industry was no exception. Often you walk away from the awkward situation with a sense of gratitude because you realize your own personality quirks are quite normal.

We had our fair share of eccentric customers at our store. One avid runner insisted on buying an untouched pair of Air Max running shoes, size 10.5. He refused to buy one if someone else had tried them on. If the paper inside the shoe box was torn, he would tell us someone tried them on and demand we return to the stock room for a new pair.

Most kids were passionate about the high-profile shoes, and they would buy whatever size we had available, regardless of if the shoes were one or two sizes too small or too big for them. A high school student would stroll in with his friends and ask for a size 12 in the new Air Jordans. On high-profile shoe release days, our team knew the exact number of each size we had in stock. All we had left was a 9.5. The response was, "I'll take it. I will make it fit." I never understood it, but it was a common occurrence for any popular sneaker. Kids and even adults just had to have the new shoes of their favorite players.

The stockroom was more like a locker room. The radio stayed cranked up to allow us to vent about difficult customers. Once you closed the door and left the sales floor, you had free reign to cut loose. It was a multi-purpose room and a safe place to yell when you were dealing with a rude customer. The nice thing was there was usually a teammate to commiserate with as you unleashed your rant of the day. Depending on the day and the customer, sometimes they laughed at you, and other times, they joined in and laughed with you.

Colorful Coworkers

I met a colorful cast of characters during my two-year stint and a couple of them remain dear friends twenty-five years later. Here is a closer look at the personalities and a few stories that originated from simply selling sneakers at the Fayette Mall.

Rob King

Rob was a sales associate who grew up in Charleston, West Virginia. He had started at The Finish Line during high school as a part-time sales associate. Prior to landing the job, he was already a fan of sneakers, and the job just reinforced his passion for them.

An older gentleman taught Rob exactly how to maximize his units per transaction. The plan was simple, but yielded powerful results, and he practiced it for years after that fateful coaching session. When a customer decides to purchase shoes, do not give them back; just point to where the cashier is located. The sale might be over, but the opportunity to add multiple items is just beginning. Hold onto their shoe box as you genuinely thank them for the purchase. Then lead them to the checkout. This casual walk past the socks, hats, and T-shirts is your chance to show the customer other products and suggest add-on items. Last, you put the shoe box on the checkout counter and thank them once more. It is a simple system, and it all hinges on carrying the box to the checkout and taking a little more time to interact with the customer along the way.

Here is how I would describe Rob: uber-competitive, a great teammate, constantly smiling, with a big heart and a personality to match. Rob was an authentic shoe geek, and he knew more about brands, technology, special editions, and what new products were on the horizon than anyone else on our team. Rob played point guard on his high school basketball team, and he was one of our top leaders on the sales floor. A great sales associate quickly adapts to the customer's personality and can talk about anything. Rob put his customers at ease with his friendly tone and attention to detail. His ability to listen patiently to their wants and needs was key to his success.

Our friendship was cemented by overnight business trips to Louisville, Kentucky, and Indianapolis, Indiana, to assist other Finish Line stores. Our favorite trip was when the city of Indianapolis hosted the NCAA Men's Basketball Final Four. The entire city was filled with enthusiastic sports fans, and the store was packed every day. The hours rushed by, and we did not have time to stand around.

Of course, being in our twenties, we stayed out late and enjoyed the city's nightlife. Those nights and the stories that arose from it still make me laugh and smile today. We were young, and our bodies required little sleep. After all, we'd just had to stand on our feet for eight hours and talk about running shoes with customers. When the workday ended, we still had energy left.

Because Rob was usually the top salesman on our team, other stores would invite him to visit and conduct some unofficial sales training by allowing other employees to watch him in action. One particular trip provided another valuable life lesson for Rob. The store manager had worked in our Lexington location and asked Rob to visit his store in Tennessee to show his staff how to sell more sneakers and multiple items per transaction. At the end of Rob's shift, the manager handed him a mop and a bucket of soapy water.

Confused, Rob commented, "Why in the world are you asking me to mop? You asked me to come down here to show your staff how to sell, not how to mop the floors."

The manager replied, "Rob, you are correct. However, if my team sees that the #1 salesperson mops the floor just like anyone else, it will teach them a lesson far more valuable than a creative sales tactic."

Rob nodded in agreement and mopped the floor. He never forgot the lesson, and it reminded him of the importance of teamwork and not letting your ego get the best of you.

Rob was the type of coworker you looked forward to seeing when your shift began, because you knew he would make you laugh and help the day go by faster. Rob was a dedicated friend inside and outside the store to me and others too.

In his current job at Astorg Auto, Rob routinely wins sales contests at the Mercedes-Benz dealership. Instead of being excited about a high-end running shoe, he now shares his excitement for luxurious cars, some surpassing the $200,000 price range. I am not a car guy, but something tells me if I stopped by to visit Rob, I would walk out of the dealership with an expensive new ride. After all, he leads the sales team in after-market purchases.

I am proud to call him a friend, and I admire his success. When I scan Facebook and see his sunny poolside photos from his latest incentive vacation, I simply shake my head and smile. I knew he would win the contest before it even began.

*Rob King working at The Finish Line
in Charleston, West Virginia.*

Jimmy K

Most of my interviews for the book were conducted by phone, and Jimmy Khounlavong was no different. It is always good to reconnect with old friends. The first five minutes we reminisced about our college days and the time we worked together selling shoes.

Because his name is longer than what we were accustomed to, we called my friend Jimmy Khounlavong simply "Jimmy K." But the nickname was more than an end run around the challenge of pronunciation. In the south, giving someone a nickname is a term of endearment, a critical component of developing meaningful friendships, and can be argued to be a natural part of life. Jimmy wasn't immune to it. Neither was I. You can only imagine the number of derivatives of "Tosti" that exist to this day.

Growing up as a Lao American in eastern Kentucky was difficult. Being a minority in a homogenous area of the country can have its challenges. Discovering sports and sneaker culture changed the direction of Jimmy's life. These passions became a medium for friendships, an outlet for expression, and the launch pad for a career.

Jimmy's career began humbly with a part-time job at his local Finish Line store in Ashland, Kentucky, while he was still in high school. He was instantly hooked, and when he transitioned to the Lexington location during college, his view of the sneaker world expanded even further. As he talked to more customers from different walks of life, he realized he had a gift for encouraging customers to open up and talk—whether about the latest Olympic race, a recent basketball game, or, better yet, what they wore on their feet. Sport brings people together, and Jimmy found himself having honest conversations with strangers that never would have occurred outside the mall environment. Age, socioeconomic status, ethnicity, and nationality were irrelevant, even if for only five minutes.

For sneaker fans, remembering a good shoe is like hearing a great song that you forgot about. They recall the day, the moment, and the impact the shoe had on their lives. Shoes received titles such as "the Flu Game," "Concords," "Space James," and the list goes on and on. It would be unfair to call sneaker collecting a hobby. To collectors, sneakers are much more than an everyday purchase.

Jimmy's passion for sneakers, coupled with his gregarious nature, made Jimmy our top salesperson. His smooth voice and demeanor could have landed him a career in broadcasting. Jimmy was quick on his feet and had an uncanny ability to make people feel comfortable. Moreover, he was a student of the game. He constantly researched the latest brands and newest technologies, and he knew how to apply the knowledge to best serve our customers. When selecting running shoes, there are basic technical questions one should ask to correctly assist an individual's specific needs. Because there are different body types, running styles, and biomechanics involved, it is best to learn the needs of the person first, then find the right technology, fit, and cushioning necessary for the person's intended use. Are they a heel or a forefoot striker? Are they a neutral runner, or do they over-pronate? Add style preference, and the customer is at risk of experiencing the paradox of having an excess of choices that they do not know what to buy. And buying the wrong thing is almost worse for the store–customer relationship than buying nothing.

Finding the right shoe for each customer was a matter of pride for Jimmy. Jimmy excelled at listening to the customer's questions, and he put effort into understanding their needs and mindset before blurting out a long-winded and boring technical response. Establishing a relationship was always at the forefront. Just making the sale was never his motive; his goal was always to form a relationship. To do that, he focused on the happiness and satisfaction of the client. It was about making The Finish Line the customer's go-to source for sneakers for the next decade. Return clients would ask for Jimmy by name when it came time to buy the next pair of shoes for themselves or family members.

Jimmy parlayed his love of sneakers and servicing the athlete into a career at Nike for over sixteen years. During his time at "the Swoosh," he experienced a variety of sales, merchandising, and leadership roles. He also worked in his dream categories, such as basketball, running, and sportswear. While at Nike, he lived in Chicago, Detroit, Portland, and Los Angeles—that last one as general manager of Nike Sportswear Los Angeles.

Jimmy experienced success at each stop with Nike, and he loved every minute of it. Being able to give back to the culture and community that welcomed him was truly a full-circle experience and an accomplishment he is immensely proud of.

Jimmy K sporting his Nike Air Max running shoes.

Jon Andrews

Jon and I worked at TFL with Rob and Jimmy K. Jon was filled with positive energy, and considered a hustler, but in a good way, not lazy at all. Jon was a pleasure to be around and could make someone laugh without trying. Bad days were a rarity when he was around, and his can-do attitude stood out amongst our team members. Jon and I were also roommates for a short time. Jon was an avid gamer and made me look foolish in *Super Mario*

Kart and the uber-popular *James Bond GoldenEye 007* game. Somehow, he moved seamlessly from room to room, warding off the animated villains, while I remained stuck in the corner pointing my weapon at the ceiling and spinning in circles. It was pure entertainment for Jon, and I do not blame him for cackling nonstop at me during those memorable late nights.

Jon grew up in South Bend, Indiana, and was an avid University of Notre Dame fan, as well as a big Adidas and soccer guy. Everyone enjoyed working with Jon because he was a nice guy and smiled often. He also happened to have damn near perfect handwriting, which came in handy for updating the shoe names and styles on The Finish Line's shoe wall.

I remember that the first $180 shoe was a Nike product. Anfernee "Penny" Hardaway's new shoe was called "Foamposite." We all knew the high price point would generate complaints if any part of the shoe was defective or wore out too quickly. The price was eye-opening for shoe geeks and sales reps across the industry. Nike is known for investing time and money in research, and this shoe was an expensive one to bring to market. The price was justified from a business standpoint, but the customers were not as concerned with the research involved, nor even the hefty price tag. The shoe was immensely popular, and no other basketball shoe looked like it.

Jon and I reminisced about the sinking feeling we used to get when a regular customer walked in carrying a Finish Line bag. We knew what that meant: a return. Returns were dreaded because the transaction negatively impacted your sales goals for the day. Nothing was worse than a slow sales day when three of your regular customers decided to stop by the store to return a purchase.

He also reminded me about the Rain & Stain display hat. Rain & Stain was a waterproofing spray we carried and politely recommended to customers. It came in an oversized aerosol can. We had a display hat that was treated with Rain & Stain, and we would spritz the hat with water to show the spray's effectiveness. When water hit the hat, it instantly created gigantic bubbles and rolled off.

Jon is a good buddy of mine to this day and can always make me laugh. When we talk, a Finish Line reference is often mentioned, along with a hearty laugh. He is a talented artist and created the cover art for this book, as well as for my first book, *Who We Meet Along the Way*.

*Me and Jon Andrews eating breakfast
in Lexington, KY March 2024.*

John McCarty

John McCarty was one of the store's Assistant Managers. He was a highly respected shoe industry veteran. I remember he possessed an immense mental catalog of old-school, iconic shoes and athletic apparel. He could rattle off the names and price points of any shoe from the past decade. It felt like he had a sneaker history degree and a minor in athletic brand T-shirts.

John's expertise was matched by his big personality. He grew up on a thirty-acre farm in eastern Kentucky. He had a booming voice and was loud by nature. I think he missed his calling as a football coach, specifically the offensive line. Whether he was aggravating a close buddy or correcting a rookie employee, the volume of his voice was intense and frightening at first.

He was hilarious and friendly, but brutally honest. One prime example of this was his photographic memory of the shoe wall and what shoes were available in our stock room based on the remaining sizes. After we closed each night, one of us had to restock the shoe wall while John counted the cash registers and prepared the nightly deposit. John's good buddy Derek joked how much he hated when John was the closing manager and he got stuck with restocking the shoe wall. It was pressure-packed, and Derek knew what to expect when he misplaced a shoe or forgot to pull the correct style or new color that should be on display. Like a snarky game show host, John would walk over to the shoe wall and, with no remorse, start flipping shoes and tossing them on the floor, saying, "Wrong, wrong, wrong!"

John had lofty standards and wanted our team to take pride in our store. Perfection meant something to him and he wanted us to follow his lead. Even though it frustrated Derek more than anything, the coaching propelled him to a newfound attention to detail. The following year, Derek's hard work and commitment paid off. He won the prestigious Manager of the Year award for the entire company. He called his friend and former boss, John, to thank him because he is convinced that he wouldn't have won it without John pushing him to be the best.

I also remember his personality and genuine appreciation of life itself. It was a simple, yet insightful mindset. In addition, he was a passionate fan of rock and roll and seemed to live life to the fullest and did not take crap or mince words with anyone, ever! If you are John's friend, you never know what he will say next, but you are always glad you are there to hear it.

John currently lives in Lexington, Kentucky, where he has worked in the Coroner's office for the past twenty-five years. It is a tough job and not suited for everyone. John and his department deal with death every day. As you might imagine, some days are worse than others, but what he sees and encounters is not easily discarded. He shared a powerful description with me about his job and life itself: "I've been in tiny shacks and million-dollar mansions, but people should know that grief doesn't care about the amount of money you make."

John is known for his tough-guy exterior, but this job has changed his emotional outlook on life. When he is at work, he focuses on the task at hand, but when he finishes his shift, he goes to concerts, hangs out with friends and family and just has fun in life. Often, he will tell someone on scene, "Listen, you don't know me and the reason we crossed paths today is for a terrible reason, but you are my family today."

He still cranks his tunes up loud whenever he can. The only difference for this shoe junkie is that after four knee surgeries, he officially made the conversion from Nike to Brooks. As he put it, "I now choose comfort over style." He told me he owns twelve pairs of Brooks running shoes. To my fellow sneakerhead, I applaud you for what you taught me during my time at store #136. I am proud of you for what you do for the Lexington community, one challenging day at a time.

John McCarty enjoying down time at the office.

Andy Brumett

Andy was another memorable teammate of mine. He was soft-spoken, nice to everyone, and possessed an encyclopedic knowledge of Nike's most famous spokesman, Michael Jordan. Andy has an impressive collection of the popular Air Jordan basketball shoes and has spent hours studying articles and combing sneaker websites to stay on top of special releases, color variations, and collector news. To say Andy is a dedicated collector is an understatement. Let me explain why. When a new edition of Air Jordans was released, Andy bought three pairs: one to leave unopened for preservation and investment purposes, one to wear for basketball (in rotation with other shoes, in order to last longer), and one for casual wear.

A decade ago, he estimated his current collection of sneakers topped 1,000 pairs. He has them stored in various climate-controlled storage areas in different cities. I had to ask him the obvious question: which pair is his favorite? I gave him an easy out and told him he could list his top four. Here they are, in no order:

- Air Jordan XI. This is an often-mentioned fan favorite because of the sleek look and style of the shoe. The Concord variant, with its black patent leather, could be referred to as the tuxedo of sneakers.

- Air Jordan III and IV. When these were released, there was nothing like these shoes on the market.

- Air Jordan VI. This is the shoe Michael Jordan wore when he won the first of his six NBA Championships.

These days, Andy and his wife, a professional equestrian, run a multi-faceted horse boarding and training facility in Indiana. Her primary focus is the English riding style. Andy jokingly told me she doesn't say too much about his gigantic shoe collection because her passion isn't exactly cheap, either.

A small sample of Andy's Air Jordan collection.

Campus Concepts
Baltimore, MD 1997-1998

Campus Concepts

BRANDON TOSTI
Sports Marketing
Regional Manager

312 North Charles Street
Baltimore, Maryland 21201
(410) 625-0044 • Fax (410) 625-0065
btosti@campusconcepts.com

This innovative sports marketing company was based in Baltimore, Maryland, but employed regional sales representatives across the country. As I look back now, I realize the owner was ahead of his time as it related to corporate sponsorship and integration to reach the coveted college-student demographic. The company started with basic bulletin boards located inside campus recreation centers. Campus Concepts covered the cost of the boards, and each campus agreed to post a small sponsor advertisement on the left side of the board. The remaining 80 percent of the space the university could use as the campus recreation manager saw fit.

Each month, the university took photos and submitted them to the corporate office as part of the fulfillment effort. This was proof to the sponsor that their national ad was indeed included for the month or two stated in their contract. These boards reached thousands of college students in campus recreation centers across the country. The sponsors did not care about rankings or which conference the school's football team played in. They cared about impressions and converting students to lifetime customers.

The next national promotion involved credit cards. The days of setting up a table and a vinyl banner in the student center were long gone. Credit card companies were trying creative methods to reach the college market. This concept had a slight twist: it featured a Pop-a-Shot basketball game. The plan was to lure students into the game and attempt to get them to sign up for a new credit card. The promotional return was not as high as we hoped, and six months later, 80 percent of us were laid off and the company shifted to a new program.

Now, those static bulletin boards are digital and rotate corporate ads every thirty seconds. I must give the owner of Campus Concepts credit. In 1998, well before digital advertising and social media, he realized the potential of the college market, and he devised a creative method to break into it long before others did.

For six months, I would load up my 1992 Buick Regal with a fold-up Pop-A-Shot basketball game and headed north to various college campuses. I covered twenty-two schools across Kentucky, Ohio, Michigan, Indiana, and even one or two schools in Pennsylvania. I spent five lonely nights per week on the road during this time. Being an extrovert, I found the hardest part was eating dinner by myself four nights a week. Sometimes, I would meet the Campus Recreation Director for a beer, but they often headed home to spend time with their family. An older friend of mine in sales gave me some good advice. He told me to bring a newspaper to dinner to help as a distraction.

To pass the quiet nights, I would call friends and coworkers. I had nothing to tie me down or worry about back home, but I missed my friends and looked forward to Friday night when I knew I would be home, even if it was short lived, because I might leave on Sunday afternoon if the next campus included a long drive.

Cell phones at this time were still large plastic blocks with flimsy antennas. Cell phone minutes were costly, and when a consumer exceeded their monthly allotment, the rate quickly jumped from cents to dollars. Text messaging was non-existent. I vividly recall paying close to $500 for my cell phone bill one month when I'd made four six-hour drives.

One perk of this job was the occasional free ticket to see a game while I was in town. Once a University of Michigan student gave me a ticket to a home football game. The Big House, as their stadium is affectionately called, is a spectacle. It was and still is the largest college football stadium, with over 100,000 seats. The Detroit Red Wings of the National Hockey League had won the Stanley Cup the previous season, and they were featured on the field during the halftime show. It was the Northwestern University game when Michigan cornerback Charles Woodson made an incredible one-handed interception. Die-hard sports fans will know the play I am referring to; it is worth searching for it on YouTube. Woodson would win the coveted Heisman Trophy later that season.

The week after that game in Michigan, I passed on the opportunity to see an Ohio State home game. I hope to return to the Horseshoe someday, but that week, all the travel had caught up with me and nothing sounded better than sleeping in my own bed.

My view for the University of Michigan football game.

What I Learned About Sponsorship

Sponsorship is commonly defined as a brand spending money with an event or an entity to receive recognition or a benefit for the investment. It allows consumers an opportunity to interact with brands at sporting events, music festivals, and other large events. Sponsorship industry veterans often refer to it as *bringing the brand to life*. The technical term is "sponsor activation," and typically includes some type of on-premise display, tent, or exhibit. Contests, games, and conducting giveaways are common themes.

I spent most of my career in sponsorship. I thoroughly enjoyed it because of the creativity involved and the people I worked with. The experience prepared me for quick thinking as it relates to conflict resolution, brand awareness, and understanding what sets a brand apart from its competitors.

Every product has a target demographic or market the brand is trying to reach. Companies invest major funds in behavior research, sales reporting, and other performance indicators. A billboard advertisement on a highway or a mobile app does not provide the same effect as a memorable interaction or branded souvenir a fan receives at an event.

Companies are constantly attempting to position themselves to be the brand of choice for the younger consumer. They invest significant amounts of time, research, and money trying to understand what drives consumer behavior, especially at the critical eighteen to twenty-two age range. Part of the push comes from the reality of the maturation process. This is the first time that college students must purchase their own laundry detergent, deodorant, toothpaste, and shaving gel. When I was in college, every residence hall student received a welcome box with a sample size of all these products.

The intramural sports program provided a new way for sponsors to reach young consumers. The wide variety of sports offered corporate sponsors the chance to be selective in which area they invested marketing dollars and sponsorship programs on respective campuses.

Sponsors were not looking for a simple billboard on a football field or an oversized poster inside a student recreation center wall. They wanted direct access to the students, and campus recreation served the purpose well. This program provided it to a coveted demographic.

Sponsorship is powerfully unique and difficult to understand if you are not engaged in it. When a company buys a radio or website ad, it is a simple business transaction. The company creates the ad and discusses the length of the promotion, then the media team runs the ads for the agreed-upon amount of time. They send a post-event summary to illustrate the number of times the ad ran and other relevant statistics such as number of viewers, audience reach, and impact.

A sponsor activation is an experience designed to be memorable. It allows brands to come to life and encourages consumers and fans to interact, touch, and hear about the brand. This can be accomplished by sampling new products, contests, or a simple chat with a fan at the event. Brand ambassadors or street team members engage with fans with no pressure, which encourages them to ask questions and learn more about their favorite brand or one they are seeing for the first time.

Sponsor activations typically include large, colorful signs and tents designed to attract people. It can also include oversized, branded vehicles. Creativity plays a major role, and the activation footprint creates memories which are often shared on social media platforms.

Companies spend thousands, and sometimes millions, of dollars on sponsorships each year. The initial investment begins with a contract negotiation and the right to be associated as an official sponsor with the event or team. Then the real work begins in the form of a sponsor activation because the brand must create an eye-catching way to highlight the brand to the customer base and event attendees.

The best activations are interactive, where a patron can touch, see, and hear more about the new product. If a beverage company launches a new flavor, the public might be hesitant to purchase a twelve-pack without knowing if they will like it or not. Sampling at events eliminates this barrier because the serving size is free and is two or three ounces. Not to mention, if it is a positive experience, they are likely to tell their friends about the new product and encourage them to buy it at the store.

Another intelligent move by the company was to incorporate sponsor assets as branding opportunities. Campus recreation budgets were limited, in most cases. Now, the recreation directors had access to new equipment including yard markers, basketballs, flags, and end zone markers. Corporate sponsors were not just buying advertising space on a banner or a photo. Their investment directly benefited each campus and increased awareness, and one might say popularity, of the recreational sports program offerings. Colleges could upgrade existing programs or create new opportunities with the incremental funding provided by sponsorship revenue.

Recreation center managers share best practices with their peers, just like any other industry. If it can work on one campus, then it is a safe bet it will work well on others too. Success is contagious, and it did not take long for word to spread.

Other relevant industry buzzwords are *recognition* and *recall*. This measures participants' memory as it pertains to what they remember about advertising, sponsor signs, and on-site activities. Studies conducted by sponsors were positive and proved the partnership was achieving marketing goals. It is important for brands to align themselves with customers and convert them into loyal fans.

Once the company cracked the code and gained a foothold through the campus recreation departments, the owners expanded programming options and integrated additional sponsors while maintaining professional relationships on campuses across the country. They were the industry leader and kept thinking of new methods and ways to expand the current business concept.

It wasn't restricted to traditional sports. Fitness and exercise are a major component of college life and provided yet another avenue for corporate sponsors to integrate into the daily life of college students who routinely worked out. A creative incentive-based program stemmed from this opportunity and helped students across the country stick to their fitness routines. Naturally, a national event was the next step in the process.

When the sponsorship contract expired, the sponsor chose to invest in other programs and properties. It made little sense for Campus Concepts to keep a high number of regional representatives on the payroll. This was the first time I heard the words, "Your position has been eliminated." Unfortunately, it would not be the last time.

This was the first disappointment and setback of my sports career, and I was heartbroken, confused, and frustrated. Luckily, I still had an apartment in Lexington and did not have to move to a new city and start over. I cannot imagine having to move to another city after such a short stint, but it does happen.

Although I did not love every aspect of the job, it would provide a base of knowledge of corporate partnerships I would use in the future. I enjoyed visiting college campuses and added memorable life experiences. Just when I thought I caught my break, I took a step back and started over. I felt a combination of embarrassment and failure, even though the circumstances were out of my control.

Me at the company's headquarters in Baltimore, Maryland.

One of my roommates still worked at The Finish Line and told me they would welcome me back. I knew I wanted nothing to do with selling sneakers again, because I had left the job for a reason, and partly because I was already feeling as if I had failed. A direct backward step was the last thing I wanted. But it was good that I had not burned that bridge. I ended up working as the backroom manager, handling inventory and weekly deliveries.

On the surface, it was a mindless job. I was happy not to deal with the public and the stress of worrying about my sales numbers. My job utilized different skills, such as thinking ahead and visualizing the future use of space. We packed the stock room shelves from top to bottom and shoe boxes wrapped around the room like a maze. Every two weeks, we shifted the shoes to make room for new styles, trendy fashion picks, and additional color schemes. Part of my job was to make this life-size *Tetris* game make sense, which required leaving ample space for the inevitable shift that was waiting for me less than a week later. The backroom was small. When our shipments arrived, we temporarily stacked the shoes in the emergency exit hallway we shared with other mall stores.

This job provided me with three things: a stable and predictable forty-hour week schedule, a low-stress job I didn't have to think about, and a safe landing spot until I figured out my next step.

> *Post-game recap: During my time at The Finish Line, I learned a tremendous amount regarding the shoe industry. The lessons ranged from technology to fabric and style choices. Other valuable skills I developed included salesmanship, visual merchandising, and the importance of providing outstanding customer service. I respected my managers and tried to learn from them. When it was time to move on, I made sure to leave on good terms, because you never know when you might need something from a former boss.*
>
> *Any job dealing with the public is tough, but it provides you with perspective on how you will treat others down the road. I am a sneakerhead at heart, but the odd hours and lack of a true office were major deterrents for me. I could have stayed and moved up as a manager and done well financially, but I was miserable, and retail was not in my future plans. When in doubt, follow your gut, because more money is not the right answer.*
>
> *Sometimes you take a chance in your career, and it does not work out as you hoped. Do not waste time questioning your decision. Learn from it and move forward. After two months of reflection, I knew I had to leave and find something I truly loved.*

Chapter 5

Grad School and the Gridiron
Center for Academic and Tutorial Services (CATS)
Lexington, Kentucky, 1999–2000

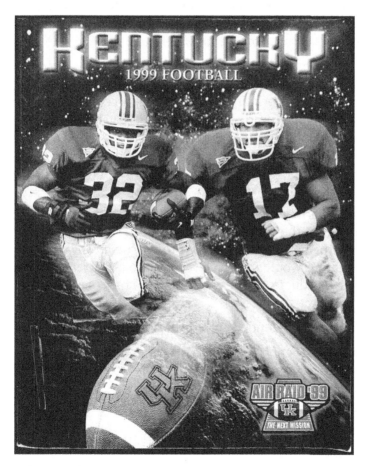

This was the cover of the 1999 UK Football Media Guide.

Pre-game: After my job with Campus Concepts was eliminated, it was difficult to work through the mental anguish and disappointment, but I realized I had worked too hard to give up and walk away. I recommitted to my original dream of a job in the sports industry and went after it.

I made the choice to attend graduate school. The graduate assistant position was a single-year position and helped me pay bills during the time I was earning my master's degree. The advantage turned out to be one of my weaknesses, which was academic related. I enjoyed school and was an avid reader, but struggled mightily during my time as an undergraduate and could not understand why. Years later, an attention deficit disorder (ADD) diagnosis changed my life, and it all made sense.

I wanted to land a job in the sports world more than anything. I spent most Friday nights at the local Kinko's (the former business print and copy center) copying and printing my resume and cover letter for different opportunities. I monitored every bulletin board in the college hallways for any new internship or job openings. My job search was anything but narrow. I would have moved anywhere, and I considered every sport except NASCAR, because I've never been much of a car guy and probably would not have fared well in an interview.

I've enjoyed learning since I was a young boy. I like to read and study the various facets of the sports industry. Once I'd regrouped after the latest job change, the next logical step was to pursue an advanced degree. My hope was that it would move my resume from the ten-foot-tall stack of recent undergraduates to the one-foot-high stack of prospective employees with a master's degree.

This would be where I ended up, but I had one or two hurdles to clear first.

My parents were generous enough to cover my undergraduate expenses. When I made the decision to attend graduate school, Dad kindly told me I was on my own, and I agreed with him.

I loved everything about sports management and opted for this program in the Education Department. Luckily, I completed the program in fifteen months, and 1999-2000 will be remembered as a fun year of my young life.

Since I spent seven years in Lexington, a new city seemed like a good option, even though I enjoyed my time in the south. I looked at three options: the University of Florida, the University of Georgia, and the University of Kentucky. I had two good friends from my Residence Hall Association (RHA) days at the University of Florida and knew they liked the campus and enjoyed their undergraduate time, but the University of Georgia stood out. I earmarked the Bulldogs as my #1 option.

I took the GRE exam, scored high enough to matter, and hustled to collect three recommendation letters. The first two were easy to secure. The third letter was a bit of a scramble, but I landed the verbal commitment and impatiently waited to hear from the admissions department. One month later, a letter arrived, and the content initially crushed me. It said that my application was incomplete because the third recommendation letter never arrived.

I quickly turned to my alma mater and figured it would be a good opportunity. During my undergraduate years, I took detailed notes, studied for exams, and struggled to earn high grades. I didn't know about my ADD disability, but it helped me in another way. I genuinely loved graduate school and read, studied more, and earned mostly A's and a B or two. I hated our Statistics class and remembered the B I received. Sports Law was my favorite class. We routinely had to read 180 pages per week. I looked forward to reading about a new case every night. Sometimes I wonder if I missed my calling by not going to law school and becoming a sports agent.

Graduate school was a welcome change for a couple of reasons. The program classes were held at night and our professors treated us like adults. If you had an issue with a paper or homework assignment, you simply called or met with them to discuss an extension. I thought part of this respect stemmed from the fact that the professors knew we, as students, were paying our own tuition, unlike party-focused undergraduate students. Academics mattered to us, and we were there for a purpose. We wanted to better ourselves, hoping to land a higher-paying job. None of us feared challenging work or lacked the discipline required. Plus, we were twenty-four to twenty-seven-years old instead of eighteen- to twenty-year-old immature college kids.

The night schedule allowed us to hold part-time or full-time graduate assistantships or jobs during the daytime hours. I immediately looked at the Athletics Department for any openings. The available internships and jobs were focused on undergraduate-level students or areas I was not interested in.

One of UK's professors agreed to meet with me and discuss my future plans. He asked me why I decided to attend graduate school. He cautioned me that a master's degree would not guarantee any advantage nor increase the probability of me securing a job. He advised me to earn the master's degree because I loved the subject and could use it later in life if the immediate goal did not work out for whatever reason. I knew in my heart I wanted to spend the rest of my career working in and around sports. The second degree would be a passion play and an achievement I could be proud of, as I would be the first person in my immediate family to earn a master's degree.

College is not cheap, and neither is graduate school. Luckily, colleges offer graduate assistantships to help gain real-world experience and make some money, too.

I began networking with professors and peers to see if they knew of any opportunities on campus. I checked the Athletics Department and all positions were filled, but someone mentioned to me that the CATS Academic Center might have an opening. I reached out and inquired about graduate assistant opportunities and was selected as a candidate.

People I Met at CATS
Bob Bradley

Bob Bradley was the long-time Executive Director of the CATS Academic Center. He began his lengthy career in academic services in 1977. The salary for his first job was $11,000 a year, with a focus on football and men's basketball.

Early in his career, Bob realized that a student-athlete's schedule was far from ordinary, and certain students needed extra help in the classroom. His passion for advising and assisting student-athletes was noticed by his peers. He fought diligently to dispel the myth about lazy athletes attempting to use learning disabilities as a cover-up or excuse for tutoring services. I admired him because he practiced transparency with campus leadership, the athletic department staff, coaches, and professors.

Bob was known for his optimistic attitude and sharp humor. Anytime a graduate assistant complained about not being able to track down a grade from a professor, he would smile at us and share his famous phrase, "I bet if I told you I had a $100 reward for the grade, you wouldn't have any problems connecting with the professor and getting it by tomorrow morning."

Years later, he realized the need for academic support was much greater as more athletes asked for help. His passion to help the students never wavered. Like most innovative programs, Bob faced detractors and critics at every turn, but never gave up on his kids.

FACTS

In 1981, Kentucky became the first university in the nation to open an academic center dedicated to student-athletes. In 1998, the center moved to its current location to Memorial Coliseum next to the Joe Craft Center. The center was privately funded by the Ohio Casualty Group Insurance and other donors. The mission of the program is to create an environment where all student-athletes have the opportunity to maximize their academic, personal, and social growth and improve their post-college quality of life. The Center for Academic and Tutorial Services has:

- 20,000 square feet of space on 2 levels
- A computer lab that houses 37 state-of-the-art computers with universal access to software.
- A study area that accommodates 60 seats in a quiet atmosphere.
- 25 private tutor rooms housing computers with internet access.
- Over 1,000 hours of tutoring completed per week.
- Over 100 tutors are employed each semester.

Source: *UK Athletics website*

Accountability and Consequences

A major part of our job required us to serve as the primary communications liaison between the coaching staff, athletes, and parents. Once a week, we met with the football coaching staff to review exam grades, acknowledge any red flags, and report any major shortcomings or attitude issues. The young men were still learning and maturing, whether they were eighteen or twenty-two years old. When the player blew off a class or appeared to not take a homework assignment seriously, the coach did not hesitate to call the player out and advise him to take care of his academic business.

If a student athlete was struggling in a certain class, we mailed a copy of a midterm letter to the parents notifying them. We wanted to keep parents in the loop rather than having them learn of the problem only after the student had received a poor or failing grade. This work was fulfilling because the parents or guardians appreciated our time and effort monitoring their child's academic efforts while they were miles away from home.

One of my funniest stories from this time involves two linemen and a broken door. Finals Week arrived, and I received a call from one of my players. "Hey, B, this is John, and we're locked inside our dorm room." I told him to knock off the funny business, remove whatever was blocking the door, and tell his teammates to open it from the outside. Apparently, there was no one within earshot to help because the student's dormmates were busy taking their exams. I pulled up John's calendar and realized that at that moment, he was missing his final exam for History 108.

I called the professor and left a voicemail, and I followed up with an email to be safe. Turns out the lock on John's door was faulty. Part of the hardware had been replaced before, because the University had it on file. We had to share this documentation with the professor to allow the student to make up the exam.

One morning, I was conducting my class checks, which we did twice a week. We would walk by classrooms to ensure no one was skipping class. Sometimes we had to step inside the oversized lecture room and look around for the student-athletes. During this class check, I noticed a crew of five football players bunched up together in the back row. In the middle was one of my players. He had his head on the desk and clearly was not paying attention. I tapped on his shoulder twice, and he barely budged. I elbowed him to get his attention, and this time he murmured under his breath, "Knock it off, man." He thought a teammate was trying to wake him. The second elbow did the trick. He slowly lifted his head, looked at me with half-opened eyes, and said, "Oh shit, it's Tosti. Sorry, man, I was out partying late." I laughed, along with his teammates, and told him to stay awake.

The Academic Graduate Assistant Pass was a free ticket to a majority of the athletic events.

I spoke with Bob Bradley, who, as I mentioned earlier, was the founder of the CATS program, and he shared some of his memorable stories with me.

Computer Glitch

One morning, Bob walked into Memorial Coliseum and noticed that over fifty kids were sleeping in the hallway. He asked if they were waiting to get tickets for the upcoming home basketball game. They told him there had been a computer glitch and all their classes had been bumped into the afternoon sections during practice times. The academic advising program had only two graduate assistants, neither of whom knew anything about advising, which meant Bob had to act quickly and devise a plan. Luckily there was one more day before classes were to start and add-drop for sections was being held upstairs in Memorial Coliseum on the concourse above Bob's office. He patiently began working through each student's schedule issues one at a time. The Athletics Director came in and asked what was going on because a group of high-level donors would be arriving soon for a meeting. Bob mentioned a warehouse on the other side of the Coliseum and instructed graduate assistants to set up there and take all the student-athletes with them.

Psychology 100

The last young man who came in had been sent upstairs to get a section of Psychology 100 that was still open. Long after all the other students left, he came back and said he had wandered around for two hours and couldn't find the table for the class he needed. Bob asked him some questions and asked to see the paper in his hand, and it turned out the student had been looking for "Sike."

Extra Students

As time passed, unbeknownst to the Athletics Director, Bob had student-athletes in all sports under his guidance. Bob's boss periodically stopped by and asked if he was helping other students from other teams. He said the students walking into Bob's office did not resemble football or basketball players. To avoid any controversy, Bob casually mentioned that he provided some advice, but not anything special. The truth was, he was helping an additional fifty student-athletes from other sports with a wide variety of academic needs.

However, Bob's boss, the Athletics Director, closely monitored the budget and was frugal. Bob approached him about the possibility of building an academic center. The AD asked what an academic center was and Bob explained. The next question was which schools had one, and when Bob told him he didn't know of anyone who did, the response was, "Well, then we aren't doing that."

AD says NO.

Bob was determined to build an academic center. He went back to his boss with the idea more than once. Finally, the Athletics Director asked Bob if he understood the meaning of the word "no." Bob decided the next time he ventured into his boss's office, he might be searching for a new job. Later on, out of the blue, the boss called and asked about the center Bob had previously mentioned. The AD responded, "You know, the academic thing where the kids can study and stuff." Bob was stunned because the next directive involved meeting with the Construction and Design office on campus and requesting initial renderings.

The Center for Academic and Tutorial Services officially opened as the first true full-service academic center in the spring of 1981. When it first opened, the UK coaches told Bob that their friends coaching at other schools would call and ask for more details about the services and programs that were offered. They referenced it as a constant reason for losing kids to UK in the recruiting battle. Parents were enthused about the academic support because they worried about their kids succeeding in college off the field.

In 1998, the finishing touches were put on a new three-million-dollar renovation of the old Coliseum swimming pool, converting it into the new CATS center. Thanks to a one-million-dollar donation by The Ohio Casualty Insurance Group and their CEO, Lauren Patch, the Athletics Department could move into a new 20,000 square foot facility.

Bob's career with UK Athletics began in 1977 and ended with his retirement in 2018. Thousands of student-athletes have been served by the program and its staff. The employees who dedicated their time and energy over the years were, and remain, incredibly dedicated. In addition, CATS was a rewarding place to work because the student-athletes respected the opportunity and support they were given.

Barb Deniston

Early on, Bob recognized a high number of athletes were struggling with reading deficiencies. UK had a master's degree program in reading, and his next strategic decision entailed adding a new reading specialist to the center's roster.

Barb Deniston, a graduate student in the College of Education Curriculum and Instruction department, was working on her master's degree in literacy. Bob called the dean of the college and said he needed the top student, which was Barb. Initially she was hired as a graduate assistant; eventually, she was promoted to full-time. Bob told me this was probably the greatest hire of his career.

Barb had taught elementary school for three years. When she was ready to expand her academic knowledge, she started on her master's. Her original plan was to finish the master's degree, then leave UK the following year. Accordingly, when she was offered the part-time position at CATS, she signed a one-year contract with no benefits. In time, Barb developed one of the best reading programs in athletics and created a program to work with student-athletes who generally struggled with academics.

Twenty years passed. When I started working at CATS in 1999, Barb was my direct supervisor. Reading and study strategies were her specialty, and outside of CATS, she provided a wide variety of tutoring and reading help to high school students, as well. She taught me how to deal with high-pressure situations and how to extinguish the proverbial fires we encountered on a weekly basis.

There is never a one-size-fits-all in conflict resolution. I've seen her speak softly, be stern, and even yell when it was required. Sarcasm was another tactic, but she used it only on special occasions.

Her job was difficult because she oversaw sixty football players. During her career, she had heard outlandish excuses, and even some absurd ones. Barb cared deeply about academics. She did not tolerate excuses and was not interested in why a student-athlete did not finish a homework assignment. Her version of tough love was a combination of caring and bluntness.

She often attended football practice to assess her students and understand if they were having a bad week. One time she marched onto the practice field to prove a point to both the coach and a player. It wasn't a promotional stunt, because in her mind it was imperative for her to be viewed as part of the coaching staff and be respected as such.

Barb understood that everyone responds differently to adversity and expectations, based on a wide range of factors. Part of it stemmed from the reading assessments and screenings she performed. Early in her career, one of the football coaches shared a bit of wisdom he learned from the recruiting trail. It was to sincerely listen when someone else is talking. This allows you to develop a deeper understanding of where the person is coming from and what their body language is telling you, but you must pay attention.

Barb spoke of the long hours during her early years in the job, but she added that it never felt like work. The job and the small CATS team allowed her to be involved with other areas. She spent most of her weekends with the UK coaching staff, recruits, and their families. Each recruiting visit included coordination between multiple departments. She tried to look at each player not simply as a football standout but as a person. How did they treat their parents, how did they speak to the coaches, to others on campus? This provided Barb with insight into the player's attitude and what she could expect if they came to UK.

Barb showed me the importance of reading people and forecasting potential scenarios if I didn't act upon my gut. She did a phenomenal job reminding students that athletic talent is just one aspect of life, and that all kinds of unforeseen things can happen, including not making it to the NFL or incurring a career-ending injury. A football scholarship, she told them, is a safety net with insurance of the most important kind: a valuable education and the confidence that comes from learning to be a good student. In academics, as in sports, you must put in the work and effort to reap the reward.

Barb's success at UK led to job offers on other campuses. Some were with athletic departments. Being an educator at heart, she did not rank a higher salary or a fancy title as a top priority. She told me about a certain interview where the football coach said, "Well, we cannot have a woman in the locker room." Barb kindly responded, "It is never a problem at UK. I knock, announce myself, pause, then walk through the locker room." She mentioned sexism was not common in the academic side of sports, and this incident led Barb to a key realization. She felt like she could be a leader and not worry about discrimination and small-minded attitudes if she remained at UK.

Barb knew she was making a difference when the student-athlete's confidence changed and he proudly shared a test score or an improved assignment grade with her. For most athletes, the game-winning touchdown feeling only lasts a minute or two, but their college degree lasts forever.

Christine "CJ" Jackson

Christine and I knew each other from our involvement with the Residence Hall Association (RHA), UK's campus leadership group. Christine swears I was the one who coined the nickname "CJ." Everyone liked it, and it stuck. We worked on various leadership programs and attended conferences together, but after the first two or three years of college, we lost touch, which happens on a campus of 24,000 students.

When I began working at CATS, I was delighted to find that Christine was a graduate assistant there. I was glad to be reunited with an old friend, and I looked forward to learning from her as we began our jobs together. Better yet, we shared an office and the responsibility of managing the academic services for the UK football team.

CJ taught her students the importance of setting and communicating clear expectations and accountability. She did not get emotional or upset when something went wrong. She routinely handled her business in a professional manner—she was always early for meetings, for example— and expected her football boys to do the same. I felt as if I should have warned the student athletes to know what to expect, because I knew she did not tolerate excuses or laziness. She was tough yet fair. I knew her players were getting a Momma Bear who would hold them to a high standard and teach them a valuable lesson about being responsible for your actions, good and bad.

CJ was the mother of two young boys, which provided a glimpse of what my future might hold. I listened intently when she offered sage advice on parenthood because she never held back. Years later, after my wife and I had kids, it seemed as if everything she told me came true.

Christine "CJ" Jackson

CJ and I both received an autographed football
as a thank you gift from Coach Hal Mumme.

Anthony "Champ" Kelly

Champ was one of the thirty student-athletes I worked with during the school year. He played multiple positions on the football team, including defensive back and wide receiver. He took great pride in his academics and often took the initiative to schedule extra tutoring to ensure his grades would remain at a high level. A model citizen on and off the field, Champ quickly became one of the team's best community ambassadors and just a fun person to be around.

A decade later, our paths crossed in Denver, Colorado. Champ was working for the Denver Broncos as the Assistant Director of Player Personnel. He invited me to tour his office in Dove Valley, where the team's headquarters is located. It was a nice gesture and one that he did not have to make. His office had oversized LED TVs and dry erase boards everywhere. This is where detailed player notes and stats would normally be displayed, but I was visiting during the offseason, which meant they were all clean with lots of empty white space.

Champ's next career stop was when he accepted a similar job with the Chicago Bears. When I was in Chicago for the popular IEG Sponsorship Conference, we tried our best to connect, but it didn't work out. I still appreciated the fact that he was willing to set aside time for me, because I know how demanding NFL front-office jobs are. Later, I called him to ask for a networking favor, and he happily obliged. Champ exuded pure class and integrity in every aspect of his life, and I appreciated his support. He is a loving father, a philanthropist, a devoutly religious man and one heck of a talent evaluator in the NFL, who I bet will be a General Manager soon.

In 2010, he and his wife, Stephanie, started their foundation, Heart Power Inc. The foundation's focus is C.H.A.M.P. Camp, which is a free football camp for underprivileged kids held in multiple cities. The acronym stands for Character, Heart, Attitude, Motivation and Pride, which perfectly describes Anthony "Champ" Kelly. The speakers cover more than just football, and the kids walk away with a smile and a bit of valuable life advice. I stopped by to visit and chat with him during one of his camps in Denver. Everyone could see the excitement of the coaches and players as they rotated among the different stations. His nickname is fitting because he is a true champion in everything he does.

Champ Kelly and his family at C.H.A.M.P.
Camp (Las Vegas 2023).

*Derek Homer, one of my former students, with
me and my son at C.H.A.M.P. Camp.*

Michael Stone

Michael is a Kentucky native like me. He bled blue with all his heart. Michael was born and raised in Powell County, Kentucky, about half an hour east of Lexington. He worked as an Academic Graduate Assistant at CATS, and his work ethic impressed me because he never complained about staying late to get the job done the right way. He was a perfect employee because of his pride in the university.

Michael is a skilled storyteller. We always knew we were in for a doozy whenever he walked into our office and shut the door. In his own words, storytelling in Appalachia has long been a way of passing down history. The same stories are repeatedly told with such attention to detail that it is almost as if they are written. I also remember that Michael was great at impersonations, and that he knew how to work a crowd.

Along with his work at CATS, Michael routinely volunteered to help other teams in the UK athletics department. If the volleyball team needed a scorekeeper, Michael was there in a heartbeat. If the baseball team needed extra water coolers transported from the training facility, he gladly offered his services, never expecting credit or praise.

His unselfish attitude even turned into a part-time job for the softball team. He was asked to step in as the public address announcer for one game. To no one's surprise, he was a natural, and what began as a simple favor quickly turned into a season-long commitment. When the season ended, he was presented with an oversized card displaying the team's appreciation for his time and effort. Nothing was mentioned regarding his accent, but he jokingly told me someone must have appreciated it.

Today Michael lives in Lexington, Kentucky, and is the visiting team liaison for the SEC (the Southeastern Conference). He has proudly held that job for twenty-three years, the longest in the conference's history. I have serious doubts if his record will ever be broken. During a recent job performance review, his supervisor discussed all the tasks he performs outside of his day-to-day academic responsibilities.

Other volunteer opportunities have come his way. He sits courtside at Rupp Arena for every men's basketball home game and operates the scoreboard. Nothing like having 24,000 rabid fans watching your every move, just waiting to voice their displeasure if you make a mistake. No, thank you! I smile whenever I see him on a national broadcast. It is a detail-oriented task that requires pinpoint accuracy because one second can be the difference between two points or a turnover.

Michael puts his students' needs first. He is a father figure, a cheerleader when needed, and the no-nonsense coach when someone stumbles or slacks off on a group project. I hope his athletes realize how deeply he cares about each of them even after they've graduated and moved on to start their careers.

The only problem with his love for all things UK athletics is that, once the fall months roll around, it means he is working games on both Saturdays and Sundays. Michael has never asked for, nor does he expect a penny for this time and effort.

Me and Michael Stone meeting for lunch in
Lexington, Kentucky, to tell old stories.

Chris Stewart

Chris Stewart is a North Carolina native and a basketball guy at heart. Naturally, his students at CATS were the UK men's basketball team. He had an easier time with class checks than the rest of us because it is not hard to tell whether a 6' 10" player is in the room or not.

"Stew," as we called him, was a monster of a man. He stood 6 feet 8 inches, weighed 240 pounds, and was in great physical shape. I've never seen someone eat as much as this guy did. However, everything he ate was healthy and nutritious.

Stew is an intelligent and outgoing person. I found him fun to hang out with because he loved to debate anything sports related. I sometimes wondered if he should have been a lawyer, based on his powerful vocabulary and debating skills. Stew could carry a conversation about anything—the stock market, international diplomacy, or the latest Fortune 500 company shaking up its industry. Stew had played college basketball at Division II Lenoir-Rhyne in Hickory, North Carolina, and he never hesitated to remind us of his strength on the basketball court, not to mention his love for the Carolina basketball team and his beloved Tar Heels. Stew would hurt no one, but we still had to earn every rebound.

He was the social planner for our group at CATS. Anytime we had a good story to rehash from the night before, we headed to his office. He would start off the session laughing at the top of his lungs and imitating one of our favorite professors. Twenty years later, he keeps all of us connected with "Happy Birthday" texts. Whenever a major sports-related story breaks, he is the first to respond and ask for our feedback.

I knew early on that Stew would succeed in whatever career path he pursued. He was the consummate professional: highly intelligent, detail-oriented, and driven without needing to step on someone else to achieve his goals. Stew currently works as the Chief Partnership and Impact Officer for the Verstandig Family Foundation.

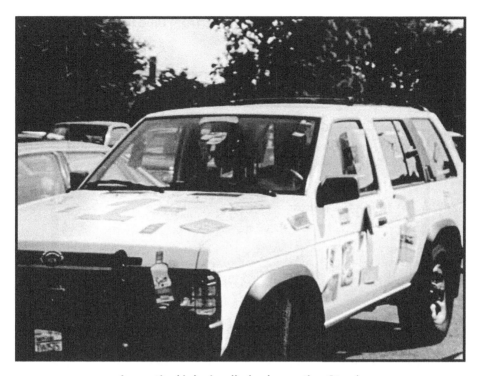

A practical joke I pulled—decorating Stew's
SUV to resemble a NASCAR vehicle.

Michael Boudreaux

Michael "Mike" Boudreaux hailed from Baton Rouge, Louisiana. His Cajun drawl was straight out of a movie. Three kids, two of whom were twins, meant he was a busy married man. He was a proud LSU alum and got married at a young age, compared to our crew. Mike's family are longtime supporters of LSU, but he was looking for a change, and UK seemed like a good landing spot. He was also an Academic Graduate Assistant at CATS when I worked there.

I listened intently and appreciated it when he shared his fatherly advice with the other guys. Boudreaux was a math whiz and had majored in accounting. He has worked as a CPA for twenty years now. This guy was cool under pressure, but he would let it go from time to time and tell you how he really felt about topics.

Brandon and Beth,

Hey – I hope the honeymoon went well in Costa Rica! I wanted to thank you both for making everything so easy for your out-of-town guests. We enjoyed the Rockies game, and Stoner and I were able to pick-up $25 Broncos tickets ten min. before kick-off on Sunday. You guys are both great people and I am really happy for you. Y'all always have a friend in Louisiana and you're both welcome any time. Enjoy married life and I hope to see y'all again soon.

Your friend,
mike Boudreaux

A thank-you card from Mike Boudreaux.

*Left to right: Chris Stewart, Mike Boudreaux,
and Michael Stone at my wedding.*

Unexpected Road Trip

My favorite memory with this group was a road trip that came together at
the last minute. Usually, those are the best kind. Mike Boudreaux wanted
to see and experience a true Kentucky high school basketball game. It was
March, which meant regional tournaments were taking place across the
state of Kentucky. I mentioned that the basketball team at my alma mater,
Paintsville High School, was playing in the 15th Regional Tournament and
it was a 1 hour and 15-minute drive from Lexington. The guys bought in,
and we took off down the Mountain Parkway, headed to the mountains of
eastern Kentucky.

We walked into the stuffy cracker box gym, and before we sat down, Michael Stone looked at me and said, "What are your school colors, and what is the mascot?" Next thing I know, this crew of grown men lets out an ear-splitting cheer of "Let's Go Big Blue, Let's Gooooooo Tigers!" We were enthusiastic, and more than fans glanced at us with a weird look. We did not paint our faces, but you would have thought we were parents or enthusiastic teachers from Paintsville. After the game ended, we jumped in the car and headed back to Lexington for work the next day. That morning began with a closed-door retelling of our adventure.

We worked together during the day and went to class at night. The group felt more like brothers than students who shared night classes. Michael Stone, Stew, and Boudreaux flew to Denver for my wedding, which defined our friendship and their character. Twenty years later, we keep in touch.

Keith Sayers

Some people carry themselves with poise and confidence that simply radiates from them with little effort. Keith Sayers was this person for me. Within seconds of meeting him after one of our classes, I walked away impressed. He was businesslike and an astute professional in the way he presented himself.

Originally from the small town of Northfield in Vermont, Keith played soccer in high school because his school did not have a football team. He also played basketball and baseball. Keith earned his undergraduate degree from the University of Vermont. His plan and goal were to land a job in the National Basketball Association (NBA), which was not an easy task. The problem was that a minor league basketball system did not exist, yet everyone wanted athletic trainers to have professional league experience. Switching tactics, he got his foot in the door with a minor league baseball team and hoped to use that experience to transition back to the NBA.

His first athletic trainer opportunity came from the Milwaukee Brewers baseball organization and one of their minor league teams based in Ogden, Utah. During the offseason, Keith kept busy working with Weber State University's athletic teams, including women's soccer, indoor track and field, and the men's and women's tennis teams.

The hard work paid off when he was promoted to the Class A Milwaukee Brewers farm team, which was in Beloit, Wisconsin. The team played what is commonly known in the baseball industry as a "minor league long season," which runs April to September. The schedule was a grind and required him to live out of a duffle bag for over half the calendar year. During a span of 180 days, the Beloit Snappers played 168 games!

One advantage of working in Beloit was the proximity to the major league team. The Milwaukee Brewers played an hour away, which meant the trainers could occasionally drive up for a game. From a professional perspective, it meant Beloit was often where major league players were sent for short-term rehabilitation assignments, especially pitchers.

Keith often met major leaguers, and most of them were friendly and engaged with the team staff. Ironically, they wanted to talk about life, employees' hobbies, or pretty much anything but baseball, because baseball was their job.

Rehab stints were stressful for athletic trainers because they were required to submit post-workout reports to the team. Some pitchers were on a strict pitch count to avoid aggravating the injury or rushing the player back too soon. Don't forget, a pitcher's arm was part of a multi-million-dollar contract. It was devastating to watch a pitcher who was scheduled to throw twenty pitches stop after the third one due to pain. The athletic trainer knew something was wrong and dreaded relaying the information to Milwaukee, even though it was a common occurrence.

After enduring multiple seasons of the intense travel schedule with no opportunity for advancement, Keith returned to school to earn his master's degree. Milwaukee granted him the option to switch from a long season class A team to a short season team to allow him to pursue his graduate degree.

Keith chose UK because it was in the south, which in his mind meant warmer weather. Also, UK's sport management program had a good reputation. Keith's graduate assistantship was aligned with the professors in our department as a teaching aide. He was the rational and level-headed voice when our group went astray. Keith knew how to have fun, but also understood when we needed to focus on academics. He kept us out of trouble more times than we would like to admit.

Keith Sayers, me, and Mike Boudreaux
at my apartment in Lexington.

Post-game recap: I encountered a diverse group of people work-ing at CATS. I dealt with incredibly talented athletes, learning disabilities, and people whose home environments and family dynamics were different from what I grew up with. I learned a great deal about respecting others and gained a deeper under-standing of society by walking with someone else in their shoes. It was a lesson in perspective and a reminder to be grateful for my experiences and the people I met along the way.

Chapter 6
Small-Sided Soccer & Big-Time Hoops
3v3 Life
2000–2002

HOST COMMUNICATIONS
9100 W JEWELL AVE, SUITE 200
LAKEWOOD, CO 80232
303•989•4084 ext. 35
FAX 303•989•0539
btosti@summit3on3.com

BRANDON M. TOSTI
National Sponsor Relations
Regional Event Director
Summit Sports

SUMMIT SPORTS A division of Host Communications

Pre-game: I had one class left to complete my graduate degree, and it was my practicum, which is a formal name for a 300-hour internship. I prepared for the mental game of chasing the elusive sports job. Flashbacks of late-night runs to Kinko's to copy and print my customized cover letter and resume filled my head.

I accepted an internship with Summit Sports and Events and was ready to see where it could take me. I wanted to make a good impression and secure a full-time job at the end of the internship. It was priority #1. I felt I had exhausted all my options in Kentucky and the southern region, which made it easier to stomach a long-distance move. It was a great opportunity to expand my contacts in the western half of the country. I packed my car and made the seventeen-hour trek on I-70 to continue chasing my dream.

During my formative years, I visited both Arizona and Colorado, and I became enamored with the western spirit. The Colorado Rockies were especially appealing to a young boy who had grown up in the hills of eastern Kentucky. After college, I was determined to move west to either Arizona or Colorado.

Graduation was on my radar, but I needed to complete an internship to fulfill my master's degree requirements. I applied for internships in twenty different states, ranging from junior golf tournaments to one of the famous college football bowl games. Each week, I checked numerous job boards in our building and every sports job website I could find. My hard work and sheer determination finally paid off when I received a fateful phone call from Colorado. Little did I know what a huge role this small mom-and-pop sports event company would play in my life for the next twenty years.

The internship in Colorado presented a dilemma. It was a travel-heavy opportunity with twelve other interns. Having spent months on the road while at Campus Concepts, I was ready for something slower paced. I felt an office position would provide me with a better opportunity to make a lasting impression and hopefully land a coveted full-time position. The national soccer director changed his mind after my interview and decided to place me in an office-based role, which provided flexibility for me and the company. The decision was easy because I simply followed my heart and the chance to chase my dream of living out west.

A copy of the Summit Sports employee handbook.

*Me (right) and my friend Thomas at the end of
a long drive from Colorado to Kentucky.*

Me (left) and a couple of our roadies (summer interns).

*Jennifer Tabbert (left) and I (right) with one of our interns
after wrapping up a tournament in Wichita, Kansas.*

Summit Sports and Events: The Origin Story

Summit Sports and Events was based in Lakewood, Colorado, a western suburb of Denver. The company produced the country's largest 3v3 soccer tour, visiting sixty-five cities. In addition, the company ran the 3-on-3 "Roundball Ruckus" national basketball tour and the "Let it Fly" 4v4 flag football tour.

Dan Cramer and Cris Carrico, both accountants, were the owners of the company. Both men played vital roles in my career development, and their story is one that needs to be told. Before I get into what I learned working at Summit, you need to know how the company came to be. The story provides a blueprint for aspiring entrepreneurs of how to build a company from a single event to a multi-city national tour.

Dan Cramer

The story of Summit Sports and Events begins with Dan Cramer. Dan grew up in Lakewood, Colorado, a quiet suburb fifteen minutes west of Denver. He was a child of the early '70s, when kids played on one team from Little League through high school, which allowed chemistry to play a role in the confidence and comfort level within the squad. Familiarity with one another's tendencies provided an extra layer of security because you knew how your teammate would react in every situation. Hyper-competitive traveling youth teams would not take over the sports industry for another thirty years. Teamwork truly meant something then, and Dan's group of teammates had a long history of playing baseball together. This familiarity helped the Lakewood Tigers capture the Colorado State High School Baseball Championship Dan's senior year, a triumph he savored with his childhood buddies.

Dan was a good baseball player, but basketball was his true love. His high school coach loaned him a key to the gym, and Dan spent his nights shooting jump shots until 11:00 p.m., yearning for improvement and consistency. He played as much as he could: alone, with friends and family, and with other players from across the city.

Dan was recruited by some Division II and NAIA schools to play basketball. The University of Denver (DU) was the only D-I school to recruit him to play basketball, so he chose Denver. The Denver Pioneers were not affiliated with a power conference, but they played at a high level of competition against UCLA, Florida State, and other big-name schools. UCLA and Florida State faced off in the finals of the NCAA tournament that year, and the UCLA team led by Bill Walton won the NCAA National Championship.

As a sophomore in college, Dan earned a spot in the starting five, which was no small accomplishment. Back in the 1970s, college players did not leave early for the NBA. They played for four years, and most underclassmen had to wait two years or more to start.

Dan was a point guard, and his job was to run the team, score when needed, and play defense. In a game versus Southern Mississippi, Dan's coach took him out after he missed a shot. As Dan sat on the bench, he was not happy with the coach's rash decision. Dan was, and remains, a fierce competitor, and his stubbornness took over. He decided he would show his coach what he was capable of. He decided that the next time he went in, he was going to shoot the ball every chance he could. Dan re-entered the game with ten minutes remaining in the first half, and he scored twenty-six points in ten minutes. In the second half, Dan picked up where he left off at halftime and stayed hot, scoring twenty-four more points. The final box score listed fifty points, and he'd shot only two free throws, which remains a school record for the most points scored in one game. Keep in mind this was 1973, well before the three-point line came into play.

After his illustrious hoops career at DU, Dan had a tryout with the Denver Nuggets, but did not make the team. He took his talents to Europe and played professionally for the Dutch professional basketball club Nashua Den Bosch. The club won eight of the ten championships, played in the EuroLeague, and competed against other champions from other countries in Europe. One season, Nashua Den Bosch advanced to the finals and lost to a team from Italy with NCAA scoring champion Johnny Newman. Dan also played against some former NBA players.

One of Dan's favorite places to play was in Tel Aviv, Israel. The power-house club Maccabi Tel Aviv, a multi-time EuroLeague champion, was a worthy opponent. It was an intense place to play, as the games were held in a sold-out arena packed with screaming fans. Moreover, the court was surrounded by armed guards. Dan recalls that during warmups, the guards routinely played head games with the opposing players, pointing their machine guns at them and pretending to pull the trigger.

Dan's shooting skills continued across the pond. He averaged close to twenty-eight points a game for a decade and found himself on a winning team most of the time. His nickname was "The Flying Dutchman." Years later, he would be inducted into the Dutch Basketball Hall of Fame. He was known as a sharpshooter and played mostly as a shooting guard, with a great outside shot. Too bad he didn't get to play with the international three-point line.

Basketball was Dan's career for his first three years in The Netherlands, but he realized that one day he would return to the United States and would need a job. When he graduated from DU, he had been offered a job with the big-five accounting firm KPMG. He contacted them to see if he could work in their international office in The Netherlands while also playing basketball. They were happy to have him join their team. Dan worked forty-plus hours a week on top of his basketball commitment and continued to win championships. When he returned to the United States, he had a full-time job with KPMG.

Dan was well known in the metro Denver area. He hosted a regional Colorado high school sports highlight talk show, and this opened doors to local leaders, coaches, and athletes. It also placed Dan in the right spot to take advantage of the sports explosion that was a few years away. The head coach of the Denver Nuggets was the colorful and eccentric Doug Moe. His son, Doug Moe, Jr., walked into Dan's office one day and asked a simple question that would change Dan's life forever: "Are you Dan Cramer? I hear you are the mayor of Denver. Will you help me run a basketball event?"

Dan jumped at the opportunity. That day put him on a new trajectory to another career in the sport he loved—this time as an owner instead of an athlete.

Roundball Ruckus 3-on-3 Basketball

The back of a Roundball Ruckus tournament T-shirt.

In 1989, Dan and Doug Jr. organized the first "Roundball Ruckus," a 3-on-3 basketball event, and it was a massive success. As part of the event, Dean Smith—yes, that Dean Smith, head coach of the University of North Carolina Tar Heels—led a clinic for the youth in town. This was in part because Doug Moe, Senior, had played under Coach Smith at Chapel Hill.

Soon after, Dan realized he could turn this into a business. He called a marketing representative who worked for Coca-Cola in Salt Lake City, Utah, and pitched them on the possibility of sponsoring a large basketball tournament. They jumped at the chance and signed on right away. The Salt Lake City event was even larger than the Denver one. Dan knew he was on the right track. For two years, he continued working for KPMG during the day while building his new business venture on the side. Slowly, he established his event company, one city and one tournament at a time.

Dan had several things going for him as an entrepreneur. He was proficient with numbers and the accounting rules, as well. He also understood the value of cash flow and how mismanaged overhead and administrative expenditures can catch up to big dreamers and poor planners, dashing dreams and emptying bank accounts.

The traditional business model, in an ideal scenario, is to manufacture a product, promote it, and then sell it twelve months a year. The event business is seasonal, which presented both challenges and opportunities. Dan was not afraid to invest time and energy in this business venture. Some entrepreneurs create new lines of business; Dan simply expanded his reach into middle school sports.

Dan's experience and knowledge of the media world, combined with the burgeoning sponsorship industry, meant that he was a savvy entrepreneur with a product everyone wanted. Sports are often referred to as having universal appeal, and basketball is one of those sports that crosses demographics and geography. Hoopers hoop everywhere, and you can always find a good pickup game if you know where to look.

After hosting a round of successful basketball tournaments, Dan had an epiphany: If 3-on-3 basketball was this popular, maybe the same format would work for soccer. All four of his kids played soccer at the time and Dan knew it was a growing sport in the US. The 3v3 soccer format began with some PVC pipe and a sketch on a napkin.

The initial feedback was overwhelmingly positive, filled with smiles and overjoyed parents. The games were high-scoring affairs fueled by youthful energy. From a developmental perspective, the format forced the players to hone their skills because hiding amongst the other ten players was no longer an option. Not to mention, with the smaller field and the absence of goalies, anyone could score a goal once they crossed the midline!

The first tournament was held in a park on the east side of Denver. Dan worked with a local soccer club, and the event fielded 250 teams. The first corporate sponsor for Dan's company was Kellogg's. This relationship led to a beneficial one with King Soopers, the largest grocery store chain in Colorado.

As the popularity of small-sided soccer tournaments increased, Dan made the proverbial leap from his safe and predictable accounting job to that of CEO and small business owner. He convinced a coworker, Cris Carrico, to join him on this quest, as Cris was also an avid basketball fan.

Cereal Bowl

Early on, Dan realized he wanted to include everyone, all levels of athletes, not just the elite or superior gifted ones. This powerful decision yielded more than just monetary gains. It provided opportunities for kids of all ages and abilities to play in a fun tournament and make memories for a lifetime.

Football was popular in Colorado middle schools, but the postseason tournament was a small bracket, and when a team lost in the early rounds, their season was over. Dan thought he might lift spirits and provide the kids with one more opportunity to play another game or three, depending on their success.

He created the Cereal Bowl, a consolation tournament for all the teams eliminated from the playoffs. The tournament provided much needed cash flow for TC Cramer Sports. They produced soccer and basketball tournaments only in the summer months, which meant revenue would stop in the winter months. As any business owner will attest, the simple football tournament concept kept the proverbial lights on in the office and in the hearts of young men who loved the game of football. Think about it, what coach would not want one more chance/opportunity to teach his kids another life lesson?

Colorado winters are typically mild, believe it or not. However, it snowed almost every Friday night before the Saturday games. I have vivid memories of shoveling yard lines and markers early Saturday mornings. Those kids did not mind and loved suiting up like the cold weather NFL teams you watched on Sundays. I, as a native Southerner, quickly learned the importance of ski clothes, layering, and genuine winter boots.

Dan had an uncommon piece of sports memorabilia in his office. It was a framed scoresheet with frayed edges from a basketball game against the UCLA Bruins. The final score of the contest was UCLA 82 and Denver 46. The legendary Hall of Fame Coach John Wooden signed the piece of paper with the following, "Sorry for the outcome, Dan. Great game!"

A photo of the final score sheet from the DU-UCLA game in 1972.

Cris Carrico

Cris was the co-owner of Summit Sports and Events. He and Dan Cramer were accountants in downtown Denver before deciding to leave the stable accounting gig to start an event company. To this day, Cris is one of my favorite bosses and a trusted mentor. His zest for life and adventure was apparent from my first conversation with him. He loves life and is not afraid of hard work and trying new business concepts. Cris has been a skilled listener and supportive coach from near and afar.

His enthusiasm and belief in others are a special gift, not to mention his eternally optimistic attitude. If I ever need a confidence boost or a quick reminder to keep things in perspective, Cris is the one I call. I often tell others I would gladly run through a brick wall for this man and have tried to mimic parts of his management style in my career.

Despite the title of co-owner, he was the first one to jump in when needed. I can remember Cris often scrambling to drive twenty minutes during rush hour to drop off ten T-shirt boxes at the somewhat nearby FedEx office. It felt like clockwork, and you never heard Cris complain. He would drop whatever he was doing, sprint to his oversized Dodge Ram truck, and return an hour later to churn through another night of work in the dog days of the Colorado summer. At least there was little humidity and no mosquitoes, another best-kept secret about the Centennial state.

To understand where his love for sports originated, like most good stories, you must start at the beginning. From the early age of two, Cris sat on the bench with his father, who was a high school football coach. He was by his side at every practice and rarely missed a home game, dressed in his uniform, even though he would not set foot on the field or court for another five years. It did not matter because he was a coach's kid and LOVED every minute.

Basketball was his first love, and Cris spent his free time working on his game at a city park. During his time in high school, Cris had developed a coaching mentality and the ability to get a feel for a team's chemistry or lack thereof. He was never the most talented athlete, but he was viewed as a leader. His coach's defensive philosophy was to full-court press and play tough man-to-man defense if the opponent was fortunate enough to break his vaunted press.

When Cris went to college, he excelled in football more than hoops and attended Eastern Illinois University as a quarterback. He was 6 feet tall and 165 pounds and moved to fullback his sophomore year. He had a reputation for grit, effort, and determination, and was not afraid to hit anyone. Cris was fearless and his teammates held him in high regard for his motor, which never seemed to slow down.

After graduation, Cris landed his first job with the accounting firm KPMG in Decatur, Illinois. Soon after, he accepted a transfer to Denver, Colorado, where he met his business partner, Dan Cramer. The two quickly bonded over basketball and Cris was a frequent participant in Dan's early Friday and Saturday morning adult league. Cris mentioned the impeccable character of these men and how he trusted them to watch his children with no reservation.

In the early years, Cris and Dan worked twelve hours (8 a.m. to 8 p.m.) for the accounting firm, then switched gears and focused time and energy on building the grassroots event management company, one 3-on-3 basketball tournament and city at a time. I asked Cris, "At what point did you think, or realize, you might be onto something big?" "Never," he emphatically responded. "We were undercapitalized for years and our goal was to have fun. During this time, the NBA was pretentious, and we were basketball guys to the core. We wanted to enjoy sharing our love for the game, one tournament at a time. We noticed Gus Macker's success and thought we might eventually make a living from it someday, but we had no ego, just a deeply rooted passion for the game."

The wildest section of this story was the support of the accounting firm. Cris tipped his hat to Dan's ability to generate revenue for the company, which meant the two basketball junkies could get away with more than others. Dan was a rainmaker and he kept adding clients each year. Cris mentioned that the office equipment provided different support for the event business early on. He vividly remembers that the office had four copy machines, one strategically placed in each corner. Cris and Dan would press 999 copies and sprint to the next copier, then repeat the process for hours until they reached their goal of 10,000 flyers. They summoned the IT Department to repair the printers more than once. Something tells me this would not be an option in today's world.

One of his best attributes was his push to improve our processes. Cris was a student of the event management world and was not afraid to ask questions and learn from his competitors. The city of Spokane, a midsize city on the eastern side of Washington, held the world's largest 3-on-3 basketball tournament, and had done so for a number of years. Cris researched the tournament and created a one-page document for our Event Managers. It made little sense to pay for a high dollar consultant, but it mattered to Cris, so he designed his own training presentation for us.

The Spokane Hoopfest sheet was a staple in our office moving forward, both as an inspirational guidepost and a reminder of how far we still needed to go with our own tournaments.

Spokane Hoopfest's Recipe for Success:

Solid foundation from day 1

Commitment to be the Best!

Strong Leadership and Direction.

Excellent Volunteer Base

Community Support at every turn.

Location, Location, Location.

Spokane Hoopfest Sponsorship

Two (2) title sponsors at $7,000 each	$14,000
Seven (7) major sponsors at $6,000 each	$42,000
Eight (8) Food/Beverage/Merchandise sponsors at $5,000 each	$40,000
One-hundred twenty-three (123) court sponsors @ $600 each	$74,000
Total sponsorship	**$170,000**

Operating Committees to run a successful event:

- Set-up and breakdown
- Contests and Festival
- Court Monitors/Referees
- Food Court/Water/Gatorade
- Game Management
- Information/Scoreboard
- Registration
- Site Manager
- Site Maintenance/Trash
- Team Marketing
- Awards
- Merchandise
- Parking/Security
- First Aid

Cris often claims his proudest accomplishment of the little event business was the sheer number of young people who took a chance on our tiny company and achieved amazing things in their respective careers. I speak for his former employees when I say that we were the lucky ones.

My Summit Internship

I started in May 2000 as a summer intern and managed our national sponsor program. The word "program" implies we had multiple sponsors, but our national 3v3 soccer tour consisted of a single corporate sponsor, Sunny Delight. Toward the end of the summer, as the tour grew in popularity, other sponsors called our owners to discuss multi-year agreements and a significant increase in sponsorship fees. If I recall, Sunny Delight paid an estimated $400,000 for the naming rights of the tour. Got Milk? Negotiated a two-year deal worth close to $1.5 million.

$5 Lunch

I never knew why, but once or twice a month, Dan would walk into my office and offer to take me and a teammate to lunch. This was a big deal because Dan was a businessman first, and not friendly to everyone in the office. Numbers ruled his world, not emotions. These lunches were always one of two locations: Subway, or a popular mom-and-pop Italian restaurant called Cafe Jordano. Either way, a sandwich was only $5 and change, but it was a kind gesture that stuck with me and something I continue to do with rookie employees, particularly on their first day of work.

Lunch with Dan was more than a quick meal. It was a chance to learn, ask questions about business, hear his thoughts about his faith and life. He would listen to my ideas and impart years of his knowledge as to why an idea would or would not work. I am sure I thanked him back then, but I want to include it here to be safe. I want him to know how much his generosity meant to this Kentucky kid who had moved 2,000 miles from home for a job.

Speaking of food, Dan had a voracious appetite. Cris and I often jokingly referred to him as a lion. He consumed calories fourteen hours a day. Ninety percent of the time it was healthy food, but he enjoyed a candy bar here and there, as well as his favorite fast-food chain, Chick-fil-A.

On one occasion, Dan and I were in New York City, and he wanted to show me around. We walked nine blocks, caught a movie, and then popped into a convenience store that was still open at 1 a.m. I distinctly remember Dan bought a slice of pizza, a cup of yogurt, a bag of potato chips, and an apple, and he devoured it all before we reached the next block.

The next morning, I woke up to Dan grunting and breathing heavily. At first, I wondered if he was having a heart attack. No, he was up at 6 a.m., knocking out thirty pushups and sets of sit-ups. Remember, I was the young lad in this story, twenty-six years old, full of zest and ready to take on the world, and he was the experienced CEO who four hours earlier had crammed a greasy slice of New York's finest pizza and other healthy snacks in his belly. I glanced at him, shook my head in disbelief, and pulled the sheet over my head and tried to get thirty more minutes of sleep.

Dan's accounting background helped and hurt him occasionally. Some of the egotistical executives did not believe him when it pertained to operating expenses. He understood the value of a buck and in his first Hoop It

Up meeting, he slashed the operating budget by $2 million in five minutes. The ability to analyze financial documents such as budgets and balance sheets was his forte, but he ensured the company stayed focused on cutting costs and operating lean.

7-11 Friday Morning Run

We had a Friday morning ritual in our office: a run to the 7-11 across the street for Gatorade and Clif bars. It was a welcome pick-me-up, especially as we were young and sometimes spent evenings hanging out and drinking with our teammates, excluding Dan and Cris. I blame the Fat Tire two-for-one beers at our favorite bar, Govnr's Park. Every Friday at 10 a.m. like clockwork, we made the slow stroll through the office to ask who wanted to walk over to 7-11, but for some reason, we never thought to ask Dan before we left. Without fail, he would slide open his small office window, his cell phone lodged between his shoulder and his ear, and yell at me to grab him a bottle of chocolate milk. I used to wonder what the person on the other end of the phone thought about it. It was funny and predictable.

As the summer internship was ending, I asked about full-time job opportunities with the company. Dan and Cris were thinking of hiring someone to manage the milk account with its newfound sponsor revenue. Lucky for me, I was their number one candidate.

I was excited and eager to accept the offer, but an interesting storyline developed in the meantime. As I was mentally preparing to drive back to Kentucky and pick up my belongings to make the move to Denver, a job opened with the UK football team. It was a recruiting coordinator position, and I had the inside track because of my familiarity with the coaches based on my graduate assistantship the prior year.

Everything was falling into place! I still had to participate in an interview and win the job. Keep in mind, I was working soccer tournaments and driving a Budget truck from Colorado, which meant I did not have a suit and tie with me. After all, the purpose of the trip was to stop by my old house in Lexington and tie up loose ends, then move to Colorado the following week. I called the coach and told him I only had khaki shorts and a golf shirt, but I knew the standard attire for any job interview is a suit. He understood my dilemma and assured me I had nothing to worry about and to come on in.

The Assistant Coach was honest with me about the peaks and valleys associated with prime-time collegiate athletics. He told me, "Son, I know people at the University of Miami, Michigan State, Purdue, and Notre Dame. If we win, I can help you move up the ladder." Then with a dramatic and intentional pause, he made sure I was looking him in the eyes and cautiously said, "If . . . we . . . win."

I did not have the luxury of mulling the offer over for weeks. It was more like four days. It was tempting: my heart had bled Kentucky blue since I was six years old, plus I would be able to return home. Finally, after three years of networking and endless job searching, it seemed I would be able to start my career with my alma mater. What a perfect ending to what was a rocky and uncertain start.

I took time to think about the possibilities of where my next job could be and what Bowl game we might play in. Ultimately, I declined the football job offer. The job in Colorado paid only $26,000, but I felt the job in Kentucky was not worth the risk: I did not want my potential to hinge upon a coach and his record when I had no control over the team's success on the field. It turned out to be a wise decision. The following season, the UK Wildcat football team went 1–10, and—you guessed it—the entire football staff was fired. My bet paid off, and not just in monetary form. Anytime I share this story, people comment on how smart I was making the right decision. I quickly correct them: I simply made the decision that was best for me, and, luckily, it worked out. I have also made my fair share of decisions that did not end well.

One of our tournament registration forms.

Office Environment

The dress code at Summit was very casual. We rarely held meetings with outside clients in this space, and everyone was under thirty years old. Flip-flops, basketball shorts, and sometimes even tank tops were all acceptable attire. That job was the lowest paying one I have ever held, but it is still my favorite one. The people and the experiences played a major part in my life. Looking back, we were like a Silicon Valley startup, just without the millionaires, Ping-Pong tables, dog lounge, and fancy coffee bar. In addition, we did not have a Human Resources Department, but we were mature for our age and encountered no major issues.

Lunch Hour and a Half

Most companies have a strict lunch hour rule, but that was not the case with Summit Sports and Events. It was a carnival, free-spirited atmosphere. There was a basketball hoop outside for impromptu 3-on-3 games, and daily lunchtime group bike rides.

Everyone worked long hours, particularly during the summer months, which meant an extended lunch period was never frowned upon. Our bosses knew the number of hours we spent on the road and in the office. There was no need for timesheets or a time clock to punch in and out. They were lenient and supportive of our taking extra time off when needed.

Warehouse

The warehouse was a fun trip and a break from the madness. Sometimes an impromptu game of basketball would break out, although we had to dodge pieces of equipment and cartons of sponsor products. Warehouse excursions were a stress reliever filled with comedy, and sometimes an extra T-shirt, razor, or bag of Corn Nuts. Without fail, we helped organize the T-shirt stock, soccer equipment, and other event supplies when we stopped by.

One summer, Irish Spring soap was a tour sponsor. When the tournament season concluded, we had four palettes of soap left, and the company told us to keep the product rather than incur the expense of shipping it back to their warehouse. No one in our office bought bar soap for two years.

Technology

We printed 15,000 paper registration forms for each market. This was before social media, and online registration technology was still in its infancy and was expensive to implement. It was also difficult to trust the numerous companies that seemed to pop up out of nowhere. This meant every team registration form was received in the daily mail run and processed by hand. Our Team Services Department logged names, processed payments, fielded customer questions, and did the troubleshooting for registration issues.

T-shirts

During Summit's heyday, we printed well over 100,000 T-shirts per calendar year. This process was often harried and far from perfect. The timeline, in theory, was for us to send the graphic files to the printer by the Monday prior to the upcoming weekend's tournament. Keep in mind, at any one time, we were printing T-shirts for five or six tournaments every weekend.

A commonly used term in the sports and entertainment industry is "logo soup." It is used to describe a sponsor asset where ten or twenty logos must be included in one spot. The title sponsor's logo is the largest and sits at the top, but the rest of the logos seem to get lost in the mix. It was a nightmare to deal with, and sixty-five different tournament designs were not easy to maintain. Every city had different sponsors, soccer club names, and dates that had to be triple checked.

Budweiser offered a cash prize for this adult tournament.

Bracketing Team

Another group of employees and interns played a crucial role in our tournament operations. The bracketing team planned every tournament schedule by age, gender, and skill level. Yes, they had a template, but it was a multi-day and tedious process, supported by coworkers and summer interns.

The group began the process with a pencil and sheets of paper, creating a round of games for each age group, including field number and the playoff bracket. Next, the plan was inspected by two or three employees to identify errors and fix any double bookings of fields. Other factors to consider in bracket development were the number of fields available at the complex, the number of teams, and the hours of daylight. It was a complicated and tangled matrix of planning and shuffling to fit as many games as possible in a limited window.

Once the bracket had been approved, it was entered in the computer. Then the brackets were saved on a computer disk and rushed to FedEx to be delivered overnight to whatever hotel the event's director was staying at. This usually occurred on Thursday afternoon. The disk was crucial because it included the templates for each tournament and allowed the Event Director to make changes as needed, then print updated brackets heading into Sunday afternoon's playoff round. Event directors were sometimes forced to make changes with a Sharpie or attempt to find a Kinko's nearby if we had time. The Sharpie option was the last resort.

Our scoreboards on site were atrocious: flimsy and downright awful looking. They were cheap fiberglass squares that sometimes hung from the side of a 10 ft. × 10 ft. tent. It is easy to criticize twenty years later, but they functioned well for hundreds of events with few complaints from coaches or parents.

Logistics

At the start of each summer, the company would reserve six fifteen-foot Budget trucks. Each month for three months, interns (we called them roadies) would take two trucks out on the road for much of the summer. The event director would fly to each city while the roadies transported the equipment by truck. In retrospect, this was a questionable plan. Basically, the company was giving twenty-one-year-olds the keys to trucks filled with soccer equipment essentials. To this day, I am in complete awe that a serious wreck did not occur, that I know of.

Truck Schedule

The schedule was a tricky and delicate decision because we never wanted to compete with a historic festival or other long-standing sports event in town. We were guaranteed to lose in that scenario and made a point to heed the local soccer club's advice. Trust me, we only made this kind of mistake once.

Another challenge was routing our six Budget soccer trucks in a stream-lined and efficient manner while crisscrossing the country. Mostly, trucks were strategically assigned to one region, such as the Northeast or the West, but occasionally there was an unavoidable long haul from Chicago to Las Vegas and back to Little Rock the following week.

04/29/02	Truck #1	Truck #2	Truck #3	Truck #4	Truck #5	Truck #6	Truck #7
APRIL 6-7						Las Cruces	February 2 / 3
						Austin, TX	February 9 / 10
APRIL 13-14						Phoenix, AZ	March 9 / 10
APRIL 20-21	South Florida	El Paso, TX				St. George, UT	March Fri15/Sat16
						Las Vegas, NV	March Fri29 /Sat 30
APRIL 27-28		Tucson, AZ				Nationals-Disney	January 18/19, 2003
MAY 4-5							
MAY 11-12	Port St. Lucie, FL	Austin, TX					
MAY 18-19	Tampa, FL	San Antonio, TX					
MAY 25-26	Memorial Day Weekend						
JUNE 1-2	Orlando, FL	Salt Lake, UT(Fri/Sat)	New Orleans, LA	Minneapolis, MN	Knoxville, TN		
JUNE 8-9	Birmingham, AL	Tulsa, OK	Houston, TX	Cedar Rapids, IA	Springfield, IL		
JUNE 15-16	Nashville, TN	Wichita, KS	Dallas, TX	Portland, OR	Omaha, NE	Fort Collins, CO	
JUNE 22-23	Atlanta, GA	Kansas City, MO	Philadelphia, PA	San Diego, CA	Jacksonville, FL	Seattle, WA	
JUNE 29-30	Lexington, KY	Detroit, MI	Buffalo, NY	Denver/Littleton, CO	Long Island, NY	Grand Island, NE	Chicago/Tinley Pk, IL
				Fri 28/Sat 29			
JULY 6-7	Los Angeles, CA	Des Moines, IA					
JULY 13-14	Louisville, KY	Milwaukee, WI	Pittsburgh, PA	Cincinnati, OH	Harrisburg, PA	Denver/Thornton, CO	Chicago/Lisle, IL
JULY 20-21	Albuquerque, NM	Madison, WI	Boston, MA	Indianapolis, IN	New Castle, DE	San Jose, CA	Columbus, OH
JULY 27-28	Sacramento, CA	Lincoln, NE	Cleveland, OH	St. Louis, MO	Virginia Beach, VA		
AUG 3-4	TX Reg-San Antonio	Toledo, OH	Springfield, MA	Baltimore, MD			RM Regional-Vail, CO
AUG 10-11	FL Regional-Orlando	OH Regional-Dayto	ME Reg-Knoxville	MW Reg-Lisle, IL	Syracuse, NY		
AUG 17-18	NE Regional East Brunswick NJ						
AUG 24-25			SW Reg-Tucson, AZ	Midland, TX			

A copy of our 2002 truck schedule.

Me adding yet another coat of field paint.

Fundraising Partners

Like most youth sports organizations, soccer clubs were constantly searching for a quality fundraiser to earn money and support the club to offset operational expenses. In each tournament city, Event Directors negotiated an exclusive marketing partnership with a prominent local soccer club. For every team registration we received, the club earned a small commission. It was a sliding scale, with an incremental dollar amount increase for every one hundred teams. This helped achieve local support and spread the word throughout the city and surrounding areas. It was common for teams to drive from up to five hours away to participate in our tournaments.

Friendships Beyond the Pitch

The best part of this job was the people we met. We traveled to each tour city for marketing and planning meetings in the offseason and developed tight-knit friendships with the soccer club volunteers. The Davis family in Louisville, Kentucky, always insisted that I stay at their house instead of a hotel. I did not mind because my contact was a bourbon aficionado, and he had a game room in his basement. On one of my visits, my flight arrived in the early afternoon, and I watched the host's two sons for an hour before he got home from his office.

Sometimes cities provided us with gifts, such as the homemade beef jerky and tequila we received from Albuquerque, New Mexico. Every tournament stop had its own story. Our team often joked we lived a mix of the carnival and rock star life without all the bad stuff.

National Tour Format

The tour had three segments: local, regional, and national. The top five local teams from each age group qualified for the Regional Championships. From there, the top three teams qualified for the World Championship Finals, which were held at Walt Disney World in Orlando, Florida, in mid-January. We tried to select popular tourist destinations for the regional events. For example, our Rocky Mountain Regional

Championship was held in Vail, Colorado, a popular ski town and wonderful location to spend a summer weekend. The selection process was strategic: the goal was to identify a popular destination within a six-hour drive of other major cities so that families could extend their visit by a day and turn the trip into a mini-vacation. This approach also landed me business relationships with tourism chambers and convention and visitor bureaus.

Media Partners

Since we were a traveling circus, we needed a media partner in each city to help promote the event throughout the metro area. We signed promotional contracts with in-market radio and TV stations. The contract amount ranged from $7,500 to $16,000, depending on the size of the market. Generating revenue beyond the team registration fees was important because the expenses to mount each event were considerable. Remember those Budget trucks I mentioned earlier? Not only did we have to cover insurance and gas for the trucks, but we also paid for hotels seven days a week, and a daily meal stipend for up to fourteen interns.

In exchange for their licensing fee, the media partner could sell nontraditional advertising to local businesses and retain 100 percent of their sales. In the radio industry, this was commonly known as non-traditional revenue (NTR), because it was not part of their typical ad sales program. Our soccer tour proved to be lucrative and valuable for media partners that understood the value of packaging and creating localized content. One partner from Chicago generated close to $1M in revenue.

Like most small companies, we struggled with trying not to expand too fast. It seemed like every small town wanted us to bring the national tour to their area, and we had to review each request in consultation with Dan or Cris to gauge whether the market would support our bottom line. A common trap new businesses fall into is thinking too highly of their product and accepting a loss the first year or two that is greater than what they will be able to make up in a reasonable time frame. In our case, we had done the work to be reasonably confident that the larger 500-team tournaments could absorb some of the loss until the tournament grew.

Our national tour concept was attractive to cities of all sizes. Each local soccer tournament was turnkey. Our team managed all the logistics, which allowed the media partner to focus on packaging advertising buys into sponsorships. Moreover, our format appealed to smaller media markets because it gave them the chance to be part of a national tour. Our competitors ran a small number of events in a small number of states, but their events were viewed as one-offs, with no opportunity to advance and play more teams.

Milk Mustache Photo Booth

You have probably seen the famous "Got Milk?" ad campaign, which has been around in various forms since 1993. The public relations agency behind the campaign identified their top forty media markets and visited our tournaments in those cities with their famous milk mustache photo booth. I learned a tremendous amount about media planning and promotions by working closely with the PR agency's team. Prior to arriving in each city, they identified the top radio and TV outlets in the market, then worked hard to secure interviews and live footage from the tournament site as often as possible.

It was valuable to educate kids on the health benefits of drinking milk, but it was equally important from a branding perspective and the opportunity to reach their target demographic. Hundreds of smiling kids running around a soccer complex with souvenir Polaroid photos of their milk mustaches was branding at its finest.

Regional Offices

At its peak, Summit Sports and Events produced close to 120 events per calendar year. As the demand for events grew, Dan and Cris decided that although Denver would continue to manage the majority of the events, the best option was to open two small regional offices, one in the Midwest and the other on the East Coast. The cities selected were Lincoln, Nebraska, and Boston, Massachusetts. The offices were based in strip malls. I give Dan and Cris credit: it was a major point of trust having twenty-somethings operate regional offices thousands of miles away. I do not think Dan and Cris ever made a check-in trip to the Lincoln office.

Ten months of the year, our contact with the regional offices consisted of phone calls and emails. Occasionally, the regional staffers would fly to Denver for sales training, which was highly anticipated by everyone. We were a large, occasionally dysfunctional family. The regional tournaments were our family birthday gatherings, and the World Championship event at Disney was our family reunion.

Kenton Jurgensen

Kenton Jurgensen, one of our Lincoln staff, was a member of the Army Reserves and was finishing his undergraduate studies at the University of Nebraska–Kearney. He was searching for an internship when he stumbled across our little event company. The job paid $250 per month, which supplemented his income from his other job at OfficeMax.

Kenton's unofficial attire was "Roundball Ruckus" polo shirts and event T-shirts. He wore these three to four days a week, along with a tournament-branded bucket hat.

I remember Kenton was organized and could be trusted to get any task done. His military background had prepared him for life and it was evident. He knew when to have fun but made sure everyone on his team finished their daily tasks first.

Innovation was important at Summit Sports and Events, but so was efficiency. Every dollar was important to our company. Retail distribution of registration forms was a reliable source of business for us, but Kenton had a great idea to ensure forms were being distributed in the right places and quantities. He began stamping a special code inside each registration form so they could track where registrations had come from.

Kenton said there was no time to goof off from April to October. Now, November and December might have been a different story, and the office hours unofficially changed to 8:00 a.m. to 3:00 p.m. Our team joked about how the regional offices rotated between playing card games and Nintendo tournaments each week during our offseason.

Kenton Jurgensen

Chad Menking

Chad Menking, our other Lincoln associate, had a superpower: the ability to calm angry participants down before a disagreement turned into a full-fledged fight. He was the one we sent to neutralize arguments and bad attitudes. No one wanted injuries stemming from a fight, nor the bad press that would have come with it. You might think Chad must have been a menacing figure. He was in good physical shape, but he was average height. It was his tone, not his looks, that made the difference.

Chad told me the job was like having a Spring Break every weekend—a new city, a new group to party with, and another event to bring to life. "It was the best job in the universe." As we talked, he reminded me of our hectic summer schedules and how we were literally all over the country. His biggest takeaway from the job was the friendships he made, and I would have to agree with him.

Cozad, Nebraska, is a small town, but they loved our basketball tournament. They routinely had 100 teams in the tournament, which was a high number for basketball. During one of Chad's first events, he encountered a bracketing error, and he knew he had to find a solution. He called our Senior Event Director, who responded, "Just run to Kinko's tonight, fix the bracket, and print a new one."

Chad replied, "Uh, I am in the middle of Nebraska! The closest Kinko's is 200 miles away!"

Chad also recalled his winter trip to Colorado, when my wife and I patiently taught him how to ski. We stayed behind him and made sure he did not injure himself. I had forgotten about that day, but it was a good memory to laugh about and a reminder that coworkers become more than just teammates.

Me and Chad Menking horsing around in Denver.

Matt Ruxton

Matt Ruxton was an undergraduate student at University of Massachusetts, where he worked on the largest student-managed 3 on 3 basketball tournament in the northeast. The Haigis Hoopla Tournament, named for a courtyard on campus, included 500 teams of all age groups his senior year. It was well supported by local corporate partners and media outlets.

Matt started working for Summit Sports for $100 a weekend as an Event Assistant. He said the event production experience prepared him to handle anything in his future jobs, especially irate parents and coaches screaming at him every other weekend. Their frustration usually stemmed from a bad referee call or a mistake in the playoff seeding.

As a mom-and-pop event company, Summit Sports and Events operated without normal business rules and did not have safeguards in place such as rules for expense reports. A tiny basketball tournament in Burlington, Vermont, changed that in a hurry.

From time to time, we ran small events. We knew building a successful event takes time, and not every tournament starts in year one with 300 teams. The Burlington event had a great location—Matt said the city closed a main street downtown to host the event—but the size of the tournament, only thirty teams, would not contribute much to the company's bottom line. Unfortunately, the tournament finished in one day instead of two.

After the tournament ended, the Summit staffers found a local bar, where they commiserated and drank a toast to pulling off the smallest tournament in the company's history. The problem was, they drank multiple rounds of beer. When they submitted their expense report on Monday afternoon, Matt was almost certain the beer cost more than we had made on registration fees for the tournament. The following week, a company expense report policy was quickly implemented. If I ever make it to Burlington, I will raise a glass and toast the town, the Boston office, and those thirty teams.

After Matt left Summit Sports and Events, he landed with Special Olympics Massachusetts in the event division. Matt liked the fact that the job combined sports and giving back to the community. I asked him what year he started, and he said proudly, "2004, the same year the Red Sox won the World Series." Spoken like a true sports fan.

Matt is currently the Vice-President of Sports and Operations at Special Olympics Massachusetts. Matt loves his job and appreciates the coaches, volunteers, and athletes who make a difference across the state. He fondly remembers the first large-scale Special Olympics event he worked on. A frazzled, panting coworker ran up to him and said, "This is crazy. Why are you so calm?" Matt grinned and replied, "I've worked a ton of events—believe me, this one is easy."

Me and Matt Ruxton caught up during our family's vacation to Boston. (June 2023).

Tim Barry

Tim Barry arrived at the Massachusetts office six months after completing his undergraduate studies at the University of New Hampshire. He had just finished an internship with the Fleet Center, home of the Boston Celtics.

When I spoke to Tim about his time at Summit Sports and Events, he referenced the amount of faith and trust upper management placed on his unproven shoulders at such a young age. It inspired him to do a great job and work diligently on every event detail. Looking back, he was proud that the Boston office had produced 35 percent of the company's revenue, which was significant for a couple of twenty-somethings with undergraduate degrees and a small number of internships under their respective belts.

Tim appreciated the fact that he and Matt got to manage every facet of the business. One minute they were on the phone pitching a sales presentation to a New York City radio station general manager, and the next, they were arguing with a referee assignor or reserving port-o-lets for five future tournaments.

I spoke to our teammates in Boston and Lincoln on a regular basis because of my day-to-day sponsorship fulfillment responsibilities. We put out proverbial fires and solved problems. I dreaded Monday mornings because I knew I would be on the phone with the PR agency for Got Milk? discussing what hadn't gone well over the weekend and how we could improve our processes moving forward. We created a basic event checklist for all the Event Directors, yet somehow, there was an excuse for why someone had not set up the fifteen-foot inflatable milk bottle at the tournament site.

The job was tough and not for everyone. The summer months were a grind and required hard work from interns and full-time team members. If you could not handle this type of work, you were quickly exposed. The event days were long, hot, and humid, and you had to rely on a small team to facilitate each tournament.

Tim shared his thoughts on his experience with Summit Sports and Events:

> "At a pivotal time in our early adult lives, we sacrificed key summer activities for a "career" —much to the surprise and amusement of our friends, who often made more money and had easier jobs. For us there were no weekend excursions, no camping trips, and certainly no impromptu cookouts with friends or last-minute beach trips. However, the responsibility we had and the vision of the future was what drove us to these unorthodox roles.

The Event Director position provided a foundation to excel and made us overqualified for our next jobs. The amount of responsibility and trust Dan and Cris provided to the event directors was remarkable. We had freedom to make mistakes, solve those problems, and, most importantly, learn from them."

As Tim reflected on the job, he realized that managing a regional office at twenty-four years old was kind of crazy. Building budgets, hiring, and managing ten seasonal staff, balancing finances, negotiating contracts, marketing and running thirty-plus events in only three months--the amount of responsibility given to the event directors was impressive. He had this to say:

"There were weeks we had an event in three different states that I was ultimately responsible for. What an amazing opportunity we were given, not only to prove ourselves, but to learn the facets of running your own business! And what an incredible opportunity to learn what type of person we were and what type of leader we were."

We also reminisced about our unforgettable experiences from the road. An unexpected benefit of the job was seeing all sorts of places we would never have had the occasion to visit otherwise—places like York, Pennsylvania; Oneonta, New York; and East Brunswick, New Jersey. Tim enjoyed taking the interns to Niagara Falls and to the Anchor Bar in Buffalo, birthplace of the buffalo wing. In Pittsburgh, which he ranks as a highly underrated city, they rode the funicular and ate at Primanti Brothers.

Another of Tim's favorite road stops was a pirate-themed bar in a Bangor, Maine hotel—two places he never, ever thought he would be. Sometimes the unexpected and quirky experiences are what makes a job memorable. Above all, the best part of his job was meeting his future wife. Neither expected a lifetime together would be the outcome, but here they are, twenty-plus years later!

I believe Tim said it best: "The people who worked hard and did so with hustle and a positive attitude, I wanted them on my team. Looking back, I could look left or right and I knew my teammates had my back." I could not agree more.

Tim Barry working at a charity golf tournament.

Training Event

Before we turned this wild group of college kids loose on the road, we met with the group and explained what to expect on the long days and nights. The training event was held Memorial Day weekend in Fort Collins, Colorado, which is seventy miles north of Denver. Every truck and intern team worked this event and then on Sunday morning, everyone went their separate ways, traversing the country, one city and gut-busting story at a time.

For the full-time staff, this was one event we looked forward to because we had ample help, which allowed us to relax and stay out too late, creating memories and stories we tell to this day.

*My good friend, Brian Tatum, and his
truck after a long road trip.*

Me working the fastest kick booth at a tournament.

Hoop It Up 3-on-3 Basketball National Tour

**NBA Hoop It Up Sponsor Photo
Checklist**

- Take the majority of the pictures on Saturday.
- Be sure the camera is set at the highest quality (three stars).
- There are only 40 pictures on this setting, so only take one picture per request below.
- Check off each request after photo has been taken and turn in with event reports.
- Take photos from a sponsor perspective and take nice, clean shots. Make sure there is no garbage or other none sponsor related items in the background, etc.
- This is a digital camera, so you can always review and erase the picture if it didn't turn out!

- Dunk contest (make sure inflatable is in background)
- Dunk contest. (make sure inflatable is in background)
- Dunk contest
- Dunk contest
- Dunk judges holding up numbers
- Crowd shots (wide angle)
- Dunk Winner

- Tank set-up
- People playing Crunch Time event
- Crunch Time tent and announcer
- Thirst stations and people getting
- Thirst stations and people getting
- staff passing out samples
- signage on top gun courts
- prize distribution, winners picking up GEB bars

- Participants playing game
- Participants playing game
- Wide angle shot of event set-up, goal and inflatable
- Tent area
- Tent area
- Participants playing Spin-to-Win game

*My client development team binder and
event photo checklist for sponsors.*

The Spokane Hoopfest held the title for the largest 3-on-3 basketball tournament, but Hoop It Up was the country's most popular and largest grassroots basketball tour. It was based in Dallas, Texas, and was developed by Streetball Partners International. Host Communications acquired the company and built its own event division.

The next company to be acquired was Summit Sports and Events. I was invited to meet the Dallas-based sponsorship team and see an event in action and see how they managed their corporate sponsorship program. The event was held in Miami and it fell on my birthday weekend in late April.

The first thing I noticed was the sheer size of the event footprint. Almost every Hoop It Up event was held at a pro stadium based on the open space and flat surface. Everywhere you looked you saw a basketball court and hoopers.

My first stop was the Sponsorship Village to see the various activations, which included Jeep, New Balance, and Gatorade. The Jeep and Gatorade activations were professional, colorful, and stood out for the right reasons.

There was downtime between games and a good distraction was the opportunity to test drive a new vehicle. Jeep had designed an off-road course with elements that provided the driver with a glimpse of the technology or features on the vehicle. One area illustrated the suspension as you crossed over a long section of coarse, braided rope. My favorite section was the braking area. It was designed to showcase the braking capability of the vehicle. There was a fake mountain that interns hid behind and then threw Styrofoam boulders in front of the Jeep as it rounded a blind curve. The reactions were hysterical. I gladly volunteered to work. It is still one of my funniest work memories.

The Gatorade station was impressive both in size and appearance. You could see it from a long distance and knew what was inside the transparent fiberglass receptacle. It was an industrial-sized tank you would expect to see on large farms. If I recall, it was a team effort. We mixed the Gatorade powder with a stirring stick the size of a rowboat oar while someone else was filling the tank with water.

Me working at the Miami Hoop It Up Tournament

Mark Schreiber

Mark was a long-time employee and primarily a basketball director, which made sense due to his height and playing career. In high school, he was a McDonald's All-American and was recruited by major basketball programs, such as North Carolina State University, University of Maryland, Oklahoma University, University of Nevada Las Vegas, University of Missouri, Georgetown University, and the University of Southern California.

Mark declined a scholarship offer from Maryland because it was too soon after the death of their superstar guard, Len Bias, and he did not think the coaching staff would be stable at that point in time. Mark was a big Tar Heels fan and yearned to play for a great program. Unfortunately, Mark did not get to live out his dream due to a freak accident that occurred his junior year. He was at a high school party with friends when a fight broke out. Mark tried to step in as the peacemaker and attempted to separate the melee. Another individual walked up behind him and struck him in the head, knocking Mark out cold. However, Mark had much more than a concussion to deal with, because he spent ten days in the hospital in a coma, resulting in the left side of his body being temporarily paralyzed. In addition, he lost thirty pounds in two weeks. The incident resulted in a fractured skull and a bruise on the brain, which swelled and rotated one-quarter of a centimeter, resulting in the surgeon needing to drill a hole in Mark's skull to relieve the fluid pressure on his brain.

This all resulted in months of intensive rehabilitation, where Mark learned how to walk again. Luckily, he made a complete recovery and regained his ability to walk and play basketball, but a Division I basketball career was no longer an option.

Mark is grateful for life and the experience. He played two years at Washington State University under Head Coach Kelvin Sampson, with part of the time being a redshirt year to rehab and learn basketball again, then played at a junior college in Arizona. Mark finished his basketball career with two years at the University of Northern Colorado, but basketball was no longer in the cards for him at the high level he was playing at before the incident.

Standing at 6 feet 10 inches, Mark was an intimidating figure and had the deep, booming voice to go with it. In reality, he was a kind soul and an astute numbers guy. He took me under his wing and taught me to monitor my event budget, and how to negotiate and maximize expenses, down to pennies on the dollar. I appreciated his support and knowledge of the event industry. A $600 line item might be the difference between my event breaking even and a commission check.

Mark started off on the basketball side of the business with Cris and Dan, then added soccer years later as the company expanded its reach. He made an impression with his attention to the financial side of the business and was promoted to National Basketball Tour Director. The company soon after negotiated a contract to host the National Championships in Springfield, Massachusetts, near the National Basketball Hall of Fame, and the staff toured the facility, which Mark said was highly enjoyable.

Trip Back to KY

Mark accompanied me to Lexington, my "college stomping grounds," as the saying goes. It was my first basketball event as the Event Manager and he wanted to support me, which meant he took two days out of his work schedule when he did not have to. Mark wanted to add his comment to this section: "One of the things that made you successful in managing your events was your ability to communicate with all involved. Soccer and basketball are of significantly different demographics, but you could connect with sponsors, referees, local workforce, and most of all, the players. You never approached a conflict with a confrontational attitude, just killed them with kindness."

Looking back on his time spent with Cris and Dan, Mark is grateful for all the things he learned and the opportunities presented to him, including visiting cities he probably never would have visited otherwise. As a truck-driving intern, Mark visited Chapel Hill, the home of the University of North Carolina. He stepped inside the Dean Smith Center, commonly referred to as "the Dean Dome," and also snapped a photo of the building from the outside.

During our trip to Lexington, even though it goes against his Carolina blood and loyalty, he was fortunate enough to set foot on the Rupp Arena court. In his own words, "I visited two of the top blue-blood basketball schools with so much tradition and history; I want to say thank you!"

Mark went back to college to earn his MBA and is currently living in Denver, where he works as a Financial Analyst for a local medical insurance company, and is raising two wonderful children as a single father.

Mark's certificate from the McDonald's
All American Basketball Team

Adam Germek

We hired Adam as a summer intern for our national soccer tour. He attended the University of Tennessee for his undergraduate degree but finished his master's at Mississippi State University. A former Summit Sports and Events intern recommended him, and I am grateful he did.

Germek, or "Ger-mack" as we called him, has unlimited energy and is one of the hardest-working people I have ever met. No task is insignificant, and he will stay until the job is finished, even if that means staying behind while others are off partying. I have picked up bags of trash with this guy and negotiated five-figure contracts by his side. His energy does not waver.

He has this uncanny ability to flip a switch and go from goofing around with buddies to the sharp sales guy in two seconds. It is truly amazing to see it in person. I cannot tell you the number of times we were on a sales trip and stayed out too late, and it's as if he transforms into a superhero sales guy as soon as we mention it is go time. If I were a business owner, he would be my "can't miss" pick.

In real life, he is a fierce competitor, a lightning-quick athlete with a long arm span and great jumping ability. Off the field, his fantasy football skills are legendary. He researches more than anyone in the league combined. Adam knows that the Dallas Cowboys third string running back is getting married next month and his pet iguana's name is Charlie. He is in the play-off hunt every season and has won multiple championships. Yours truly barely makes the playoffs, and the two times I reached the Super Bowl, I lost both contests to Tom Brady. I still wonder why I endure the punishment of this goofy game, but it is a fun way to stay connected to a group of good buddies.

Adam and I shared a memorable road trip one fall. Our company had a satellite office in Lincoln, Nebraska. Being the college football fan I am, I wanted to see a game at Husker Stadium, and asked our coworker if he had any way to secure us two tickets. It turned out we were free to travel the weekend of the Oklahoma versus Nebraska game. The Oklahoma Sooners were ranked #2 in the country and the Nebraska Cornhuskers were ranked #3. We had a free place to stay and cheap game tickets. For the sports fans, you know the memorable play from this game and why it stood out. Nebraska's quarterback, Eric Crouch, handed the ball off to his running back, then Crouch casually jogged to the left sideline as if he was done with the play, but suddenly turned upfield and sprinted thirty yards to catch the pass from his running back. The Sooners missed the defensive assignment, and the Huskers won the game.

The trip started with a pit stop at 7-11 to load up on snacks. I bought my usual Gatorade, one pack of gummy bears, a bag of pretzels, and a Snickers. I walked back to the truck and as Adam entered the vehicle, he started chucking bags of candy into his seat. After the third bag of gummy worms zipped by my head, I thought that was the end, but I was mistaken. He bought traditional ones, extra sour ones, Starbursts, and Mike and Ikes. This guy spent $25 on candy and I loved it. He is the only person in the world who loves gummy candy more than me. For his fortieth birthday, his wife made sure he had a gummy candy bar.

Adam has a strong background in event management and sponsorship sales. He has been successful at every stop and currently serves as the CEO for Special Olympics in Tennessee. Adam currently lives in suburban Nashville, Tennessee, with his wife and two daughters.

*Me and Adam Germek at a 2019 sponsorship
conference in Nashville, Tennessee*

World Championship

The sixty-five-city tour culminated during late January at Disney's Wide World of Sports Complex in Orlando, Florida. We helped fill a major gap in their facility schedule, and they welcomed us with open arms. A company the size of Disney understands the importance of cash flow in an off month.

My first World Championship, I flew with everyone else. We redeemed Frontier Airlines miles to offset some of the cost, because flying twenty-four employees was not cheap.

The following year, I had planned on flying again with my teammates. My girlfriend, Beth, who would become my wife, had moved to Denver earlier in the year. One day in the office, one of the senior executive directors asked me if I wanted to take Beth this year.

I said, "Absolutely!"

"Great!" said the senior event director. "The only way she can go is if the two of you drive the Budget truck to Orlando."

Earlier I mentioned the fifteen-foot Budget trucks our event interns drove. But this event required a twenty-four-foot truck. This thing was a beast, and of course it had a governor on the engine, which meant our top speed was 66 mph with a downwind. The trip was 27 hours one way and covered 1,842 miles. My teammates who made the trek in the past let us know it would take three long days. Beth and I talked about it and decided to give it a shot. I remember Dan Cramer told me with a serious face, "If you two survive this trip, then you'll get married. It will be a test, trust me." He was not wrong.

We pulled out of Denver with sunshine and mild temperatures, but our fortunes changed as soon as we crossed the Texas state line. Between the sideways rain and potholes the size of moon craters, we felt like we were on a 4x4 Jeep tour without the proper suspension (or seat belts, for that matter). My wife inherited her father's short temper as it relates to driving. Dumas was the name of the city where we encountered the rough conditions and where our patience quickly faded. We pushed on and stopped on the other side of Amarillo, where we called it a night.

Day two's goal was New Orleans. We arrived at our hotel and made our way down to Bourbon Street for some sightseeing and fun. I had been to the city before and enjoyed playing tour guide as we explored the French Quarter. The next day would be our longest day of travel, so we reluctantly stopped sightseeing early and got some much-needed sleep.

The next morning, we woke up early and hit the road. We pulled into Disney World and shared a sense of relief and excitement. We threw our suitcases in the hotel room, then joined everyone at the hotel pool for some relaxation and well-deserved downtime. I bet we swam and hung out at the pool for three hours.

The championship days were a blur. We would arrive on site around 4:30 a.m. The days were filled with sunshine, along with griping coaches and parents. Since our entire company was working at this single event, we placed our Event Directors strategically based on their strengths. Our bracketing all-stars worked their magic and triple-checked every division, while our customer service team calmed down livid coaches who had lost their minds over a questionable call or a loss. Thankfully, I was on a different committee altogether and avoided the headquarters tent where the madness occurred.

Our return trip started out smoothly, until we reached Natchitoches, Louisiana. It was Beth's turn to drive while I napped. Everything was fine until we blew a tire. Beth heard the loud pop and braced for a bumpy ride. Luckily, we were by an exit, so she took the ramp and pulled into a gas station. I slept through all the commotion. When we hopped out of the truck to inspect the damage, we noticed three tires had blown out, not just one. This was not the way to start our return trek. Thankfully, there was a Popeye's restaurant attached to the gas station, so we ate lunch while we waited for the mechanic to arrive. We lost four hours of travel time, and neither one of us said a word for the next hour.

The silence was short-lived, though, because of a work-related issue. It turned out someone had forgotten to unload some Major League Soccer (MLS) All-Star ballot materials, and of course we needed to overnight them as soon as possible. We scrambled to find a FedEx location, then rifled through the truck to find the materials. The unexpected stop meant more lost driving time, but at this point we were committed to making the long haul as short as possible. Things were not going well and I wondered if we would survive the trip home. What else could go wrong?

Luckily, the remaining portion of the trip was relatively calm. We pulled into the Summit Sports and Events parking lot, exhausted but excited to be home and out of the monster truck. We went home and slept well that night. Beth returned to her normal job, and I waited for my teammates to fly home to unload all the equipment, one box at a time.

My 3v3 World Championships event credential

Me and Brandy Chastain at our World Championship
at Disney's Wide World of Sports

Moving On

One of my vacations while at Summit Sports and Events was backpacking in the western part of Colorado. I was having pain in my left knee, but I attributed it to wear and tear. However, when my knee gave out while walking down the stairs at the rental house, I knew something was wrong. It turned out I had a meniscus tear.

I met with the orthopedic surgeon and the plan was to remove the damaged tissue and be on crutches for two to three weeks. My last day with Summit was in late August, and I had my knee surgery the following day. I remember waking up from the operation, groggy and in an immense amount of pain. I felt like I was an actor waking up from being drugged because the clock on the wall was slowly moving in and out of focus. Try as I might, I could not fully wake up. I gratefully accepted another pain pill from the nurse and napped a bit longer before I was discharged.

My follow-up appointment was filled with positive news. The surgeon had reattached the meniscus to my bone to preserve the paper-thin tissue. This meant I could avoid arthritis and other hassles of having my knee being bone on bone at thirty-one years old. The only bad news was this meant I would be on crutches for eight to twelve weeks.

Other than physical therapy, I was home alone on the couch for eight weeks with too much down time. I rented a video game system from Blockbuster for a month, but since I am not much of a gamer, it got old quickly. I turned to reading and slowly began my job search. I had been in this spot before, and once again, the number of sports jobs in Denver was slim to none.

NikeTown

I eased back into the workforce and took a part-time sales job with NikeTown, Nike's retail store in downtown Denver. A retail job had not been part of my plan, but I was a longtime Nike fan, and the job served its purpose.

I worked with at least thirty different people during my time at NikeTown, which is not surprising as retail is a business with a high turnover.

However, two of them stood out and became my friends for life: Lawrence Matthews and Steve Nelson.

Lawrence "Law" Matthews

Law is one of the funniest people I know. He grew up in New Orleans and attended the University of Nebraska, but settled down in Denver, Colorado. He is one of those guys who is good at every sport. I played hoops and flag football with him, and he can hold his own. He sees the court and field like a point guard or quarterback and is not afraid to let you know what play is coming next. He is truly that talented. I was envious of his ability to excel on and off the court.

Law can and will talk trash with the best of them when needed, but he usually does so with a big grin on his face. His favorite brand and company is Nike. He is loyal to the swoosh brand and knows a bit about every color swatch and limited release, and he unapologetically cheers for almost every sponsored athlete, both male and female. Law is intelligent and can hold a conversation about anything with anyone he meets, which is another reason I appreciate his friendship.

He and I talk about life and tough societal issues, including race and politics, as well as Air Jordan shoes and current Nike business topics. No topic is off-limits. I believe everyone needs a friend like Law. I enjoy our talks because he makes me laugh every time. I know better than to argue with him for too long, because he is well-spoken and has done research. He should have been a lawyer because he relishes a heated debate, but we still enjoy the friendly banter.

When it came time to announce the title of my first book, I wanted to do something fun and different. Keep in mind this was during the COVID-19 pandemic, which meant I could not travel anywhere, and neither could my friends. Thanks to technology, we adapted and followed the world's lead. I set up a Zoom call and had three friends play a *Wheel of Fortune* type game to guess the book's title while others on the call watched. The three friends I chose did not know each other, which made it even better. Law was the first friend I asked. The other two were Justin Manna and Mike Arthur.

Justin and Mike each guessed one letter. Then it was Law's turn. He guessed W and then solved the puzzle: "Who We Meet Along the Way!" Justin and Mike shook their heads in disbelief, and I couldn't believe it, either. We all laughed. The other two immediately claimed Law had somehow cheated.

Back in 2011, my beloved UK Wildcats made it to the Final Four. I had ample vacation time and found a cheap flight, and Law generously offered me one of his extra bedrooms. Everything was falling into place—that is, until I came down with a mild case of pinkeye. Even with medicine and doctor's approval, I decided it was not worth the risk to get Law or anyone in his family sick. I sincerely thanked him then and do so again now. He is a Tar Heels fan, and though his heart bleeds a different blue, he remains one of my good friends.

Steve Nelson

NikeTown had three managers, but Steve Nelson stood out among them, for a good reason. His best quality was that he understood how to motivate people, even when someone was having a bad day or not feeling 100 percent. In addition, he was an astute student of Nike history and was passionate about the brand's culture and truly lived it every day. He often ended our staff meetings with one of Nike's maxims.

These principles are meant to give a sense of direction and purpose to employees at all levels of the corporation:

- It is our nature to innovate.
- Nike is a company.
- Nike is a brand.
- Simplify and go.
- The consumer decides.
- Be a sponge.
- Evolve immediately.
- Do the right thing.
- Master the fundamentals.

- We are on the offense—always.
- Remember the man [the late Bill Bowerman, Nike co-founder].

Source: Nike.com

Steve's nickname for me was Coach. I was taking a break from coaching youth basketball at the time, but I appreciated the nickname. After I left NikeTown, Steve told me he had enjoyed working with me because of my positive attitude and because, with or without the official title, I was a leader.

Steve was never satisfied, and he encouraged all of us to work hard until the last minute of each shift. If you set a personal or store record for sales that day, he would walk by, high-five you, and say, "Let's try to get one more sale." He did not come across as pushy, or like a tough coach; he was teaching us a life lesson to never settle. His favorite quote was, "Act like your pants are on fire and you can't put it out!"

Each morning before the store opened, we held a team meeting to review sales goals, new product launches, and any store layout changes. Steve closed every meeting by reading an inspirational Nike quote. True, we were simply selling sneakers and sweatshirts, but his energy and belief in us made us strive for greatness. Steve, thanks for pushing me to be the best version of myself and for reminding me that whether you are selling the latest Air Jordans or a discounted T-shirt, keep hustling, because impressive sales numbers are temporary, but chasing greatness never goes out of style.

Me, Law, and Steve at a Denver Nuggets game.

Post-game recap: I learned more about business at Summit Sports and Events than most of my other jobs combined. It was my favorite job and paid the least amount of money. The level of trust at our age and the room to make mistakes was something not available with other sports jobs. We joked we were poor rock stars traversing the country, visiting new cities and states each week. The travel, whether it was by truck or plane, was enjoyable and where most of my favorite work stories originated.

The NikeTown experience taught me the importance of company culture. The inspirational quotes and photos of famous athletes were not just for attention. It meant something and every employee, regardless of their role, knew and understood the reason why.

Chapter 7
Small Team, Major Impact—Metro Denver Sports Commission
April 2003—November 2004

Brandon Tosti
Director of Membership & Marketing

1550 17th Street, Suite 600
Denver, CO 80202
303-615-7490
Fax: 303-615-8490
brandon.tosti@denversportscommission.com
www.denversportscommission.com

Pre-game: After being sidelined with knee surgery for four months and spinning my wheels while enduring another lap in the retail world, I was thrilled to return to a traditional sports industry role. One of my mentors, Rick Hatcher, a Sports Commission veteran and former Division I baseball coach, helped me get the job. I was eager to learn the inner workings of a sports commission and the impact it has on the city and citizens by hosting sporting events of all sizes.

The Metro Denver Sports Commission is a 501© (6) organization. It was established by a local Denver businessman, Rob Cohen. He was not the first person to act; he acknowledges and praises the group of individuals who had established a prior sports commission.

Metro Denver Sports Commission: The Origin Story

Fast forward to 1989. Rob Cohen, originally from Wichita, Kansas, relocated to Denver after graduating from the University of Texas and working short stints in Dallas and New York City. He is the Chairman and CEO of the IMA Financial Group, Inc., an integrated financial services company.

In 2001, the Big 12 football Conference was interested in moving its championship game to Denver. The initial inquiry bounced from the Chamber of Commerce to the Denver Broncos Football Club to the Convention and Visitors Bureau, but no one took advantage of the opportunity. Each entity had time consuming projects on their respective plates.

The missed opportunity inspired Rob to act. A basketball guy at heart, he knew other cities hosted events and he wondered why Denver, with its natural beauty, 300 annual days of sunshine, and multiple pro teams could not do the same.

Determined to explore his hunch, Rob drove eighty miles south to Colorado Springs and met with the United States Paralympic and Olympic Committee executives. The meeting proved to be beneficial and educational on multiple levels. The major takeaway was the city of Denver should form an entity to successfully host mid- to large-scale sporting events. This would garner attention in the sports world and move the city of Denver into the forefront of potential event hosts.

After two years of tedious research and phone calls to other sports commissions across the country, Rob prepared to launch the business concept in Denver. The process included budget building and adjustments during that time. The first step was to meet with high level executives with each local professional team, then secure initial funding for operating expenses. He had three requirements for each team:

- Place a high-ranking team official on the Board of Directors.
- Contribute financially.
- Support the bid event process once the newly founded organization began working on future events.

Rob shared some important lessons he learned from establishing a sports commission from scratch. He stressed the importance of building a capital reserve fund, to have funding readily available when a major bid presents itself. You do not want to waste time and resources scrambling to raise another round of money just to bid for one event. Another piece of advice is to allocate 10 percent to the event bid budget from every event the commission produced. Again, you are building a cash reserve naturally with one eye on the future. Preparation is important in all facets of life and the event business is no different.

The Board of Directors consisted of a powerful combination of successful and well-connected business leaders and sports executives. Each professional sports team in the city held a board seat, which meant I worked with most of them on special projects and day-to-day operations of the organization. The Board also included athletic directors from the local universities. For someone of my age and with limited experience, this job felt like a networker's paradise. After reading certain names in the newspaper or sports business journals, I was now eating lunch and discussing event bid documents once a month with these men and women.

Since the organization was still in the infancy stage, fundraising became a top priority for long-term security and general expenses. Rob generously donated office space and covered other general operating costs, which helped the commission in its early years.

My Time with the Commission

I came on board with the Metro Denver Sports Commission (MDSC) in 2004 as Director of Membership and Marketing. I managed our membership database, which meant I logged every donation we received, whether it was $50 or $5,000. My role focused on the lower-level funding opportunities, primarily the $50 to $500 range. It began with the individual sports fan, and we built a small database of $50 donors. The Colorado Rockies generously donated multiple pairs of tickets, which were a nice premium for anyone who made a $50 donation to the MDSC. The long-term incentive was the opportunity to purchase tickets to the 2008 NCAA Frozen Four, which would be held in Denver.

Like most entities responsible for fundraising, we had a strategically designed committee. It consisted of two commercial real estate professionals, a former White House cabinet employee, and younger professionals who were eager to make a name for themselves.

Our lead fundraiser operated on a different level than I did. He would call me to let me know about a meeting with four of his friends or business associates. Three days later, four $1,000 checks would arrive in our office. My coworkers jokingly referred to these meetings as thousand-dollar lunches. It appeared easy for him because he was asking wealthy locals who could afford to donate that amount and not think twice about it. By contrast, $1,000 was darn close to a mortgage payment for me and my wife. It was a tight circle of successful businessmen and businesswomen who supported each other. They were all deeply engaged in more than one community nonprofit, and they truly cared about the long-term growth of the city and the sports commission. Seeing our lead fundraiser in action showed me the importance of making the ask—a lesson that would benefit me in the future.

Part of our fundraising strategy was the opportunity for the donors to get involved at the ground level before we secured a major sporting event. After that, the MDSC would no longer be a secret. Both companies and individual sports fans would want to donate to secure premier tickets. The MDSC was establishing a foundation for the future. We needed to know who supported us when we had zero events and know that they were friends of the program for the long haul.

A Super Bowl or World Cup is the kind of prize event every major city wishes for. First, we had to prove that Denver was a capable event host. Perhaps the Can-Am Police–Fire Games piqued no one's interest, but they provided an economic boost and led to more prominent events. Eventually, when Denver scored bigger events, donors who had supported us early on were in a prime position for priority access to event tickets without having to beg or promise favors.

Of course, probably the most sought-after sporting event for cities is the Olympic Games. Rob Cohen knew Colorado had declined the bid for the Winter Games in the early 1970s. But this was a new millennium. Rob organized an exploration committee and cautiously moved ahead with research into what was required to host an international event of Olympics caliber.

Rob and the committee members visited Turin, Italy, during the 2006 Winter Games. It was a great trip, and the group learned a tremendous amount regarding transportation and logistics. Rob shared a funny story with me about that trip. After a long night, the group stopped by a small restaurant to enjoy some authentic pizza. When it came time to order, the waiter stopped by the table and screamed, "No dough! No dough!" Rob and the crew shook their heads in disbelief. How does a pizza parlor in Italy run out of dough during the Olympics?

The Bid Process

Most large-scale sporting events are awarded to cities based on a bidding process. The preparation process is lengthy because it is a combination of creative and analytical elements. The event owner needs to understand the host city's capabilities, as well as any potential weaknesses. Airport size, ground transportation, number of hotel rooms, the distance between downtown and the venues all play a pivotal role. If the host venues are seventy-five miles apart and the airport does not have adequate community support, the event will choose another host city.

A bid application can be thirty to forty pages in length, and it is accompanied by recommendation letters from state and city officials, including:

- the governor
- the mayor
- the CEO of every pro sports team
- tourism bureaus
- sports commissions
- chambers of commerce
- athletic directors and head coaches at local universities
- executives of well-known companies headquartered in the city

The support letters are not promotional fluff or meant to be an ego boost for anyone involved. They include important facts and figures about the city's venues, transportation options, number of hotels downtown or near the venue, and even restaurants. In addition, each city partner provides a sales page touting their respective expertise. Someone must also invest time ensuring the presentation has accurate contact information and a consistent look and feel from the cover page to the final page. This includes formatting, style, graphic design, concise text, and professional photos.

These factors play a significant role in the bid process and can make or break a bid's success. Large-scale events fill hotel rooms, and there might be another convention during the same time. Event organizers are savvy leaders and know the tough questions to ask. They investigate everything that might impact the look, feel, and ultimately the success or failure of their event.

Economic impact is a popular buzzword used in the sports tourism industry, but it carries a deeper meaning to city leaders, sports executives, business owners, and citizens. When a city hosts a regional Little League Baseball tournament or a premier-level marathon, the event attracts athletes, coaches, and families from other states. Most of them must rent a car, stay in a local hotel, and eat at least two meals per day in a nearby establishment, and most will spend additional money on tourist activities. This provides a short-term boost to the local economy and an increase in tax revenue. Furthermore, some cities implement a hotel or rental car tax because tourists are traveling for business or leisure, and they will not scoff at five extra dollars on their bill.

Local Organizing Committee—(LOC)

The purpose of a Local Organizing Committee is to manage the event logistics, including transportation, hospitality, ticketing, venue operations, marketing, and a legacy project. The legacy piece is important because it pays tribute for years to come and provides a reason for the citizens to remember the event's financial impact. It is also used for storytelling and public relations purposes. Smaller committees are created to efficiently delegate the responsibilities and administrative legwork needed for event planning and implementation.

All these efforts require expertise, knowledge, determination, teamwork, and an understanding of who can get things done on short notice when the need arises. It is a wide-reaching network that unites for the good of the public and the city. A committee role is not about padding your resume; there is ample work to be done, and it takes a group effort.

My Mountain West Conference credential.

Special Events

To survive, a nonprofit organization such as the Metro Denver Sports Commission needs funding from large corporations and midsize companies as well as individuals. Special events are a popular funding mechanism. They create unique opportunities for supporters who are tired of the predictable chicken dinner or golf tournament. Creativity was one area I felt good about and knew I could contribute to with a myriad of options.

The Hard Rock Cafe was one of our partners, and the restaurant was a natural fit for a small event. I think the first event I proposed was a Halloween ball called "The MVP Masquerade." My idea was rejected, and I understand why, but I was attempting to appease two board of directors with whatever we decided on, which was a challenge. It was difficult to get the group to agree on the format and theme of the party. There was also pressure since it was one of the commission's first special events.

One of the popular corporate fundraisers across the country was a simple event known as "Jeans Day." Most companies required dress slacks five days a week, but Jeans Day allowed employees to wear blue jeans if they donated $5 to the nonprofit. It was wildly successful because it was easy to implement in small or large offices, and employees raved about the opportunity to dress casually for one day.

Sneaker Week: Genesis of the Idea

Five dollars was a great price point because everyone could donate that amount. For weeks, I racked my brain and scoured the internet searching for a clue or a concept I could build on. I finally stumbled across Sneaker Day, which was a copycat of the jeans program and was part of a sports nonprofit located on the East Coast. My supervisor reached out to the nonprofit and received permission to use their idea if we changed the name. Instead of Sneaker Day, we had Sneaker Week.

I loved the idea of having the event last more than just one day. Companies could allow employees to wear sneakers for one or five days for the $5 donation. However, the extra days allowed me to develop other opportunities to engage our donors and get them excited about Sneaker Week.

The Sneaker Week logo was designed by a board member.

Sneaker Week

Growth Plan

2004 – Kick off the 1st annual Sneaker Week – 15,000 participants

2005 – 25,000 participants

2006 - 35,000 participants

2007 - 45,000 participants

2008 - 60,000 Kick-off party held at Invesco Field

SNEAKER WEEK

"The can't miss event of Denver!"

The goal is to start with a single day format and turn it into a weeklong event.

Monday – Recycle old shoes at Niketown – Regrind used to build new courts.

Tuesday – Charity/Celebrity Basketball Game at DU or Pepsi Center

Wednesday - Speaking Panel - Dick Vitale, Rick Reilly or John Feinstein

Thursday – Black tie affair - Tuxes and Tennies

Friday - Camp out night/Sports movie festival - Participants camp in the outfield of Coors Field or Invesco and watch sports movies.

My aggressive plan. I've always been a dreamer.

Our advertisement appeared in a local sports magazine.

Sneaker Week Add-Ons

The second step was finding something to correlate with the week's festivities. I reached out to athletes and celebrities to ask them for a pair of unworn, autographed sneakers. Part of my logic was that the unique request might benefit us in the long run. Autograph requests for photos, jerseys, balls, bats, and flags are common, but sneakers were something different—and sometimes being different matters.

The list of shoes we collected from athletes and sports related celebrities included:

- University of North Carolina Tar Heels Men's Basketball Coach Roy Williams
- Tamika Catchings, USA Senior Women's Basketball Team and Indiana Fever
- Aron Ralston, avid mountaineer and author of *Between a Rock and a Hard Place*
- New York Jets Quarterback Chad Pennington
- Major League Soccer Commissioner Don Garber
- Smashmouth, rock band
- Big Head Todd & the Monsters, rock band
- Gary Gait, Colorado Mammoth lacrosse player
- A professional bowler
- A professional golfer
- Retired NBA players

OFFICE OF THE VICE PRESIDENT
WASHINGTON

April 5, 2004

Dear Mr. Tosti:

On behalf of the Vice President, thank you for your letter asking him to donate an item for the auction sponsored by your organization.

Recognizing the Federal personnel principle that employees should not use their offices for private gain – even for the gain of a private charitable organization – White House policy discourages the contribution of auction items. The Vice President makes a voluntary practice of observing this White House policy.

Although the Vice President cannot send an item for your auction, he sends you his best wishes for a successful event and for the continued good work of your organization.

Sincerely,

Cecelia Boyer

Special Assistant to the Vice President
For Correspondence

Mr. Brandon Tosti
Metro Denver Sports Commission
1550 17th Street, Suite 600
Denver, Colorado 80202-1657

I took a chance and sent a letter to the
White House requesting shoes.

The first year of the Sneaker Week program, we raised $30,000 with the help of twenty companies. The following year, we eclipsed $75,000. Sneaker Week was one small part of my job, but I was passionate about the potential of the program, both financially and from a promotional perspective. It allowed us to talk about something other than sporting events to non-sports fans.

I did not know it then, but this was a direct correlation to my undiagnosed ADD. When I am passionate about a project, I struggle to focus on anything else and I expend most of my energy on it. It remains this way until the next big thing strikes my interest. I often say ADD is a blessing and a curse because it allows me to express my creativity, but it must be something I strongly believe in. I had other job responsibilities to tend to, however, Sneaker Week was my proverbial baby. Right or wrong, I did not believe anyone else could match my excitement and passion for the project.

USA Basketball Liaison

To prepare for the 2004 Olympic Games in Sydney, Australia, the USA women's basketball team embarked on a four-city tour, and Denver was one of the locations chosen. Preparations were slightly rushed because of timing, but we could not turn down the opportunity to host and support such a prominent event. We spent weeks implementing grassroots marketing plans and cold-calling youth basketball coaches to drum up ticket sales and support for the team.

I was assigned as the USA team's liaison for the week. I escorted them between their hotel and the practice venue each day, but that's not all. I also assisted with other general questions and needs that arose during the week. The women were extremely competitive and phenomenal athletes. Their quickness, especially on the defensive end of the court, was hard to comprehend. I had a split second to feed an entry pass; if I hesitated, the passing lane was no longer open, and I had to reverse the ball to the point guard and reset the offense.

The altitude did not faze them at all. Everyone was in top physical condition, unlike me. Keep in mind, not only was I out of shape, but I also had not played full-court basketball in years. My face was three shades of red.

During one game, a USA Basketball team official asked me if I needed a breather because he jokingly said I might not make it to the end of the game. There was no way I was subbing out of this unique opportunity. My legs hurt for three days afterward, but it was worth it.

The event was the highlight of my time while working for the MDSC and I honestly did not think I would ever top it in my career. Soon after, I detected a change in my relationship with my supervisor. There was something going on, but I could not pinpoint what. We were never close, but now every interaction seemed short and pressed. We rarely agreed on business strategy: his job was to raise funds for the organization as quickly as possible to ensure long-term financial stability, whereas I was focused on building relationships and membership retention.

Later that year, in September, I married my longtime girlfriend and went on a wonderful twelve-day honeymoon to Costa Rica. When I returned to work, I was informed I was not the right fit, and the organization would move forward without me. Actually, I was told I could resign, which was unnerving and felt like a shady attempt on the part of my boss to protect his image with the board of directors. I politely declined and told him I would allow the situation to truthfully unfold. The experience was painful and emotionally draining, even for an optimistic person like me. It was tough to endure, but luckily my wife was strong and fully supported me.

Despite the fact I was only thirty-two years old, I knew the city of Denver was a small circle regarding relationships. I bit my tongue and handled everything in a mature manner. You never know when you might need someone's help down the road, and I try my best not to burn a bridge in my personal or professional life. I do not exchange Christmas cards with my former boss, but when we cross paths it's always businesslike and cordial. I know he would take my call if I needed something, and the same goes for me.

Before I left, I requested a meeting with Rob Cohen to discuss my departure and my concerns about the way it had been handled. I spoke with a formal tone, and despite my nerves, I calmly presented my list of topics and questions. Rob listened intently and made two general comments. He said he might agree with me on a point or two, but his closing statement was one I will never forget. He said it was important for him to keep his word to the executive director, and one promise he had made was that he would not interfere with personnel decisions. We shook hands, and Rob told me to keep in touch in case he could ever help me in the future.

Looking back, it was a simple decision and the proper way to handle it. I did not cuss and scream at him, nor did I make an emotional scene. I am glad to report that Rob also kept his word to me. Our business friendship is intact twenty years later. Rob is kind enough to take my call and meet with me when I am working on a new project every few years, which would not have been the case if I had handled my exit interview in a different manner. By the way, during my interview with him for this book, Rob told me he disagreed with the decision to let me go.

> *Post-game recap: One important lesson I learned from this experience is that creative freedom is vitally important for my job satisfaction and overall happiness. From then on, whenever I interviewed for a job, I asked the interviewer if the job would allow me to utilize my creativity. I knew that anyone with the desire to temper my passion in this area would be wasting my talent and time. I confidently declined the opportunity and knew to look elsewhere.*

> *The other important takeaway is that the experience strengthened me emotionally. I learned that everyone is not built like me. I was no longer afraid of a terrible boss, an egotistical one, or being let go from a job. It was liberating. Sure, in the moment, it hurt like hell. I had done nothing wrong but was embarrassed and felt awful telling my wife I lost my job weeks after our wedding. It is not an experience I would recommend. But the strength and resolve I gained from it proved beneficial in the long run.*

*Me and the 2004 Olympic women's
basketball team in their hotel lobby.*

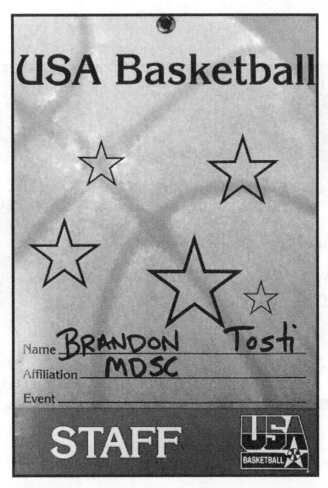

My USA Basketball event credential for the week.

Chapter 8
Flying Solo
November 2004—November 2005

Pre-game: The experience with the sports commission left me shaken for a bit. For years, I had taken pride in my work ethic and positive attitude. Now, I found myself unemployed and disappointed yet again. Deep down, I knew I wanted to start a company. The timing seemed right, and my wife and I were in a space where it made sense. The financial risk was minimal, other than the lack of a steady paycheck. Plus, I had a hunch about youth sports and how sponsorship could help local teams. I was curious to find out if I was right, and I took my shot.

After my time with the sports commission, I was not sure which direction I wanted to go. The holidays were quickly approaching, which is when companies shift their focus away from hiring new employees. It is never a good time to be searching for a new job. I took time to ponder what kind of job I would pursue next.

My former boss from the MDSC forwarded my name to someone he knew at a local TV station. I took the sales interview, but my heart was not in it. I left knowing my urge to start my business was not going away and I needed to pursue it.

I talked it over with my wife, who fully supported me. She felt like this was the best time if I was going to make the leap as an entrepreneur. It helped that we did not have kids yet and one of our two cars was paid off, but we had just returned from our honeymoon in Costa Rica. There is never a suitable time long to lose a job, but this was a tough pill to swallow. She said she could support us for a year and then we could reassess our situation. I knew I had to try because years down the road I would wonder, what if?

I lacked confidence and knew little about entrepreneurship. I bought a $10 small business reference book and reached out to some of the MDSC board members who owned small companies for advice about hurdles I might not foresee.

The most valuable information I received was about the importance of time. If I had fifty hours a week to dedicate to my company, what was the most efficient and productive area? Business development and sales are top priority and easy to jump into, but the ancillary pieces of a company are important, also. When you work for a large company, someone else handles marketing, promotions, HR, and even the website. I was in a constant tug of war with my brain, checkbook, and emotions. I was torn about where to invest my time.

Now I had the green light, the big question was the type of business I would start and what was I good at? Up to this point, I was comfortable and familiar with corporate sponsorships. I also understood how to create sales packages and could decipher the industry jargon. Last, I had a lot of amount of contacts and knew several decision makers with local companies. These were all advantages for me as a salesperson.

I noticed every sports league was conducting some kind of fundraiser for what seemed like eleven months out of the year. I remember my parents buying light bulbs, popcorn, and magazines to help my school and sports teams in the 1980s. What if there was a way to add a professional touch to the soccer club's fundraising efforts?

It hit me. Practically every youth sports organization needed funding but lacked knowledge of the sponsorship industry. Sure, a mom or dad can volunteer to write and send letters to twenty different corporations asking for money. Most local companies are bombarded by sponsorship pitches from every professional sports team in town, every local college, every resort and concert promoter and performance venue. The big players submit a well-researched and developed sponsorship plan with demographic information and other relevant consumer insights. Youth sports organizations were missing the most important piece of a sponsorship pitch: What's in it for the sponsor, and how do you properly ask for sponsorship? My plan was to secure sponsorships for youth sports clubs and programs in exchange for a sales and consulting fee. I had visions of representing a large number of youth sports clubs in Denver and eventually across the state of Colorado. As my client list increased, I could reduce my fees for less popular sports or clubs with smaller numbers than a soccer club.

Imagine if I controlled the sponsorship inventory for seven different youth sports organizations? If a company called me looking for basketball, I had that division covered. Volleyball, no problem, rugby? Same answer. The end goal was to create not just a database, but a portfolio, of ways to give back to the community with the traditional sponsorship brands were accustomed to. And I knew how to do this. My proposals would address how and where the brand's logo would be included and how often. It might be a local contest, in-store promotion, or a bounce back coupon. The last option is a helpful tool because it tracks redemption rates, making it easy to value that piece of the initial investment. In my mind, I felt like the business idea had great potential, but it would take time, effort, and a little luck to get it going.

My salary at the sports commission had been $32,000, which sounds low, and it was, believe me. I knew youth soccer clubs could not afford to pay a sales representative that much with no guarantee, not to mention sales commissions when I closed a deal. It was too risky. I shifted gears and realized soccer clubs *could* afford to pay me a fraction of my old salary, say, $7,000 or $9,000 per year. It would take time, but if I could secure three clients, I would be darn close to my original salary.

I knew I needed a company name that wouldn't limit my ability to generate revenue. I chose Tosti Sports & Events to have room to expand my services in case a new opportunity presented itself. A good friend of mine helped design my website in exchange for a case of Coors Light, and I paid a graphic artist $100 for my logo.

Then, I reached out to my network asking for referrals and told them about my business and what services I could provide for a consulting fee. Soon after, I met with the Executive Director of the Denver Soccer Club. A month later, I signed an independent contractor sales contract and had my first client.

Now, I had to secure a contract and start generating revenue and close some deals. I spent two days reviewing my stack of business cards. I had a good rapport with some members of the MDSC's board of directors. I called them to set up meetings and share my career news and ask for their financial support. One of the first calls I made was to a bank president. I knew banks focused on community-based sponsorships, and I thought a recreational soccer club might be an appealing partner. My meeting with the president went well and he told me he would connect me with his Marketing Director to discuss a contract and investment level. The following week, I met with her and negotiated a $25,000 sponsorship. It was a feel-good donation for the bank, but my proposal addressed their strategic business initiatives, too. For every new checking, savings, or college savings fund opened by a member of the club, the bank would donate $25 or $50 to the club. If 500 accounts were opened, the club would increase their budget by $25,000.

Based on my academic and real-word experience, I knew companies cared about one thing when dealing with sponsorships, and that is impressions, often referred to as *eyeballs* or *reach* in advertising terms. Sure, Jackson Soccer Club might be the winningest club in the state, but a company that makes organic energy bars wants to reach thousands of families if possible. The number of championships and titles is irrelevant. What matters to them is that Jackson is one of the largest soccer clubs in the state. And if I can help the company sponsor a number of big clubs, they can reach 200,000 people.

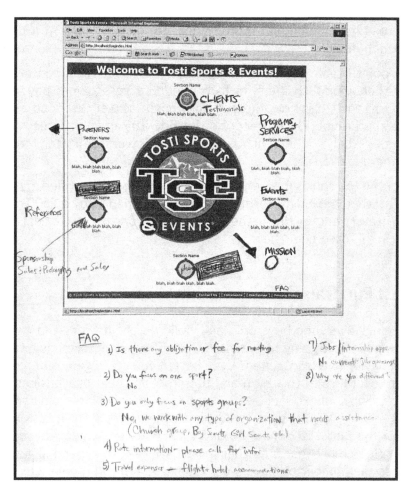

My initial notes for the TSE website.

Often, I needed to emphasize to clients that it is okay for a company to sponsor more than one club. Johnson Rental Cars wants volume regarding transactions, and the more soccer clubs on board, the better off both entities are in the future. Part of the issue was ego. Rival clubs chose not to share revenue or be associated with the same corporate sponsor. Based on this narrow-minded viewpoint, they left money on the table that could have helped all soccer clubs, not just one, and at a smaller investment level.

A key point I realized is this: A fundraiser that requires a consumer to change behavior, such as driving forty minutes across town to buy a sandwich, is a reach. It is not practical. They might as well just send a check directly to the club. The better option is to identify an action already in the consumer's daily routine, such as purchasing flowers for Easter, Mother's Day, or graduation.

One of the top sports marketing executives in Denver justified my grand thought when he told my former boss he would gladly buy a $500 dasher board in *every* hockey rink in the state, *if* he had one person to deal with—which in this case, could be me!

Florist Fundraiser

Two things everyone buys on major holidays are flowers and cards. If most families are going to purchase flowers, why not take advantage of this behavior and transaction? Even better, you could generate revenue and drive foot traffic to a mom-and-pop store and help local businesses. If a soccer club could direct 500 families to buy their flowers from a smaller, lesser-known shop, then it could be a win-win for everyone. My plan was for the florist to donate $4 or $5 per bouquet, which adds up fast. Soccer clubs, more than any other sport, have large membership numbers because the number of players per team (eleven) and the various levels of teams, such as premier, competitive, and recreational. Age groups can start at U5 and go through U18 for boys and girls.

Potentially, a club could generate $2,500 on Mother's Day. Add in graduation, Easter and Christmas. Now, the club might generate $10,000 from four holiday purchases while requiring little effort. I do not know of other fundraisers that can generate that level of money.

Putt-Putt Golf Tournament

When creating a fundraiser of any kind, it is to your advantage to include a wide potential customer base and not exclude anyone based on age or athletic ability. I took time to think of an idea that would do exactly that. The result was a putt-putt golf tournament.

I knew a local caddie who worked as the marketing director for a city-owned golf course and putt-putt course. She mentioned the option to pay per person or pay a flat fee to have the facility to ourselves. The latter was a gamble but had an upside if our attendance was decent. Once we reached the threshold, every golfer's entry fee thereafter equaled pure profit.

I sold $1,200 of event sponsorships in the form of booth spaces to home-based businesses. These were small companies run mostly by stay-at-home parents as side jobs. They could not afford traditional advertising, but $125 for a booth space hit the sweet spot. It was even more successful than I expected. We had everything from Mary Kay makeup to Longaberger baskets. I made one phone call, and the first person shared her directory with me. It turned out these businesses work together and share information and sales leads with one another.

Remember, the number one rule in event management is to check for competing events or major local established events occurring on or during your planned event date. I covered this in the 3v3 chapter. I thought I had checked the local event calendar but missed a crucial one. I had selected a busy date which was high school graduation weekend. Our numbers were much lower than expected. It was not a total bust, but I knew we had room for improvement.

Soccer Mom Contest

A local GMC and Pontiac car dealer came on board as a $500 sponsor and provided a new minivan as the focal point of our contest. The owner wanted to highlight the latest model and its new technology.

I designed a simple "Load the Van" contest but included all the new features so the moms would have to see and use them. It was a simple concept, but everyone who took part, enjoyed it and I appreciated the smiles. I also gave away prizes to the winners.

Next up was business expansion. My only client graciously called two other soccer clubs on my behalf and told him how satisfied he was with my effort.

I met with the two clubs together and the initial meeting went well. If I could sign these two clubs to nine-month contracts, I would achieve my goal and no longer stress about a steady salary. I had spent the past year getting to this point and knew it could make or break my business. A phone call from a former boss the following week set me on a different path altogether. Even though I was not a huge soccer fan, once again the sport provided me with a salary and a good job. I interviewed for the Director of Business Development position with Kroenke Sports Enterprises and accepted the offer shortly thereafter and closed the doors on Tosti Sports & Events with no second guessing and no regrets.

A parent tries her hand at the Soccer Mom Challenge.

Me and Rapidman at the Denver Soccer Club Putt-Putt event.

Post-game recap: I do not regret chasing my dream of running my own company. I learned a tremendous amount about building a business. I had to try it because I needed to get it out of my system and check the item off my bucket list. I never want to look back and regret not taking a chance. A pessimist might look at this decision and say I lost money that year and wasted time trying to launch a business. I disagree. Some lessons in life are priceless and not everyone is going to understand your motivation. It is okay. It is your dream, not theirs.

Chapter 9

The Big Leagues—Kroenke Sports Enterprises (KSE)
Dick's Sporting Goods Park (DSGP)
November 2005—May 2011
Commerce City, Colorado

BRANDON TOSTI

DIRECTOR.
BUSINESS DEVELOPMENT

6000 VICTORY WAY
COMMERCE CITY, CO 80022
P 303.727.3519
F 303.727.3536
E BTOSTI@DSGPARK.COM

WWW.DICKSSPORTINGGOODSPARK.COM
WWW.COLORADORAPIDS.COM

24 HOUR SECURITY 303.727.3737
WEATHER HOTLINE 303.727.3333

A DIVISION OF KROENKE SPORTS ENTERPRISES

STA

STAFF

BRANDON TOSTI

Dick's Sporting Goods Park

Director of Business Development

2009

Football. Fútbol. Soccer.

Pre-game: Dan Cramer helped me land my next job. He knew I was not a big soccer fan, but that was irrelevant because the job was an excellent high-profile opportunity. His advice was to get inside the walls of the company, because I was on the outside looking in. He told me to start with soccer, show them what I was capable of, then worry about trying to navigate the internal politics and a chance to work for the Denver Nuggets Basketball Team.

Introduction

Once again, I was eyeing another sports job in the Mile High City. The next skill set was nowhere on my radar, but when the opportunity presented itself, I jumped without hesitation. The Colorado Rapids were looking for a new permanent home; and, the owner, Stan Kroenke, found it on a large swath of prairie land in Commerce City, twenty minutes east of downtown Denver. My official job title was Director of Business Development. I often joked and said Zookeeper would have been a more appropriate title.

Denver has six professional sports teams. Four of them are owned by Stan Kroenke. If you wanted to work in sports in Denver in the first decade of this century, chances are you worked for the Denver Nuggets, Colorado Avalanche, Colorado Rapids, or Colorado Mammoth. Kroenke Sports Enterprises was a great place to learn the business of sports and cut your teeth as a rookie, and some were fortunate enough to advance to higher levels. At one point, I think the company had over 500 employees under its umbrella. It was the place to be for Denver sports.

I have thanked Dan Cramer before, but I want to thank him again for helping me get the job at Kroenke. My job was to sell field space and program a variety of tournaments as part of a new sports complex. The facility would house the home stadium for the Colorado Rapids Major League Soccer (MLS) team, with 18,000 seats, 24 full-size soccer fields, 2 synthetic turf fields, and 22 natural grass fields.

The Prairie Gateway project was known as one of the largest private-public partnerships between Kroenke Sports Enterprises (KSE) and Commerce City. Plans also included the potential development of future retail space.

Commerce City planned to construct new city offices for the mayor, city manager, and other officials, plus a civic center on the property. Prairie Gateway would serve as the new entrance to the Rocky Mountain Wildlife Refuge, including offices for the U.S. Fish and Wildlife Service. The project included 360 acres—160 supplied by Commerce City, and 200 purchased by KSE.

Source: Kroenke Sports Enterprises

Research Stage

It is not a common project or job to open one of the world's largest youth sports facilities in the world. I had questions, and lots of them. To tackle this monumental task, I started a list of large-scale soccer complexes in Colorado and other states. My effort focused on complexes with twelve or more fields. The only problem with in-state facilities was that they all considered the Kroenke project a direct threat on some level. I did not encounter any rude or unhelpful peers, but I soon focused my research on facilities in other states.

The first out-of-state call I made was to the Maryland SoccerPlex. The staff were friendly and quick to respond to my list of questions. After a phone conversation, I flew to Baltimore to spend time with their operations team. They were kind enough to spend four hours with me. I toured the venue and listened closely to their advice, horror stories, and justifications for their policies, procedures, and business principles. For example, there was a reason they had a cancellation rule, and it made sense to me after hearing what could, and usually does, go wrong with managing a venue, especially an outdoor one. I took page after page of notes and headed back to Denver with my head spinning, worrying about my never-ending checklist and hypothetical scenarios I was concerned about before construction began.

Construction

The facility was located in Germantown, Maryland, in a tree-lined park setting and differed from some of the other large complexes that were built in areas with little or no character. The complex included eighteen fields, if I remember correctly. One field was designated as the tournament championship field, which was a unique approach. The field was rested during the week to preserve it, and a small number of championship games were played on it during tournaments. A set of aluminum bleachers completed the look and feel of a distinguished field.

The months of research and phone calls to other venues helped me prepare for our facility's opening day. I had filled a notebook with questions, answers, and a lengthy list of action items. The last thing left on my checklist before our long-anticipated opening event was to erect forty-eight regulation-size soccer goals. The project felt like a combination of adult Legos and Ikea do-it-yourself furniture assembly. Teammates from a variety of departments helped us assemble the goals and install the nets. The first two were rough, but we created an assembly line and got into a flow. Once a goal was finished, the turf team helped us tow the goal to the endline of each field.

Instead of resting the night before opening day, I the spent evening moving soccer goals with a forklift and ensuring the last few goals were in position and staked for safety. The Rapids had had their opening day, and now it was our turn. I didn't sleep well, mainly because all the potential nightmare scenarios were racing through my head.

Managing the Facility

My job was simple: fill programming hours by booking youth and adult practice time, league play, and large-scale tournaments. The first thing we did was to sign contracts with Colorado's three premier soccer clubs and their respective tournaments. Then we began to backfill any open weekends with other tournaments and large events. Since I was not a soccer fan, I felt this approach served me well, because I was already thinking of other options to generate revenue. The soccer purists wanted me to primarily reserve the fields for soccer teams, but we had basic factors working against us. Geography was the obvious one. We were located fifteen minutes from downtown, which equated to one hour from the southern suburbs. Recreational soccer teams would not drive forty-five minutes and pay a premium price to practice soccer with seven-year-old kids for fifty-five minutes. I knew diversification was a vital key to our success.

I immediately reached out to both the largest adult recreational sports league in Denver and the smallest one. I needed all sizes of leagues to maintain my sales pipeline and build a client base for future years. I spent days researching contacts and phone numbers of adult league GMs and youth sports clubs.

I met with teams including rugby, lacrosse, ultimate frisbee, and even Gaelic games such as hurling and Gaelic football. They called me because parks and recreation departments cater primarily to youth groups, which is how it should be. My boss told me if it was PG-rated and family-friendly, then I could chase it, and that is exactly what I did. I listened to everyone, including flag football and Pop Warner football leagues. Quality fields in Denver were scarce, and our fields were pristine, safe, and brand new, not to mention the ample parking. Unlike municipal parks and recreation departments, we focused on generating revenue and lots of it.

My goal for our team was to provide the best event management service in town because we had the most expensive fields in the area. Premium pricing only goes so far; it needs to be accompanied by excellent services. Based on my event experience, I knew what headaches cause every event manager the most stress. We developed a comprehensive menu of tournament equipment that directors could rent from our department. We made it a point not to sell or push anything on them. After all, it was a huge benefit that saved time and effort. Everything was a la carte. Here are some items we included in our event tournament rental packages:

- 10 ft. × 10 ft. tents
- Golf carts
- Water coolers
- Tables and chairs
- Walkie-talkies
- Bags of ice

The bags of ice were a late addition but probably one of our smartest ideas. It was a time-saving convenience for our clients. We worked closely with a local ice vendor, who delivered a large freezer of the sort you often see placed outside gas stations. We plugged it in on Friday morning and simply called for refills as needed. It eliminated the task of sending a parent to a local grocery store or gas station to buy twenty bags of ice at a time, not to mention dealing with traffic and the hassle of finding a parking space again.

Later, we started offering box lunches that could be picked up at a central location by a parent for the entire team. This was a big hit because it was a healthy option, affordable, and available on-site. Most clubs brought three to four teams, which meant the upsell opportunity was built in with little effort.

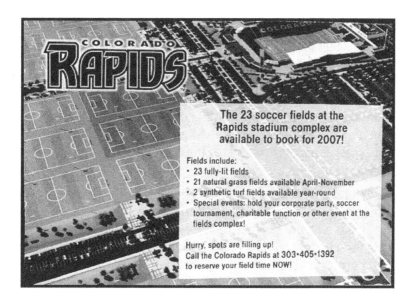

*Promotional postcard we mailed to local
soccer clubs and youth sports teams.*

Weather

Before we built one of the world's largest professional soccer venues, it of course made sense to identify affordable and under-used land with room to expand in future years. The only negative was the unpredictable and wild mountain weather in Colorado. The state is known for rapid meteorological changes. Sun can give way to wind and rain with little warning. Even lightning seems to move faster here.

The facility's architect strategically lined the edges of the field with tiny pine trees to leave a wide-open view. Thunderstorms and lightning were easy to spot miles away and everyone could see what was coming. A fatal lightning strike was my biggest fear. Even the best weather technology, well-designed evacuation plans, and clear communication strategy cannot protect you from the power of a lightning strike.

Ambulance Meeting

I worked multiple weekends for five summers at the park. There were long days and nights, but inclement weather sometimes made them seem longer. During one soccer tournament, I got caught at the fields without a golf cart nearby. Normally I would just run inside and take cover. But a gnarly storm moved in quickly, and running to the office was not an option.

The concession stand was also locked, and I did not want one of my team members to risk driving a golf cart to pick me up. I asked the EMT and paramedic if I could jump in the back of the ambulance and safely wait out the storm. We had an interesting conversation about their line of work. I was like a little kid, asking all kinds of questions about the equipment, the vehicle itself, and the various tools at their disposal.

One basic yet crucial skill is safely handling the vehicle in a wide range of conditions. There are countless things to consider while operating an ambulance. You are navigating traffic, crosswalks, children, animals, and tight spaces. Ambulance drivers are drilled on driving both forward and backward at high speeds and making last-second turns without hitting any cones during practice.

Ambulances also have various siren options for different situations. If it is a non-urgent call, the driver will use the long, slow siren. If it is a code blue emergency, they will use a quick and repetitive siren. But regardless of the speed of the siren's wail, pull over when an ambulance is approaching you and do not move until it has passed! There are little things people don't think about, whether it's driving to an accident or the adrenaline rush of saving someone's life or the emotional drain of losing a patient en route to the hospital. It was an entertaining and sobering forty-five-minute chat.

Lightning Technology

When operating a facility of this magnitude, you want to think of everything from a safety perspective, which was a top priority for our team and executives.

Since our complex was built on a wide-open prairie with little in the way of outdoor shelter, the stadium managers and I began researching lightning safety technology companies. The one we chose detected lightning and showed the number of lightning strikes and the amount of precipitation on my desktop computer screen. The best feature was the 24/7 access hotline. We could call and speak with a meteorologist at a moment's notice. This was key because it saved us time and effort. If we knew the rain was going to remain in the area for an extended period of time, we could cancel the remaining games for the night, resume the next day and avoid the dreaded start-and-stop scenario, which was annoying for tournament directors, parents, coaches, and players.

Speakers

After a season or two of stadium staff driving golf carts and waving our arms like exhausted air traffic controllers, the company invested in a PA system for the fields, which enabled us to make limited weather warning announcements, including a fire-type siren. We still had to deal with the occasional coach or parent sprinting across two soccer pitches to retrieve a $50 cooler, but the speakers were a welcome addition for our fields team. The line I taught my staff was, "I can buy you a new cooler, but I cannot replace your life, Coach! Please evacuate now!"

Since most players and parents remained in their cars during storms, the PA system allowed us to inform everyone of the storm's duration and projected path. This was a nice touch because it provided teams the opportunity to leave the complex if they wanted to without having to be concerned about missing a game once the weather cleared.

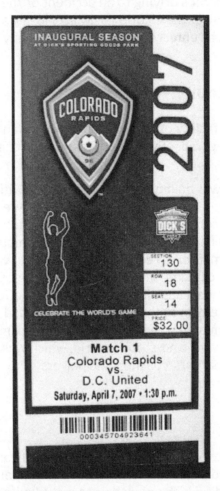

A ticket from Match 1 at Dick's Sporting Goods Park.

A Few of My Kroenke Colleagues

Josh Gross

Josh and I met because I bounced around offices when I first started with the company. Initially I started in the arena; then I was moved to the annex building across the street. I was housed in the basement along with several members of the lacrosse front office staff.

We bonded over our mutual love of college basketball. Josh is a proud Syracuse University alum. The school is well known as the leader in sports broadcasting education. A large number of the industry's top sportscasting talent and producers once attended Syracuse's S.I. Newhouse School of Public Communications.

Josh wore different hats for Kroenke, including, eventually, being the TV play-by-play voice of the Colorado Mammoth. As soon as he introduced himself, you knew right away he was either in radio or TV broadcasting. His voice was smooth—and, as I often joked, loud.

One of the things I admired about him was his ability to correctly pronounce the names of players from countries all over the world. It was important to Josh on a personal level because names are an emotional part of identity, and Josh felt it would be rude to purposely disrespect someone's name. Mangled pronunciations of names were his pet peeve. Broadcasters often receive a set of game notes that include pronunciation keys for each player and coach, but sometimes Josh would go to the player directly and ask for the proper pronunciation.

The toughest name Josh ever had to pronounce in his broadcasting career was the last name, Panagiotakopoulos, of a basketball player for the University of Northern Colorado. In the week leading up to the game, Josh rehearsed the name at home. He estimates he practiced saying it 200 times. Fifteen years later, he still knew how to say it correctly, and he mentioned he might not ever forget it.

The task of preparing for even one game requires serious commitment to the announcer's trade. Josh believes the NCAA March Madness broadcasters are the best in the business because they work multiple games in one day, with players and teams that were confirmed three days prior.

Sure, the college basketball bluebloods are easy to talk about, but the smaller, lesser-known schools present a different kind of challenge.

Jersey numbers are crucial when announcing a game. Think about your favorite player and his jersey number. It is easy to recall the number as well as the name because you pretended to be him or her hundreds of times in your backyard, making the game-winning shot. Now imagine sitting courtside for two hours with a player you just learned about a week ago and trying not to say your favorite player's name every time he touches the ball.

Further, think about team jerseys without numbers on the front. Sometimes the announcer must quickly identify the player without the visual aid of the number. Josh utilized other visual cues for these situations, such as long socks, brightly colored gloves, or hair color or length—anything that made one player different from all the rest.

Every sports fan loves to talk about sports. Josh was grateful he got paid to do it. His first radio broadcasting job paid $0. The following season, he negotiated a fee of $25 per game for webcasting. Finally, in his third season, he started earning a salary. His advice to the younger generation is to study hard at every level and act as if every game might be your last game, or the game when a future boss first hears your talent.

Looking back, Josh considered verb sheets one of his most valuable tools. This was a document that listed different verbs for every action the announcer commonly needs to describe. An announcer cannot say *dribbling* to describe a basketball player bringing the ball up the court all night every night for eighty-two regular-season games. Josh says the legendary commentators make it look easy but are true artists with their craft. They understand that their job is not to be a standout voice or personality, but rather to blend in and complement the action on the field, ice, pitch, or course.

After twenty-one years in the sports industry, Josh started his own company in March of 2023. It is a sponsorship and marketing consulting company based in San Diego, California, called One44 Group. The company name has a dual meaning. Josh's last name, Gross, is also a term meaning twelve dozen, or 144—hence One44. The number 44 is also an ode to a jersey number of significance to Syracuse University, including athletic standouts such as Jim Brown, Ernie Davis, and Floyd Little. The number was retired by Syracuse University around the time Josh and I first met.

When I asked Josh if he misses broadcasting, he said he does miss being on air, but not the prep work that accompanies it. And real pros like Josh Gross know you can't have one without the other.

Me and Josh before my book speaking event in San Diego.

J.P. Lefever

J.P. was one of our summer interns at Kroenke. He grew up in a local Front Range town, Berthoud, loved being outdoors and was a talented football player. Even though he was an imposing physical figure, his kindness and gentle personality stood out. He almost did not make the cut for an internship due to a misspelled word in his cover letter. To be fair, it happens sometimes, and Kroenke is a tough name to spell correctly. I was a tough critic regarding spelling in letters and resumes, but J.P.'s energy and engaging personality won me over. After all, someone gave me a chance in my career, and something felt right about my decision.

J.P. maintained a high level of confidence and felt comfortable in a room with team executives, players, or his fellow college interns. I told him I think it is a small-town thing. People who grow up in that environment learn at a young age to respect everyone and to never forget that they are no better or worse than anyone else. This trait was apparent from the time I shook J.P.'s hand for his interview until the day he left my office to pursue his own career.

Another thing about J.P. that stood out to me was his maturity. He knew what he wanted out of his career and was ready to tackle it one step at a time. His plan was to finish his undergraduate studies at the University of Colorado, then attend graduate school at the University of Sioux Falls. This plan hit a bump, and he had to redirect his plans. I could tell he was disappointed, but he was not deterred; he shifted his attention to the next opportunity. Optimism cannot be taught, but it is a worthy attribute for all of us to aspire to.

Hailing from Kentucky, I am a UK basketball fanatic, and I am accustomed to the old-fashioned ribbing that comes with the territory. One day, J.P. shared with me his fanhood for the Tar Heels. We were constantly talking trash to each other; it was part of our daily routine. Life led him to North Carolina, and ironically enough, he earned his master's degree in sports management from North Carolina State University.

J.P. married and settled down outside of Raleigh and is a Park and Recreation Director. He coaches youth football, and I imagine he is the kind of coach I would want my kids to learn from. When I interviewed him for this book, he rattled off names of his coworkers and what he referred to as his "coaching tree." Given J.P.'s personality and his ability to talk to anyone, I always knew he would be successful in whatever path he chose. I am proud of his accomplishments and how he carries himself, even if it is 1,500 miles away, while rooting for his beloved UNC Tar Heels beneath his red and white North Carolina State University diploma.

*J.P. is an assistant football coach at
Cardinal Gibbons High School.*

Phaidra Reed

Phaidra Reed worked for me as part of our seasonal Youth Fields Team. When we met, she was working three part-time jobs and was committed to securing a career in sports. I knew immediately that work ethic would not be an issue with her. I quickly learned she was more than capable of handling the toughest clients and anything that was thrown at her—or, in one memorable case, fell on her.

She reported for her first day of work, and I was training her that day. We jumped on a golf cart, and I drove us around the sports park as I told her about procedures, processes, and the daily operations of the facility. We threw one of the flimsy fiberglass tables on top of the golf cart to transport it to a field to prepare for that weekend's tournament. I was generally safety-minded about golf carts, but on that day, I must have taken a turn too sharply. Suddenly we lost our grip on one of the tables, and the table started sliding off the roof. Keep in mind, this was the kind of table you can buy for $40 at any local department store. Before I could hit the brakes, Phaidra leapt from the golf cart and tried to catch the table or break its fall. She tucked into a ball, rolled over the asphalt, and sprang up like an Olympic gymnast. My mind was racing; all I could think of was how I would explain to her parents how a table injured her on her first day of work. I slammed on the brakes, jumped off the cart, and ran to check on her. She was fine. Little did I know she had studied acting in college and had performed for two years in an action stunt show at Six Flags Amusement Park. She grinned and said, "Oh, I am a certified stuntwoman. That was the basic tuck and roll move. Where does the next table need to go?"

Phaidra was the first one to volunteer for any task or job, regardless of how tedious or mindless it was. When the weather turned, which was often on the Colorado prairie where the fields were built, she was the first to jump on a golf cart and drive through the twenty-four fields, instructing the coaches to seek shelter immediately. She had no fear, and she managed tasks with a smile.

Her dedication and positive attitude paid dividends when she was promoted three times at DSGP over the course of a decade. The good news is that she no longer worries about transporting tables with me.

Gabe Montanez

Gabe worked for the 24-Hour Security Department as a manager at the park. His cubicle was located just outside of my office door, and we became good friends. He was such a nice guy, very down to earth, and everyone got along with him. I admired that he had political aspirations and ran for Commerce City Council twice. People sit at a bar talking about things they would like to do someday, but too often it just remains a wish and not a dream that they chase. Gabe chased his, publicly, and I have told him privately how much I admire his courage for doing so. He may not have won the race, but he is a winner in my book.

I used to yell for him to come into my office so I could share a story with him or just vent. He was such a good listener. I felt bad that he had to endure my ADD more than other teammates did. I would constantly hop outside my office to talk about my latest brainstorm with Gabe. He was kind and would do anything for anyone. Gabe was a passionate soccer guy, and he was my go-to soccer expert whenever I had a question about a famous European player or club. He would grin and patiently walk me through the history of the club, what their fans were known for, their fiercest rival, and why people cared so much about their hometown club.

Gabe was also my roommate in Toronto at the MLS Cup and we shared some pretty good stories during the trip. For whatever reason, most of our stories involved food. There was a pizza place near the hotel called Big Slice that was open until 3 a.m., and it felt as if we ended up there every other night. It was a no-frills restaurant with a positive and welcoming vibe. One night we skipped the pizza joint, and as we were walking back to the hotel, I noticed a waffle restaurant. I *love* Belgian waffles, and this place had waffles with a multitude of flavors and toppings. I couldn't believe it! And the best part was it had a walk-up window for takeout! Are you kidding me? It was genius and I bought one with chocolate chips and bananas.

Canada is known for the Tim Horton's restaurant chain. During my time at Kroenke, I had heard stories about Tim Horton's but was not familiar with the concept. That first morning in Toronto, Gabe and I ventured outside our hotel, eagerly searching for a Tim Horton's. Luckily, we had to walk only two blocks to find our vaunted prize. I ordered a medium cup of coffee and a cake doughnut. The total was only $1.50. Gabe laughed at me and poked fun of my taste in doughnuts. He joked, "A cake doughnut? Why don't you just eat a plain piece of toast, Tosti!?"

*Me and the Stanley Cup at the Hockey
Hall of Fame in Toronto.*

Gabe and me at a pep rally in Toronto.

Back home with the MLS Cup at a Kroenke lunch event.

Nate Stahlecker

Nate and I met when I was teaching a Sports Marketing class at Johnson & Wales University. He was a model student, often asked good questions, and was never late with assignments. Nate sat in the front row, worked hard, and took advantage of the networking opportunities from two of the speakers I brought into class.

A part-time event management job was the first step in his career. He helped produce events at Summit Sports and Events and kept in touch with me afterward. Next, he secured an internship with Skyhawks Sports Academy through a business friend of mine. After a year, he reached out to me, and I hired him as part of our Youth Fields Team at DSGP. He was a little green in terms of experience, but he made up for it with enthusiasm, high energy, and a genuine willingness to learn. One of his best attributes was the ability to understand the value of customer service and the importance of solving problems quickly.

For whatever reason, Nate had a major fear of public speaking. This did not surface until one of our staff meetings. I noticed Nate was nervous and appeared flustered. After the meeting, I invited him into my office to chat. I asked him about it, and he said he'd been terrified of being called on to speak.

I told him we could work on it together. We met every Wednesday morning for thirty minutes in my office. During that time, I taught him about enunciation, the importance of speaking clearly, and how to make eye contact with teammates in the meeting. I also worked on his preparation and notes so he could rehearse what he was going to cover in the meeting.

As his manager, I commended him for having the courage to ask for help and to do something about it, because not everyone acknowledges a weakness and decides to work on it. A month passed, and he kept improving and worked on all parts of speaking. This is a valuable lesson for all junior employees entering the workforce. It is easy to identify and praise your strengths, but what is difficult is acknowledging your weaknesses and choosing to actively work on improvement. Doing so will aid your personal growth and benefit the team and the company.

Nate started as an Event Coordinator. A year or two later, he was promoted to Event Manager. In that position, he managed the Colorado Rapids Adult Soccer League, a key cog in our operations at the park and for the team. Last, he oversaw the Phish concert campground layout and logistical plan for the popular jam band's concert run at the park.

Next, Nate continued his successful path in Washington D.C., then Omaha, Nebraska, where he managed TD Ameritrade Park, the home of the NCAA Baseball World Series event. He currently lives in Denver and is the Managing Director for VOLO, a social sports company.

A funny note Nate left me about a field client
two years after an invoice was due.

Jeff Mathews

Jeff and I became friends because of good timing and the fact he helped me interview candidates for the Youth Fields Team. He was one of the longest tenured employees of the Colorado Rapids soccer team. He started with the team in the 1990s and worked in ticket sales and game day operations.

The first time Jeff and I worked together; we barely knew one another. We spent three full workdays reviewing resumes and conducting interviews—or, as I like to joke, couch time. The interviews were held on the concourse of the arena. We learned a tremendous amount during those three days about interviewing skills and what not to say. Here are some of the best stories from those sessions:

One candidate was kind, but her answer to our hypothetical situation left us shaking our heads. We started the interview with this question: "Imagine you are the Manager on Duty for the weekend. You are on Field 19, and an employee radios you and says a fight has broken out on Field 1. What would you do?"

The candidate took a deep breath and then, with a serious face, said, "Well, the first thing I would do is approach the two players or coaches and tell them to stop fighting. That is not proper behavior, and they are setting a bad example for the kids."

Jeff and I managed sheepish grins and proceeded to the next question, hoping the answers might improve, but unfortunately, they did not.

Another candidate was a highly successful radio industry salesperson whose resume was filled with exceeded goals and multiple promotions. On paper, the individual seemed to be in a great spot with the current job, so we asked why they were looking to make a change. The response started out innocently enough, with talk about what the radio industry is like from the sales perspective. Then it took an odd turn. The candidate stammered, "I need, uh, uh, I need closure, I am tired of selling airtime. I need a climax!"

Somehow, Jeff and I maintained our composure and shared a quick laugh with the candidate and proceeded to the next question. After the interview, we laughed until we cried. We seriously contemplated postponing the next interview, but somehow, we pulled it together and finished the day.

Another individual bragged in her cover letter that she had qualified for the playoffs in her fantasy football league five out of six consecutive years. Jeff and I laughed at the boast because it had nothing to do with the job. Now that I have had the opportunity to reflect on my own pitiful performance in fantasy football—making the playoffs in my Denver friends league only twice in fifteen years—maybe I should have been more impressed by the applicant's accomplishment.

The last story is about our final interview. After three years and twenty-five interviews, Jeff and I figured we had seen and heard it all. We were ready to wrap up the interview process and start deciding on my future fields team.

Since I had zero experience in running a sports facility, I knew I needed a second in command with some knowledge and experience in venue management. The last candidate really fit the bill. He was mature, a little older, and had seven years in-venue experience in Australia. We were sure we had found my event manager.

I had one more important question to ask, everybody's favorite interview question: "What is your dream job?" We anxiously awaited his response.

He calmly looked me in the eye and, with a straight face, responded, "Oh, that is an easy one. I would be a backup punter in the NFL, because you make a million dollars to sit on the bench and do nothing."

My heart sank. I immediately interpreted his response as pure laziness, and I was speechless. All I could think about was sitting through more interviews and hearing awful responses from more non-event people. Thankfully, he laughed and told me he was half-joking but stood by his creative and honest response. He got the job, and I learned how to think differently from him regarding venue management. In addition, he was a good influence on the younger members of our team, and he kept things light when we needed a comedy break.

As time went on, Jeff Mathews and I evolved a friendship based on good-natured competition and sarcasm (as you'll see in the next story). To this day, he and I still call to aggravate each other and laugh at one another like good friends do.

Me and Jeff at a Denver Broncos game in November 2023.

Kieran Cain

On paper, Kieran and I should not have been close friends. He truly loves the game of soccer; I can take it or leave it. He likes all types of cuisine and will try anything; I play it safe, sticking to grilled chicken and nothing with hot sauce or spices. But we did become friends based on our creative minds and similar work ethic. We both pushed ourselves and our teammates to do more than just what was required in our jobs.

Kieran was the Director of Marketing and Game Entertainment for the Colorado Rapids. No one could outwork him and he had an immense amount of pride in his work, as well as boundless energy and a creative mind that never seemed to run out of ideas.

He would also play a pivotal role in one of my future projects, which you will hear more about in Chapter 12. Kieran was a great teammate inside and outside of the office. I knew his marketing and public relations background would be beneficial to the project.

Kieran and Jeff Mathews had worked together for close to a decade and the three of us began to eat lunch together and talk about the company. At some point, Jeff Mathews and I were discussing future career plans. As I mentioned above, we got a laugh out of competing with each other. One afternoon, Jeff told me he was job-hunting, and I said I might do the same. He grinned and bet me that he could find a job quicker than I could. I played along; I figured if nothing else, it would make for a good story about our friendship someday. We decided the loser of the bet would buy the winner a steak dinner. Of course, we told Kieran about the bet, in case we needed a third party to intervene.

Months passed by, and neither one of us had made much progress on our exit plan. Then one afternoon when we were talking in my office, Kieran walked in, shut the door, and yelled, "I'm out of here, fellas. Where is my steak dinner?" Jeff and I were in shock because we thought Kieran, being a soccer guy, would never leave the Rapids. It turned out he'd found a job utilizing his other passion—snowboarding. Kieran accepted a Marketing Director job with Vail Resorts and would later take over the same role at Breckenridge Ski Resort.

Six months later, I would leave the company, as well. True to his word, Jeff Mathews bought me a steak dinner at the Denver Chop House.

Me, Tish, and Kieran at a volunteer project in New Orleans.

Alli Scheck

Alli and I were friendly acquaintances through our time at KSE. The first four years of my employment with the company, I reported to the managing director of the Colorado Rapids soccer team. The following year, the executives decided to split the team and youth fields into separate silos. Rather than the current setup of two directors, it made sense to create a single position to oversee both the stadium and the youth fields.

Alli and I were the two finalists for the newly created position of General Manager. I felt confident in my abilities based on my experience and the sweat equity I had invested from day one, when the facility was just a set of architectural renderings. Alli, on the other hand, had more experience with the Kroenke executives and was highly respected for her event management skills from years spent at the Pepsi Center. She was looking for a new challenge and an opportunity to advance within the company. However, neither one of us knew we were both applying for the same job.

In the end, she landed the job because of her qualifications and experience. Initially, I was crushed and angry. But she earned it and, frankly, deserved it. I tried to handle it the best I could, but I admit I was not a model employee for the first week or two. I shared my frustration and disappointment with a coworker over lunch one day, confessing that I wanted to leave immediately. One of the soccer coaches gave me the best piece of career advice I have ever received. He was from Boston and did not mince words with anyone about anything. He stared at me with a stone face and said, "Brandon, if you leave because you did not get the job, I promise you it will follow you to the next job." At first, I was stunned; I felt betrayed, as if he had failed to take my side. After I got home and took time to process his statement, I realized it was sage advice. As my friend, he was supposed to offer support, and he did—by reminding me I needed to accept the loss and learn from it.

I stayed at KSE. Alli was patient with me, and I give her credit for allowing me to work through my frustration without holding it over my head or against me. We got along fairly well, and in fact I learned important things from her. When I left my job, it was for a good reason, and it had little to do with her. She and I remain casual friends, and we keep in touch.

One of Alli's strong points was her ability to listen and create solutions. Instead of wasting time and energy arguing about a topic, she took time to listen intently to the third-party vendor and our team to understand the pain point and why it mattered to each side. Then she would bring both sides to the table, present the issue, and ask for feedback and options to move forward together. She was direct and did not avoid confrontation.

Alli routinely took detailed notes at meetings and filed them in a gigantic three-ring binder. If there was ever a question of what we had discussed or who had promised what at a previous meeting, she would flip to the tab in her binder and quickly find the answer. It amazed me. The notes were very helpful for all parties, and they were never used in a rude or snarky way. It was just the facts. Looking back, I learned a powerful lesson, and I have yet another resourceful boss to thank for it.

Alli switched career paths years later and returned to local government, as public service was something she had a great love for. She completed her master's in public administration and quickly found a job with the city of Lakewood, a western suburb. As expected by all who knew her, she did some great things at Lakewood and her success earned her a promotion followed by a new opportunity in Wheat Ridge, a cozy suburb located fifteen minutes north of Lakewood.

Allison "Alli" Scheck.

Mike Rock

Mike Rock, or "Rock," as we called him, served as the project manager for Dick's Sporting Goods Park. He managed all facets of the venue, from the construction phase to the Grand Opening. The entire process took close to two years, with countless renderings, strategic planning sessions, and budget meetings. His job was filled with high expectations, strong opinions, and some uncertainty, but Mike had a long career based in sports venues, including time spent at Coors Field and with the Oakland A's in various roles. He was the ideal person to lead this enormous project.

Communication is vital in any situation, particularly when you are spending $17 million of someone else's money on soccer fields, not including the stadium expenses. I remember Rock's calm demeanor, even when things went awry. As the project's chief, he dealt with the construction company, subcontractors, internal company executives, the wealthy owner of KSE, and the local media. He maintained a positive attitude and an even-keeled temperament and exuded calm to all parties involved.

The most important lesson Rock taught me was the importance of understanding and accepting stress. I had zero facilities experience when I was hired, so I was continually searching for answers and solutions to potential hazards and conflicts. I spent two days per week agonizing over terrible what-if scenarios.

After yet another planning meeting, Mike asked me how I was feeling and if I was happy with my venue research and progress. My anxiety and the apprehensive look on my face gave away my actual feelings: I was nervous and struggling to control a hundred different moving parts. Mike smiled his million-dollar smile, gently put his arm around me, and said, "Tosti, you will never have full control of this venue because it is too big. You cannot control everything here. No one can. What you can and should do is place your arms around it and hug the chaos." Those words sank in as I was leaving the stadium, and they still ring true years later. While I did not stop cycling through nightmare scenarios in my head, I knew he was right, and I tried my best to accept his advice that day and the rest of my time spent at the fields.

Mike Rock.

The Royal Flush and Topping Out

In stadium construction circles, there are two unique traditions that symbolize and celebrate major milestones of the project's timeline. The first one could be filed under "Strange but True," and deals with plumbing, of all things. It is affectionately known as "The Royal Flush." Before a stadium opens, it is only common sense that the hundreds of fixtures and miles of pipes must be tested in something approaching game-day conditions. The contractor recruited twenty-five people to flush the toilets and urinals simultaneously. The project manager distributed radios, and each of us walked the pristine and untouched concourse to a bank of restrooms to prepare for our role. When the call came over the radio—"Hit it!"—it was time to flush! Laughing, we ran back and forth between stalls, urinals, and sinks, pressing handles and turning faucets on and off repeatedly to test the infrastructure and water pressure.

The second tradition is a builder's tradition. It is ceremonial and occurs as the last beam is put in place on top of a structure. It is a photo opportunity for the team and sports reporters.

*My souvenir from the Dick's Sporting
Goods Park Topping Out ceremony.*

Me and Mike Downey, owner of Play Coed Adult
Sports League, on a construction tour in 2006.

Me signing the construction beam.

It sounds silly and a little awkward, but it is a fun ritual you only get to experience once or twice in your career. New stadiums are constantly being built around the globe, but a single franchise typically plays in a stadium for twenty-five years or longer. Opening a new stadium was a highlight of my time spent in the industry. The time, energy, and effort invested by everyone involved is tremendous, and the result is something fans will enjoy for years to come.

Our baseball friends downtown at Coors Field had lucked out with 71 degrees and sunshine for their Opening Day in April 2007. I had a bad feeling we would not be so lucky. Sure enough, a nasty cold front moved into the region on Friday, bringing snow, wind, and bone-chilling temperatures. "Bundling up" took on a new meaning that day. I felt so bad for all my teammates who had worked so hard for their Opening Day. The crowd still showed up, like any true Colorado fan, dressed in layers of Gore-Tex and ski pants.

Doug Fulton

Some people have big hearts, and others have the brains to match and the soul to truly appreciate what community means. Doug Fulton is one of those people, he is a prime example of what it means to be a good person. He was the Community Relations Manager for the Denver Nuggets for fifteen years, and he truly loved his job. Not only was he passionate about it, but he performed his duties at a high level and consistently over-delivered for schools and nonprofits in the Denver community. Doug knew every nonprofit in town, and I am certain he would have donated $1,000 to every one of them if it was an option. His official title was Senior Manager, Fan Development, but it could have been Community Ambassador and Goodwill Advisor.

Doug and I met and became friends shortly after I started at KSE, when my office moved across the street and I took up residence in the annex basement. He always made me laugh. I do not think it is possible to be in a bad mood when you are around him. Some people are placed in this world to spread good vibes, and Doug is at the top of that list.

Throughout the year, we crossed paths because the Fan Development department helped other teammates conduct youth clinics and camps at

Pepsi Center and Dick's Sporting Goods Park. We were connected by our dear friend, Marisa Colaiano. He and I both had plenty of memories and stories from working beside her. Marisa courageously fought complications from multiple sclerosis, but ran out of time during the summer of 2012. Doug had the unenviable task of delivering the eulogy for someone who was loved and respected by coworkers and friends. Somehow, he made it through the lighthearted yet powerful speech. It combined her passionate personality and determination perfectly. Something tells me she would have approved of his choice of words. I served as a pallbearer, as did Doug, and it was an honor I will never forget.

For large-scale fundraising events, the team would spend five months planning for the big night. The evening's program was scripted minute by minute because there was no room for error. On this special night, the spotlight was on the beneficiaries, corporate and individual donors, the players, and the staff. There was no option for a timeout if something went wrong. Part of the planning was preparing for what could go wrong and how the team would respond to it. Under Doug's leadership, his team and peers learned how to work with executives, high profile athletes, and community ambassadors.

Doug is one of those people you simply cannot forget. He works hard, has a bright outlook on life, and appreciates his blessings. We often ate lunch together in the break room, but one thing we never did was play golf together. There was a reason for that, and it had nothing to do with our schedules or the fact that we lived forty-five minutes apart. It is 100 percent because Doug is a fantastic golfer and would humiliate me, and I don't need that kind of negativity in my life.

We shared a funny moment once, and it was at Doug's expense, but it was not my fault. One afternoon, he went to lunch with a friend and brought his leftovers back to the office. Since there were a fair number of people in the building, Doug wrote his name on the outside of the cardboard container before putting it in the refrigerator. The next day, he went to the kitchen to retrieve his leftovers, but the box was gone. No note, no explanation, just vanished!

Doug was rightfully upset and frustrated. Who would steal someone else's lunch? If you are hungry, just ask. Doug would share, or loan you $10 for lunch if you needed it. Instead of throwing a temper tantrum and stomping through the office searching for the lunch bandit, Doug chose a different route—the humorous one. He patiently typed a well-thought-out and descriptive email and sent it to the entire office. I don't remember the exact wording, but it was something along these lines:

> *Doug goes to lunch with his best friend at his favorite Mexican restaurant. He ordered too much food and brought it back to the office refrigerator for tomorrow's lunch. Someone in the office opens the refrigerator door, looks at the cardboard container with DOUG'S LUNCH written on it in big black Sharpie, and proceeds to eat my lunch. What kind of animal does this to a coworker? I could understand if there was another Doug in the office, but this was intentional, and I don't understand why it happened. Please do not eat my lunch again. I was really sad, not to mention hungry, too!*

Back to the job. Doug organized three to four basketball clinics per week during the season. The various clinics allowed the professional athletes to show the softer side of their personalities, something the public does not normally get to see. The Special Olympics clinic was the largest, with close to 140 athletes. The players were emotionally moved by the attendees and would stay after the clinic ended, often playing one-on-one until the group leader informed everyone it was time to leave the court. I recall Doug proudly mentioning that, for some period of time, the Denver Nuggets was the only NBA team whose entire team—players, coaches, and staff—participated in hosting its annual Special Olympics clinic.

Another part of Doug's job was coordinating players' visits to children who were in the hospital. The medical staff did a great job of communicating what to expect prior to each visit so the players could set a tone that was appropriate to each child's situation. Doug and his team made sure to balance each group of players by assigning two veterans with a rookie, because it was always an emotional experience, and you were never sure how a nineteen- or twenty-year-old might react in that situation.

Part of Doug's job was to act as a buffer between players and the public and always keep the players in a comfortable position. This included things as simple as where to park, what to say during a media appearance, and how to set the tone during a visit or clinic.

There were good deeds performed by players from multiple teams that the media never heard about. It was not uncommon for Doug to leave a hospital visit and, within minutes, receive instructions from a player to buy four premium tickets and a jersey to be delivered to the child at a later time. It was often the player's personal credit card, too. These players understood their ability to make someone smile and made sure to give back to the community.

Doug deftly navigated language barriers, cultural differences, and attitudes in general. He shared a story with me about one player who was acting difficult at the beginning of a basketball clinic. The player made a snide comment or two to him. Doug had a good relationship with him, and he understood the player might have had a bad morning, so he knew not to take it personally. Less than an hour later, the same athlete walked over to Doug, smiling, and said he was worried that someone might get hurt because the basketballs had too much air in them. The athlete immediately grabbed a ball pump and started deflating basketballs. Funny how your mood changes when you share your love of a game with a group of underprivileged kids.

Having worked closely with athletes from around the world through hundreds of clinics, hospital visits, and other events, Doug learned how to talk to people and how to be a good person. Whether you grew up playing hockey in an eastern European country or hoops in sunny California, we are all human, and sometimes it takes a child to remind us of this simple truth.

Eventually, Doug traded in his goodwill job for a different way of helping others. He is now a successful mortgage broker and volunteers every Friday morning with a local nonprofit. He continues sharing positive stories from nonprofits across the metro Denver area. Doug and I don't get to hang out nearly as often as we would like, but we still make time to meet for lunch once or twice a year. Most importantly, he knows I won't steal his leftovers the next day.

*Doug Fulton working one of the Break
the Ice community events.*

Mascot Madness

A popular saying when someone lands a job unexpectedly is that they "fell into" it. In the case of a coworker, it was more like somersaulting into one. This individual started in 1982 in high school as a wolf, then progressed to a different animal in college, and then to the professional ranks.

For 31 years, he put on a costume and entertained fans, making over 240 appearances a year. He was a top performer and one of the premier mascots in all professional sports. Somehow, he made everything he did in the suit look easy. Keep in mind every mascot has either a large head, a massive tail, or an oversized belly to deal with and maneuver around.

The public always has questions about mascots, as did I. Let's start with the mascot's costume and the most important piece, the head. I asked him what his vision was like once the oversized head was in place. If you were the same height, he could see a portion of your face and that was it. He said his field of vision was comparable to looking through two toilet paper tubes. To see who was yelling at him and maintain awareness of his surroundings, he had to turn his head constantly. But—and this is the tricky part—he had to do it in a way that did not make the audience wonder why he was doing it so often. It was all part of the mascot magic.

The costume included more than just an oversized body. For two games at the beginning of his career, he wore oversized, floppy costume shoes. They were awkward and frustrating to run in, so he had someone glue the colorful attachments to the sides of a pair of regular running shoes, so they looked like the original costume ones.

Early in his career, he learned not to turn his legs too fast, because a young child might run into his knees. He accidentally knocked a more than one kids over the first few days but quickly adjusted. To compensate for his lack of vision, he learned to use his hearing to gauge how far away voices were as he was approaching them or vice versa.

He pushed for new and creative ways to engage fans, which helped cement his legacy in the world of mascots. To safely navigate the arena stairs and everything else, he constantly took mental pictures and counted the number of stairs as he traversed section after section in the arena. If he counted twenty stairs on the way up, he knew to touch twenty on the way back down. This was for his safety, as well as to present a seamless appearance to the fans.

A typical calendar year included hundreds of appearances outside of home games. He realized he needed to adjust some small details. The first was to create an office space with no windows so that he could dress prior to a performance and not deal with the time and energy to find an adequate room to change into the costume. The second was a branded vehicle, which allowed him to quickly change into costume regardless of the event location.

Timing and rehearsal were important to him. He had two assistants, or "handlers," as the job is commonly referred to in the industry. Their job was to keep him safe and escort him to the right place in a timely manner. The mascot cannot be late for camera shots or a halftime promotion.

The mascot's assistant plays a vital role, not only during games but at every public appearance. A good example is when the mascot autographs an item for a child, hands the pen off, and quickly transitions for a fan photo. The assistant needs to anticipate every critical move and be in the proper position for the next portion of the event. It is a team effort, because the mascot also wants to make sure the assistant looks good. He never wants to toss a T-shirt cannon on the floor or throw a Sharpie in the air and make it appear that the handler missed his mark.

The assistant also helps generate creative ideas and promotional stunts. A routine skit that occurs is when the mascot hands a famous ex-NFL quarterback a football to sign, then takes it back and gives it to a young fan. On one occasion in my friend's career, a new wrinkle was planned at the last minute. During this game, the quarterback's teenage son was with him. The idea was for the mascot to bring two footballs: one regulation size and one miniature. When the quarterback reached out to grab the regulation sized ball, the mascot handed it to his son and offered the dad the miniature ball instead. The famous dad was legitimately caught off guard, and the crowd roared with laughter.

An important piece of advice for aspiring mascots is to watch film of yourself. Study it just like an offensive coordinator would as he prepares for the next game, because your movements almost certainly look different than you think they do. A good mascot is always looking for ways to improve their interactions and see what they can do differently to get their point across.

An important detail he mentioned that fans might not think about is the amount of mental energy it took for him to work the crowd every night.

"Improv acting is exhausting," he said. He and the game entertainment team often spent two days gathering supplies and rehearsing for the next home game. Everything was based on precise timing and flawless execution.

Physical energy was also required, which meant he had to be in great physical shape. Each offseason, he rotated between running a marathon and following an intense combination of cardio exercises and a weightlifting regimen. At the end of each game, he sat in his dressing room, mentally and physically drained yet smiling, knowing he had made thousands of fans smile and forget about their worries for a night. It was not uncommon for a team doctor or paramedic to administer an IV and oxygen to him.

A large majority of professional sports teams have a mascot, and some also have a junior one for the team's kids club. The Colorado Rapids decided to try something different when the team opened its brand-new soccer stadium in Commerce City. The managing partner of the club introduced four mascots instead of one. The Rocky Mountain Arsenal National Wildlife Refuge is located less than a mile away, and the four mascots were animals whose natural habitat was in the area.

It was a strategic decision, because if you have multiple mascots in the arena or stadium, more kids and fans can be entertained at the same time. It also provides additional opportunities for community appearances at schools, charitable functions, and other popular events. Mascots are a significant part of the fan experience, on and off the court, field, or pitch. The names of the four mascots were Edson the Eagle, Marco Van Bison, Jorge El Mapache (The Raccoon), and Franz the Fox.

*Me and Rocky the Super Mascot at a
Denver Nuggets playoff game.*

Shawn Martinez

Kroenke Sports Enterprises was a major player in the Denver sports market, and the company had over 500 employees during my time there. Because of the sheer size of the organization, you met people in different departments due to the nature of the crossover from ticket sales to venue operations and facilities. Shawn Martinez worked in the Game Day and Entertainment Department, and we became friends because he also helped with the Colorado Rapids home games.

One perk of working at KSE was the opportunity to play pickup basketball from time to time on the Denver Nuggets' practice court. I honestly cannot tell you who had more fun running up and down the court, me or Shawn. It was competitive, but we both knew no one was getting called up for a ten-day contract with the team!

Shawn was born and raised on the Navajo reservation in northern Arizona. Basketball is king of all sports in Arizona, and Shawn's childhood dream was to play in the NBA. He was a point guard and talented enough to walk on and play for three years at Fort Lewis College in Durango, Colorado. He joked with me during his interview, saying, "I still made it to the NBA, but just in a different way."

Shawn's job at Kroenke was handling the music segment of in-game promotions, which made sense because he was a well-known DJ in Denver. His DJ handle is "Tribal Touch," a nod to his Native American ancestry and a subtle reminder of how his choice of music touches people.

In Shawn's mind, a DJ's responsibility is to make non-cheering fans get out of their seats and dance. Yes, it is a professional basketball game, but during timeouts and halftime, it is entertainment, and the game entertainment team wants to take each fan on a journey.

Behind the scenes, it is a major process to forecast and plan forty-one home games. The game entertainment director must take theme nights and halftime entertainers into account as they draft each game script, or "run of show," as it is referred to. The good news is there is no shortage of entertainment options to choose from.

One of the toughest challenges for an NBA game is the potential for back-to-back timeouts. The DJ must be ready to go because there is a finite window of opportunity and everyone in the arena will know if you miss it. Timing is everything!

Another important part of playing live music to 20,000 fans is ensuring no song clips include profanity. NBA games are family-friendly events, and there are multiple checks and balances to ensure that every aspect of the entertainment is suitable for all ages.

Shawn is not the only member of his family who works on the entertainment side of the NBA. His son, Austin Pawelka, started early by introducing Denver Nuggets players at midcourt when he was only eight years old. It turned into a career path for Austin. As "Paws the Music," he was one of four DJs in the COVID-19 NBA Bubble season, and he is currently the official DJ and music coordinator for the Denver Nuggets. In 2022, father and son were named All-Stars and invited to the NBA's famous midseason extravaganza.

After Shawn left the Denver Nuggets, his next career stop was Detroit, Michigan, the Motor City, home of the Detroit Pistons. Six years later, he had the opportunity for a homecoming, and he returned to his roots to continue to amplify the voices of his people, the Navajo. The twenty-year journey had come full circle, back to where life began for him.

The Phoenix Suns hired Shawn in November 2020 as their Senior Director of Live Presentation. Now he is working with the famous Phoenix Gorilla, one of the NBA's best-known mascots. As Shawn said, "A dunking gorilla is tough to beat from an entertainment perspective." Martinez brings his trademark positive attitude and infectious personality to the job, as well as a passion to keep the Native American spirit alive and at the forefront of the team's promotions.

DJ Tribal Touch will continue to spin records and make people smile one energy-infused beat at a time. Martinez stands tall for kids who look like him and hopes to be a role model for all Native Americans.

Shawn Martinez "DJ Tribal Touch" doing what he loves.

Austin Pawelka—Paws the Music

Austin began his sports career at an early age—eight years old, to be exact. The Denver Nuggets on-court product was not great at the time, and the game entertainment team thought it might be a good distraction and a feel-good promotion to have a kid announcer introduce the Denver Nuggets starting lineup at a home game. Austin's name was drawn out of a hat, and he won. At his first game, Austin calmly stepped to midcourt and added his signature growl as he announced the starters one by one, and the fans loved it. He wasn't nervous and relished the opportunity. A month later, he was invited back, and soon he was a regular contributor for the popular pre-game ritual.

As he grew older, Austin eagerly accepted new opportunities to learn the business, and he performed a variety of jobs, including the T-shirt toss, cable runner for TV broadcasts, and ball boy, which meant he helped with the team's laundry and swept the court after a player fell. In addition, he also worked as a spotter. This person's job is vital to game entertainment operations because the spotter helps relay communications to the DJ, the director, the mascot handler, and other team members.

COVID-19 and the NBA Bubble

Austin was one of four DJs selected to take part in the NBA Bubble during the COVID-19 pandemic. He said it was an easy decision. The job lasted ninety-three days and was a powerful and emotionally draining experience. For starters, Austin did not see or set foot on a basketball court for the first seven days during the initial quarantine period. Every morning began with a temperature check and a pulse oximeter reading. Three meals were delivered to his room, which was a nice touch, but it was odd not to see or interact with anyone. From a work perspective, each day was filled with Zoom calls regarding safety, operational updates, and long-range planning. The NBA consulted with top health officials at every turn. Their diligence, creativity, and research paid dividends for ESPN, the league itself, and sports fans around the globe.

The environment initially felt like something out of a futuristic sci-fi movie, but the employees quickly realized it was the safest place to be, based on the NBA's strict health procedures and testing. Once games started, everyone realized that all the highlights on ESPN SportsCenter each evening were about the NBA. The sports world had its collective eyes on Orlando, Florida. Critics wondered if the NBA could execute a project of this magnitude with a great number of factors out of their control. The league's determination, positive attitude, and partnerships with doctors and health care experts made the difference.

The league offered fitness amenities that had to be scheduled because of rigorous cleaning rules and COVID-19 policies. This helped Austin stay in shape, because it was the one constant he could control during this time. It also provided mental clarity. He said he did pushups, watched movies, and FaceTimed with his family often, especially during the first week on campus.

The need for human interaction became an issue for everyone involved. They found solace in the newly popular sport of pickleball. It became a popular way to pass the time, and the games were highly competitive, especially between the league referees. Games often stretched late into the night and were entertaining to watch.

To the general sports fan, DJing a game looks like a simple pick-and-play process. However, the truth is the DJ spends hours planning and preparing for every possibility and situation. As a game entertainment DJ, Austin must understand the flow of the game. During the first half, the home team might jump out to a large lead, but these are professional athletes with pride and athleticism, which means no lead is ever safe. The last thing you want to do is play all your feel-good party songs during the early lead, see the team fall behind, and then have nothing left for the unexpected and late fourth-quarter rally. One also needs to be prepared for the possibility of an overtime period. This does not occur often, but when it does, you need to be ready to go with appropriate songs to bring the crowd to their feet.

During Austin's first nationally televised game against the Golden State Warriors, the power to his DJ booth went out. Accustomed to thinking on his feet, he knew he had limited time to sprint upstairs and use the broadcast booth. He relied on his father's experience and advice, which meant he kept his cool and calmly handled his business and the stress that came with it.

In 2021, Austin added one more title to his distinguished list of accomplishments: NBA All-Star Game DJ. The planning and production process was wildly different from a regular season game. He had to balance sponsor ads, TV timeouts, and the unexpected reactions to what was transpiring on the court. He spent long days rehearsing timing and song choices, as well as double-checking song lyrics for profanity or questionable wording.

His DJ handle might be "Paws the Music," but this game entertainment and veteran DJ knows what is most important in his business: to anticipate the madness, embrace the chaos, and press play.

Austin with the Larry O'Brien Trophy.

Tony Kreusch—The Ice Man

Tony Kreusch was a curious kid and often wondered how things worked. His love for all things engineering led to a lifelong passion for Legos and machines. His current job title is Head Ice Tech for the Colorado Avalanche—or, as diehard hockey fans call him, the Zamboni driver.

During his college years at Colorado College, he was friends with a hockey player on his floor. One day this friend asked Tony if he was interested in a part-time job. Could he drive a Zamboni for the hockey arena? Tony replied, "Well, I can drive a tractor." After some training classes and practice laps, he was hired. This opportunity led to an equipment manager job with the hockey team. After graduation, Tony decided to stick around. He worked full-time as the Ice Rink Manager for eleven years.

His next stop was his dream job at the University of Denver. The university was celebrating the opening of their new athletic facility, the Ritchie Center. A year later, someone from the Pepsi Center, now Ball Arena, reached out to Tony to see if he could fill in for a sick employee. Tony was happy to oblige. He worked at the Pepsi Center for a week, assuming he would then return to DU and take care of the ice there. However, the employee Tony was filling in for never came back, and Tony was hired as a second driver.

Home games for Tony are a twelve-hour commitment. He arrives around 9:30 a.m. to clean the ice for both the visiting and home teams. He ensures the surface is clear of any debris and ready for primetime later in the evening. Tony has an immense amount of pride in his work and wants the Avalanche coaches and players to skate on the best surface in the league.

A new Zamboni costs somewhere between $150,000 and $200,000. The vehicle has four wheels, and its top speed is 11 mph. The machines have a twenty-year life span. There are three major differences between driving a Zamboni and driving a car:

- The driver's seat is located behind all four wheels, not positioned in the middle or on top of them.
- The right side is a complete blind spot due to the height of the machine.
- While it is a four-wheel-drive vehicle, you can and will slide if you are not careful.

The Zamboni could be referred to as the Swiss Army knife of ice maintenance vehicles. It picks up old snow from the ice, shaves a new layer of ice, and cleans the ice surface as it leaves new water in its tracks. Tony says Frank Zamboni, Jr. created the perfect machine.

For educational purposes, Tony wants fans and readers to know the ice never goes away. There is a one-inch fiberglass subfloor that sits on top of the ice and between the basketball court or lacrosse turf. Ice is forgiving, but it takes time to freeze and repair itself.

During playoff games, Tony will clean the ice more than once when possible. It helps when he has two Zamboni drivers because the time is decreased from twelve minutes of work to six and a half, which allows additional time for the ice to breathe, so to speak.

Tony is by nature a calm person, but he was almost in tears one morning after a mega pop star's concert. The artist's stage included a water feature, and somehow the system leaked and allowed dirt and debris to seep down into the ice. After conducting his routine ice check, Tony found the Head Coach and began apologizing, for fear the ice might not be perfect before that evening's home game.

Tony has been in his job for over 20 seasons and has worked over 1,000 games. The only time he missed a game, actually three, was when he was recruited to work during the 2018 PyeongChang (South Korea) Winter Olympic Games. It was a once-in-a-lifetime opportunity, so he took it. During his twenty-two-day stay in Korea, the Korean Olympic Commission provided a daily stipend, a top-notch hotel, and super food for the employees. His highlight was the opportunity to work the Men's Bronze Medal game and the Women's Gold Medal game. The best part was the fact that the medals were kept in the Zamboni room until the ceremony began. Tony estimates there must have been seventy-five or more of them, because each team has roughly twenty-four players on its roster.

With ice hockey, as with most sports, preparing the playing surface is a group effort. Tony is part of a larger team that consists of building engineers, a conversion team, and a group of backup drivers. He praised them all for their hard work and effort to bring close to 300 events a year to life.

I asked him about his favorite memory while working for the team. It was a complicated answer, and here is why. In 2001, the Avalanche won the Stanley Cup on its home ice. It was an incredible experience and a special, once-in-a-lifetime memory for everyone involved. In 2022, the team was a dominant force for most of the season, and their sheer athleticism and speed made them a strong choice to win it all. This time, the team closed out the series and won the Stanley Cup on the road—but the feeling was still a powerful one.

For the 2022 cup final, the Avalanche decided to open the stadium for a watch party for the fans. Over 14,000 fans packed the venue to watch their favorite hockey team solidify their names in the history books. After the game ended, the stadium employees who were working were able to clock out and head down to the ice for celebratory photos.

The victory lap Tony shared was different from most victory parades with fire trucks and police cruisers. As you might guess, Tony drove the Zamboni through the streets of downtown Denver. He said the crowd was seven to eight deep and electric with cheers and chants on every block.

Tony driving the Zamboni at the PyeongChang
2018 Winter Olympics.

Chris Greenley

Chris took the long route to his first job in sports, and it was a combination of good timing and pure luck. Chris was a student at Metro State University in Denver, and a classmate began a conversation one afternoon by notifying Chris that he was leaving his job with the Colorado Rapids. He looked at Chris and said, "You're a soccer guy, right? You should apply for my old job." Ironically, this conversation occurred at the beginning of a ballroom dancing class.

Chris was what people consider a non-traditional student because he was finishing his degree as a twenty-four-year-old, but the advantage of maturity benefited him in school and in other ways. Chris was known for his positive attitude and work ethic in the office. He did the jobs no one else wanted to do. It was his way into full-time employment, and he embraced the opportunity. He was only working part-time for the club, but he took full advantage of leading the Colorado Rapids Street Team, which was an innovative marketing tool to promote the team at festivals, fairs, recreation centers, and other community-based events. The job was a hot one because it was summer, and labor-intensive because the team was constantly setting up and breaking down oversized inflatables. The goal was to ensure kids safely enjoyed the atmosphere in whatever parking lot or grass field the event was on any given day.

When asked for his best sports industry work story, Chris shared a pretty good one with me. He was working with the Colorado Rapids Game Entertainment Team during the league's "Wild Wild West days," as he referred to them. A pro team's halftime entertainment program is filled with excitement and energy, and Chris was asked to assist with the mascot soccer match promotion.

There was a kids' soccer game planned for halftime with well-known mascots from the other pro teams—some fan favorites and one or two that fans may not have been familiar with. Denver Water's ad campaign was a simple one: "Stop running water, Denver!" Someone at the company chose a toilet as the campaign's mascot. Yes, that means the usual animal mascots were joined by a crystal-white toilet playing soccer with a bunch of local kids. In the toilet costume that day was an executive dressed in white running tights and a long sleeve shirt. For some odd reason, he thought it would be fun to play an active role in the halftime event.

Chris had one job, and he took it seriously. His task was to run around the field for a minute, then gently tackle the toilet. Sounds easy, right? Well, Chris thought the gentleman in the mascot costume knew what was coming, but that was not the case. Chris was dressed in his game uniform, which consisted of khaki pants and a burgundy Adidas Colorado Rapids polo shirt. The toilet entered the field from the sideline and pranced around, dodging other mascots, and waving his hands wildly. Then, seemingly out of nowhere, Chris sprinted across the pitch and accidentally caught him with a crossbody tackle that would have made an NFL linebackers' coach proud. The executive seemed surprised by the tackle, and Chris was nervous he had hurt him. The play-by-play commentator proudly exclaimed, "Denver, be sure to stop running toilets!" The mascot slowly stood up, limped off the pitch, and politely declined the opportunity to work as the company mascot at the following week's event. There may or may not be a YouTube video of the incident.

Chris takes pride in his pre-event planning for anything that might go wrong during a game. He teaches his team to double-check everything and be prepared for the worst-case scenario, including writing game scripts for extreme situations. His attention to detail came in handy during a home game when the team's ice-making machine stopped working. Suddenly, Chris Greenley and the Hurricanes Entertainment team had to distract fans for two hours with no ice!

When the ice machine failed, Chris said his team played videos from earlier in the year, historical content from the recent alumni game, and simple trivia. "But those videos are only ninety seconds at most, so we emptied that reserve fairly quickly."

After that, Chris said, "We started thinking about silly things and one of the best ones was playing solitaire on the video board. It is boring to watch someone play, so we would cut back and forth with other video content to break up the monotony. The secret is, we lost about three games before winning one, but we did not show all the losses to the fans. They only saw the win in the end. We received a big cheer, and everyone talked about it for years. Maybe more so than the ice machine failing!"

Chris praised his mentor, Shawn Martinez, for helping him identify his next stop when he moved on from the Denver Nuggets. He chose the Carolina Hurricanes, and the hockey opportunity worked out well. Four years later, he was promoted to Senior Director of In-Game Marketing and Canevision. In the fall of 2022, he was promoted again, to Vice-President of Entertainment and Production, a position well deserved after a decade of preparation.

Chris Greenley at a 2022 conference.

Cam Kelley

I met Cam through an old 3v3 soccer coworker and teammate. He and his wife lived down the hall from my friends. It turned out Cam was the Game Entertainment Coordinator for the Colorado Rockies Baseball Club. One of the neat things about the sports industry is that when you meet someone who works for another team, even though you don't know them, you can relate to and respect them because you know how hard they work, not to mention you often know some of the same people.

Cam grew up in the Pacific Northwest and was a successful pitcher. He played two years for a junior college, then transferred to Santa Clara University, where he is the current record holder for the school's baseball program. He leads the school with twenty-two hit batsmen his senior season. After he was pulled from his final game, a teammate informed him that the national record was twenty-five. His response was, "Are you

BRIGHT LIGHTS & LONG NIGHTS

kidding me? Heck, if I had known that I would have tried to hit four more batters and make it into the national record book!"

I had to ask Cam why he hit such a high number of batters. He said some were intentional, while others were due to being frustrated with his performance or wanting to stick up for a teammate who had been hit by a pitch earlier in the game. For the most part, he was just trying to throw inside. The arm and elbow protectors were getting popular around that time, so guys would lean in and take the pitch off the brace. Also, if Cam wasn't on top of his change-up, the ball would run inside and dot some guys. "Effectively Wild," he called his strategy.

He landed a spot on a single-A baseball team, but after he blew out his pitching elbow, he was ready to find a new career option. One of his Santa Clara teammates had been working with the Seattle Mariners baseball club and contacted Cam about a part-time job in the Game Entertainment division. Cam was eager to get his career started and agreed to take the job before he even knew the responsibilities. The first thing Cam did upon arriving was ask what the job entailed. His teammate responded, "You play music. I don't know the details; you just push a bunch of buttons." During the day, Cam worked in customer service; then he switched gears at 5:00 p.m.

Most fans are entertained at a pro game but have no clue the amount of work, time, and planning that goes into it. In Cam's opinion, game entertainment is 70 percent scripted and 30 percent reactive to how the action unfolds. Game day production preparation is filled with walk-throughs, meetings, and final check-ins with graphics, camera locations, and the replay operations team. It requires the coordination and effort of close to fifty employees. The next time you attend a professional sporting event, pause, then look around and think about the moving parts and hours of planning to make one thirty-second sponsor promotion come to life.

Attention to detail is crucial in Cam's job, especially in the planning of small windows of time and opportunity during a live game. One time, Cam's team played a video clip of a player who was on the Disabled List (DL) and not playing in the game. Mistakes happen. Spelling is a common pitfall. One can scour the internet to discover wild yet unbelievable gaffes involving mascot, team, or player names being misspelled, or even the wrong jersey number given. The worst case of promotional misfortune I can think of might be the time a professional baseball player was traded on a weekday and the team had planned a bobblehead giveaway for that weekend. Now they had 15,000 bobbleheads that nobody wanted.

Baseball players are known for their superstitions. Sometimes when a batter got a base hit, he would send a message to Cam to play the same walkup song for his next at-bat. Conversely, when something did not go well, the player might have a different response. One player called Cam during a game after striking out and told him to never play that walkup song again.

After a decade of working in major league baseball, Cam traded in his baseball cleats for ice skates and moved across town to work with the Colorado Avalanche. I am guessing it was a welcome change on some level, because he went from working eighty-one home games to forty-one.

He said the major difference between the two sports is the speed of the game. Baseball is slow-paced and you have ample opportunities to conduct in-game promotions. Hockey is the fastest game, but you are constantly waiting for a break in the action. This means he and his team must be ready on a moment's notice to press the play button on the music and cut the TV feed to the in-game reporter.

Another observation he referenced was the difference between baseball and hockey fans. Baseball fans are constantly fidgeting with their cell phones because there are long bouts of down-time, but hockey fans are there for the game and dislike taking part in any kind of cell phone promotion.

At the Rockies, Cam worked with Dinger, a playful dinosaur mascot. At Ball Arena, the team mascot is Bernie, an oversized Saint Bernard. The ice provides a challenge because Bernie must be agile and able to skate. Don't forget that most professional mascots have limited vision and the field of vision is usually positioned below the character's head.

Another one of my dream jobs was to be a professional mascot. Ironically, I got the chance to fill in for a Mountain West Conference Basketball commercial shoot on a random Thursday afternoon in Denver. I was the Air Force Academy Falcon, and my good friend was the University of Las Vegas Running Rebels mascot. I have been to southern Mississippi in mid-July and two different rainforests, yet nothing compares to the heat I felt prancing around in a gymnasium while wearing a falcon costume with feathers. The best part was the Rebel head had a mustache that must have been four feet wide. Anytime someone asked our tiny friend a question, she whipped around and knocked us out with her fake mustache. After absorbing the second hit, we figured it out and expected her next swivel move and knew when to dodge the 'stache.

Spatial awareness was surprisingly difficult because I could not see my feet or arms. The other fun thing about being a mascot is you can make a fool of yourself, and no one knows it is you. Do not forget the water weight you lose by sweating during an appearance. We were in a high school gym with ten people. I cannot imagine the pressure and expectations of being a mascot in an arena with 19,000 fans.

Cam Kelley working a Colorado Avalanche
hockey game at Ball Arena.

Eli Madden

Eli started in the sports industry while he was a student at the University of Minnesota. He was hired as an intern in event operations and sponsorship activation with World Power Sports Association (WPSA) Racing. He gained more experience with action sports by working for ESPN X-Games and the Dew Tour.

At the conclusion of one Dew Tour event, the team shared dinner to celebrate. Luckily, Eli was seated beside the president of the tour. It was an excellent networking opportunity, and Eli listened intently to the executive as he held conversations with the group. Soon after, he asked Eli what he wanted to do for a job. Eli replied he would like to be in the president's position one day in his career. The next question for Eli was, "What kind of sales experience do you have?" This was an eye-opening moment for Eli as he was just beginning to navigate his career journey.

A year later, he moved to Denver, Colorado, for a sales job in sports. He was not worried about landing a job with the best team or the most popular one. This can be attributed to his midwestern roots and work ethic. He referenced his and his family's experience of working twelve-hour shifts in a factory. Like most sports employees, a home game usually equates to a twelve-hour workday. Eli did not shy away from it, and he would often report to work the next morning at 8:30 a.m. even though he had the option to show up an hour or two later from time to time.

The best part of being a member of a ticket sales team is making a difference for the team because you get to see your hard work come to life. You also learn the importance of generating revenue for the organization. This is paramount for teams at any level because ticket sales, suite sales, and sponsorships are the major economic drivers for any professional sports team. The day in the life of a ticket sales representative has changed during the past ten years. Today's sales teams are on the phone 85 percent of the time, whereas in the past it was closer to 100 percent. Technology and social media have created new opportunities to communicate and reach decision makers, business owners, and fans. Today's sales staff might spend time on LinkedIn searching for new leads and contacts to call, or share a success story on one of their personal social media accounts.

Another major change has been the development of CRM, Customer Relationship Management programs. This type of technology helps track individual customers and provides a multitude of reports for sales managers, including which fans are most likely to renew ticket packages, year over year.

Eli mentioned, "Being on the front line allows those of us in ticket sales to have a pulse on the fan base. This not only teaches us what we can continue to improve upon, it also lets us build strong relationships with the fans." A good customer experience with the frontline ticketing team, maintained and built on over time, can turn a person with a mild interest in the team into a passionate fan. Eli knows this, and he constantly reiterates to his staff the importance of making quality phone calls, not just trying to rush through so you can say you made 100 calls in a day.

The focus in sales is on revenue generation, revenue retention, and filling the pipeline with new opportunities and sales leads. In the case of sports ticket sales, this work should take place in the offseason. When the season begins, the mindset shifts to implementation and execution of the sales plans that were developed three to four months prior. You lose time to hit your sales goals with each passing day, so it is important to act with a sense of urgency and work diligently in the offseason.

There are three types of ticket sales:

- **Inside sales** focus on current or previous single game ticket purchasers. This is the entry level area where most people start their careers. It allows the individual time to build confidence, learn and develop their sales pitch, execute said process over and over, and it provides the opportunity to earn his or her way to a promotion to the next level.

- **Group ticket sales** focus on six areas: nonprofits, churches, youth groups, schools, corporate outings, and performance groups such as bands, dance teams and choirs. A group ticket purchase consists of at least ten tickets. Theme nights are popular fundraisers for youth sports teams, school districts, and dance teams. The organization sells tickets and receives a percentage from each ticket that is sold.

- **Season ticket sales** focus on selling as combinations of two and four tickets as possible to every home game. Eli teaches his team to not focus on these two numbers. As an example, a company could buy eight to twelve season tickets, depending on their programming for said tickets.

Ticket sales is an attractive option for young sport management professionals, and a financially lucrative one, but the work is not for everyone. You find out quickly if you enjoy a sales environment or not. In the past, it was viewed as a stereotypical "foot in the door" type of job, but that perception has changed immensely. Teams are investing in sales teams, their software, and other helpful tools to help reach sales goals and fill the stands with passionate fans. Eli believes the goal of a sales manager is to coach, train, and develop people in the ticket sales world where they can hopefully advance to the management level or into high-end sales for the organization, such as luxury suites or corporate sponsorship sales.

Eli has been promoted four times during his fourteen years with KSE. Currently he is the Vice-President of Ticket Sales and Service for the Colorado Mammoth, the popular indoor lacrosse team. The personality trait that provides him with an advantage is that he truly cares about his sales team, their individual successes, and the organization.

Eli and I share a love for coaching others and networking to help others along their career path. We have kept in close touch, and he asked me to speak to one of his summer season sales groups. I spoke about the importance of establishing long-term relationships and helping others. We have similar views regarding leadership and the philosophy of paying it forward.

When I decided to participate in my first sprint triathlon, Eli stepped up and volunteered to be my coach. He supported me with encouraging text messages, emails, and phone calls. He also swam laps beside me and provided tips on breathing techniques. As I began the brutal brick exercises, where you transition from the bike to running, he was also right beside me for my first workout. "Brick" is an accurate description because your legs feel like bricks when you take your first few steps. Preparation and planning are crucial to success on race day—kind of like selling tickets.

Eli and me at the Oktoberfest Sprint Triathlon finish line!

Tim Gelt

A professional stadium consists of an abnormally high number of hallways and elevators. Both are designed to move staff, fans, mascots, and equipment around and through the venue. Ironically, this is how my friendship began with Tim Gelt. When I first started at KSE, I frequently used the set of elevators across from the basketball office. Tim and I crossed paths probably twice a day. I tend to say hi to everyone; I had no idea what Tim's job was, and it didn't matter. He was a coworker I saw often, and he always said "Hey" with a friendly wave. One day, when neither one of us was in a rush, we stopped to ask each other, "So what do you do?" We never worked on anything together, but we respected each other and kept in touch for years after we both left the organization.

Tim is a Denver native and grew up cheering for the Denver Nuggets basketball team. He played basketball for years during his youth, but, like most of us, he realized his days in the game were probably numbered. Back then, in his mind, there were only two paths to working in sports: you had to either coach or play. A chance meeting with a Denver Nuggets sponsorship sales account executive turned into an internship and a six-year mentoring relationship that would change the trajectory of Tim's career, even though he did not know it at the time.

During his college years at Metro State University of Denver, Tim watched with enthusiasm as a new arena slowly came to life across the street from the college. It was the Pepsi Center, which would later be named Ball Arena. It was both inspirational and frustrating, because he could see his dream court rising from the ground, but he remained on the outside looking in.

Tim's dream was to work for his hometown basketball team and with the players directly. He wasn't interested in ticket sales, community relations, or marketing. His first opportunity came in the form of a media relations internship during the summer of his junior year with the Sacramento Kings. It was a great experience that solidified his passion for the dream of working directly with the Denver Nuggets. After graduation, the mentor with whom he had kept in touch for six years offered him a second internship with the corporate suite sales department. It wasn't his dream job, but he understood the value of experience and being on the inside of the building. At the end of summer, the team offered him a full-time job in suite sales, but Tim bravely declined it because he knew in his heart it was not what he wanted to do long term.

Once again, a strong business relationship paid dividends for him. A month before the internship ended, his boss called the Nuggets PR department and recommended Tim for a job if and when they had an opening. Tim returned to campus to finish two summer classes, and in August he was hired as a media relations intern for the Denver Nuggets. He worked diligently for two years as an intern and was hired as a full-time media relations assistant.

Tim stayed in this role for three years, then was promoted to media relations manager and ultimately media relations director, where he spent nine additional years. Sometimes in life, things work out for those who put their head down, work hard, and never give up on their dream.

What Is Media Relations?

- The media relations team is responsible for information and statistics and lots of both. Local and visiting reporters and sports columnists rely on this department for storylines, tidbits, and historical facts about each player, coach, and team.

- One of the tasks in media relations is to provide game notes that highlight lead changes, shooting percentages, and other statistics.

- At the end of the day, the Media Relations person wants to make the journalist's job easier—which can be challenging because of the wide range of personalities and egos one encounters.

Game days began for Tim between 6:00 and 6:30 a.m., even though it was not required of him. The time before 8:00 a.m. was a chance to focus without distractions. It made for an arduous day, but Tim was not afraid of hard work and sixteen-hour days, and he said, "I enjoyed every minute of being paid to work in the NBA." It seemed to him that the more he was around the players, the better he was at his job.

On game day, the home team usually hosts an hour-long shootaround (a warmup of sorts for the players to get their muscles loose) around 10 a.m., after which the players are available to speak with the media. This is when the reporters get sound bites about the match-up and other storylines, especially if it is a rivalry game. Both teams go home or to the hotel, then return to the building at approximately 5:00 p.m. to begin their respective pre-game routines.

Tim enjoyed road games and the opportunity to see other cities. He also was fortunate to visit a variety of foreign countries during his tenure. The stops included Taiwan, Beijing, Mexico, and London. But his favorite league road trip was Phoenix, Arizona. It was guaranteed sunshine for two days, a plush hotel, and a jam-packed arena. The Suns staff was well known in league circles for their hospitality. When the season schedule was released, Tim would immediately highlight the two Phoenix dates because he knew those would be good trips.

Another responsibility of Tim's team was distribution and management of complimentary tickets to away games for each player, coach, and team owner. It was not difficult, but there were always moving parts and last-minute adjustments, especially for marquee games in popular destinations such as New York City, Chicago, and Los Angeles. Later on, Tim was able to add another team member to help manage comp tickets for these high-profile and popular games.

The public does not realize the amount of time, effort, and coordination that goes into each interview with a player or a coach. Anytime you see a locker room or post-game interview, it is guaranteed a Media Relations team member organized it and is standing there, two or three steps away from the camera.

The best part of the job for Tim was the people he met, including venue staff, coaches, players, and opposing team personnel throughout the NBA. He thoroughly enjoyed showcasing the players in a positive light. Contrarily, the hardest part of his job was when a player made a poor decision and Media Relations had to deal with the fallout of the situation. Sometimes, you are closer to a certain player, and you feel bad for whatever the player is going through. Another difficult aspect is dealing with losses, whether it is a five-game losing streak or, worse, consecutive losing seasons. The stress of such times is felt by everyone connected to the team.

Early in his career, Tim would hurry to complete each project, believing that speed would prove his worth. One simple mistake played a role in the rest of his career. During a routine task, he accidentally typed a wrong name on a team roster. Moments later, chaos ensued when his supervisor entered the office and berated Tim for making a basic mistake. Tim remembers the game notes being ripped and tossed in the air as the feedback was relayed. At the time, he thought it was a little excessive, but now he says the scolding was the best thing that ever happened to him. Twenty years later, Tim routinely takes the time to triple-check his work because he knows that details matter.

Tim and I worked in the Denver sports market for a combined total of forty years, which meant we knew the same people. After we both left KSE, we lost touch for a while other than sporadic contact on social media.

Six years later, I was invited as a guest of Coca-Cola to join the Colorado Rockies on their corporate sponsor Spring Training trip. It was a four-day event and well designed for guests to enjoy a round of golf, dinner with the team, and of course, a spring training game with the expected ballpark food. On game day, I scanned my ticket, checked out the team gift shop, then headed to my seat. The first person I ran into on the concourse was Tim Gelt. We gave each other a bear hug, laughing at the fact that we had had to travel to another state to hang out at a Denver team's game.

Me and Tim at Spring Training in Tucson, Arizona.

The Turf Guys

Phil McQuade

From the first time I met Kroenke's Assistant Turf Manager, I knew I was going to get along with him based on his energy level and personality. As he will tell you, Phil grew up in a social and somewhat loud family. He has one brother, who Phil claims is even more outgoing than he is, but I have my doubts.

When I interviewed Phil for this book, he shared with me that his dad swears to this day that neither of his boys *ever* mowed the grass. I almost spit out my pizza when he told me this, laughing the entire time.

Phil grew up in Broomfield, Colorado, a northern suburb of Denver. Initially, Phil wanted to be an accountant because he enjoyed math and it came easy to him. A year or two into his college days, he quickly realized there are two types of people in this world: those who love to work indoors and those who do not. Phil fell in the latter category, so he pursued a job where he could combine his love for all things sports while being outdoors. The world of turf management was a perfect match.

Turf management is not as easy as it seems. It involves dealing with diseases, watering, irrigation (pipes and sprinkler heads) and mathematics. Almost everything a turf team touches includes a mathematical equation. Before you can stripe or paint a stadium pitch, you must determine the number of gallons of paint you need to ensure the paint supplies are available. The same goes for mowing the turf. You know those mown lines on a baseball field that alternate dark and light? The angle and width of each course must be perfect. Make one mistake, and the rest of the mowing will be out of whack and the field will look lopsided. Unlike other industries, when you make a mistake in turf management, 18,000 people in the stands can see it.

What happens when a turf manager runs out of fertilizer or field paint? Everything they use is professional grade; they cannot run over to Home Depot for more. This reiterates the importance of understanding and properly accounting for supplies. When a mistake does happen, turf managers call one of their peers at another team and borrow enough to finish the current job, then kindly reimburse their friend the following week. Fertilizer is another such item; the stuff turf managers use is top grade. Zip ties and bungee balls, though, are non-specialized items that can be purchased at a home improvement store.

The turf management industry is a tight-knit group. Phil mentioned that everyone shares secrets, from the high school ranks to collegiate teams and the pros. In Phil's words, "It is not as easy as it looks, but it is an extremely rewarding job. We do more than water and mow grass. As turf managers, the two weeks before a big game are the most stressful time period. Do not forget that an NFL game might have millions of fans watching the game. If the normally pristine and perfect grass field has yellow spots and brown splotches, fans notice it, and so do the players."

The field complex at Dick's Sporting Goods Park covers approximately fifty acres. Caring for that much turf is a major task that requires a team and one irrigation manager. The "Turf Guys," as they were commonly referred to at the park, helped to maintain and groom the grass and synthetic turf fields. Yes, synthetic turf fields must be brushed to smooth out the rubber pellets because they get displaced by game play, wind, and snowplows.

Phil might be the funniest guy I have ever worked with, and that was a good thing, because we were often in conflict. Their job was to protect the grass, and mine was to book it and tear it up—and the Turf Guys liked to remind me of that, sometimes jokingly, but mostly they were serious. I know without a doubt there must have been 100 times when we hated each other. But we made it work, out of respect and thanks to Phil's humor and his colorful personality. I have told every friend who will listen that I will never work with a turf manager again in my career, but I would gladly make an exception if it was my buddy, Phil McQuade.

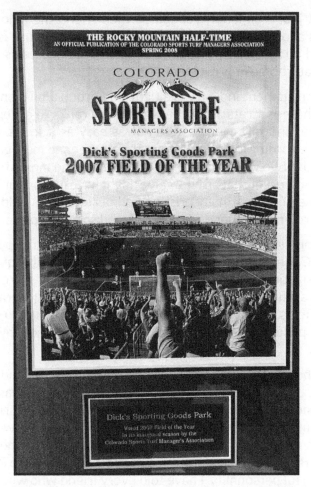

*The Turf Team's Field of the Year Award presented by
the Colorado Sports Turf Manager Association.*

Pride

Initially I struggled to comprehend why the condition of the grass was so important to the turf team. After all, it was designed for kids and adults to *use*, right? One afternoon, I was chatting with the turf manager, and he mentioned the condition of another pro stadium in town and snickered. He then described what was wrong with the field and how he'd called his old friend to aggravate him about how the field looked on television. That is when I realized turf condition is a matter of pride and ego. Turf managers see each other's work on TV when they watch a game, and they give each other grief, as good friends should.

As I alluded to earlier, in a sense I was the Turf Guys' nemesis. We battled on a weekly basis. Sometimes the issues were petty and other times they were serious. At one point, I hit my limit and said sarcastically, "It's not a grass museum!" But we always worked through the issues with humor, yelling, sarcasm, old-fashioned compromise and negotiation.

Most turf managers and team members have one or two fields to manage and only one sport to worry about. At Dick's Sporting Goods Park, we had twenty-four fields and six or seven sports leagues utilizing the fields each night.

CHSAA State Championships – May 21st, 2014

May 2014—a Turf Guy clearing snow.

Soccer Goals

A soccer goal can be a dangerous piece of equipment because kids some-times jump up and hang on the bar, not realizing that the crossbar is heavy and can tip over and crush someone. This is why we had fourteen-inch" metal stakes to secure each goal. Remember, we had twenty-four fields, and each goal had four stakes, and each field had two goals. One hundred and ninety-two stakes were pulled, tossed, and replaced in the ground every other day, which quickly became a point of contention between our two teams. This was because the turf team had to cut the grass in a spe-cific timeframe. It took time to stop the mower, pull the stakes, push the goals to the side, and finish mowing the area. It was our team's job to put everything back into place.

Schedule Central

The stadium pitch and the team's practice pitch were mowed every day because they had to be perfect for both players and coaches. However, the mowing schedule for the youth fields was Monday, Wednesday, and Friday.

Between games, the turf team focused on fungus control, proper irriga-tion, and any trouble spots on the pitch. The striping was done a day or two before the match to ensure the lines would be clear in person and on the TV screen.

Striping (Line Painting)

Clients changed each day, and of course each sport has its own require-ments for field dimensions and lines. We used white paint for soccer, yellow for lacrosse, blue for rugby, and red for flag football. Sometimes turf issues required last-minute field changes, as well. On occasion, a bad patch of grass or a small hole presented a safety issue. Other times, there was a fungus the turf team needed to clear out, which meant they had to use chemicals and keep people off that field for a day or two.

The painted lines would fade with rain and usage. To his credit, Phil would often touch up the lines, and we wouldn't know until a client commented on how nice the lines looked. Remember, we charged a premium and our clients expected high-quality fields, which includes bright, easy-to-see boundary lines. I think the record number of lines we ever had on one field was five. I was never scared of Phil, but I was nervous when I had to ask him to paint a third or fourth line on a field. Looking back, I don't know how we pulled it off, but our battles are responsible for most of my gray hair.

Wear Patterns

Each of the park's soccer fields was over one hundred yards long and fifty yards wide, but depending on which sport was using a field, we constantly dealt with varying wear patterns and trouble spots. It was common to look out at the fields complex and see lush green fields and two or three brownish-yellow circles. Certain sports tend to create small areas of concentrated damage on a field. Soccer goalies, for example, roam in one small area for the duration of the game, and they also warm up in front of the goal—which makes sense, because they need spatial awareness and familiarity with the actual playing area. Lacrosse is another one: the goalie roams the same three- to five-foot area, repeatedly digging in their cleats, rocking back and forth, and grappling the ground like a nervous tic to gain more traction. After a two-day tournament, this small area is brown and torn to shreds because the grass and the root system underneath have been destroyed. The thing Phil taught me about grass is that a little wear and tear is okay, but once you lose the crown or top layer of grass, that damage is there for months.

To counteract the inevitable damage, Phil's team routinely shifted the fields five or ten yards in one direction—east, west, north, or south. This slight adjustment provided much-needed relief for the trouble spots, giving the grass time to grow back.

Again, it was all about the customer. The complex was not conveniently located and not a block away from a large subdivision or neighborhood. I often said a recreational six-year-old team would not drive forty-five minutes to practice for an hour when the neighborhood field met their needs and was significantly cheaper. We were more like a destination. It was reasonable for our clients to expect the fields for their upcoming weekend tournament not to be chewed up.

Phil McQuade's preferred mode of transportation, the Toro Workman.

Resting schedule

Since we had twenty-four fields, we knew we could close a field to the public to rest it. I am not sure where the term originated, but we divided the fields into four pods, six fields on each pod. We rested a pod for two to three weeks, which allowed the grass to breathe, grow, and repair itself. The downtime was crucial because it provided precious time for the turf team to work on rough patches and repair the goal boxes and other high-usage areas. These wear down quickly when a field endures heavy use in a week's time. The Turf Guys were happy because they knew they could operate with no goals or clients impeding their progress or plans. It was good for everyone, to be honest, because our fields crew had to worry about only eighteen fields instead of twenty-four.

Sprinklers

Water is vital to successful turf management. Each field required varying amounts of water, which meant Field 1's sprinklers might need to run for thirty minutes twice a night, but Field 2 only needed one round of watering later in the evening. Occasionally, an adult league game would exceed their allotted time, and sometimes it was a simple oversight on the turf team, but it meant someone's kickball game ended early because of a round of unexpected showers. Most clients understood why this happened, but not everyone was calm and patient with the outcome. Remember, these were industrial sprinkler heads not small residential ones, so they were powerful bursts of water that hurt if you were close enough.

The sprinkler system, or irrigation, as the turf managers called it, was a focal point of field maintenance. The amount of water used changed based on weather, rainfall, and the severity of damaged spots. Sprinklers could, in theory, be used in creative ways. On one occasion, a local sports organization called us in a panic regarding field space for an upcoming event. We did not have the number of fields they needed, but being the nice and hospitable hosts we were, we told them we would be glad to help with our limited number of fields on one condition: they needed to remain on the two fields we assigned them and not spread out to other fields, even though it would appear they were available to use. Part of the reason was because it was an adult tournament, which was hard on the grass, and the other was simple logistics and operations. Those fields were scheduled for a rest, and we had to mow and paint them, also.

Twenty minutes after the organization arrived for their event, I received a call on the radio that their teams had moved to the other four fields on the pod, even though we had explicitly told them they could not spread out. Phil and I were frustrated and felt like the level of disrespect was rude and unprofessional. I can neither deny nor confirm that the sprinkler systems came on early that afternoon. Needless to say, they slowly retreated to their two assigned fields. We may or may not owe a certain national rugby team across the pond an apology.

Communication Process

This piece was crucial to the success of the complex. Phil and I began meeting daily to discuss striping requests, field issues, problem spots, and client complaints.

Change was inevitable, and my team notified clients as soon as possible when their field number changed for the evening. This was important because it impacted multiple teams and leagues, particularly if we had painted Field 12 for lacrosse and Field 21 only had soccer lines.

An Unexpected Asset

A byproduct of having a large athletic complex was the vast number of parking lots on site. Alli Scheck and I realized we could generate a small amount of revenue by renting or selling empty parking lot space to various customers. It started when one of the trucking companies called us during the National Western Stock Show, which is held in January. The gentleman needed a place to stage his empty horse trailers, and we had ample space available.

The Weirdest Voicemail of All Time

I remember I checked my voicemail one Monday morning, and I had a message from a gentleman who said, and I quote, "Hi, Brandon, I am calling to inquire about the use of your parking lots. You have the most beautiful parking lot I have ever seen." The man was a local representative of Sports Car Club of America. Our complex was under one of Denver International Airport's flight paths, and he had seen us from the air and noticed a sea of gray, or asphalt, in this case.

Sports Car Club of America

The Rocky Mountain Region of the SCCA hosted car racing events on our asphalt on Sunday afternoons. The interesting fact is how they laid out their racecourse. They used baking flour to sprinkle the lines and curves throughout the parking lot to create a customized and highly visible race-track. One by one, each car would navigate the course for time. It was temporary, cost-effective, and safe for both the asphalt and the environment.

These car races required little to no manpower or oversight on the part of our staff. The SCCA folks were professionals, easy to work with, and they cleaned up after themselves, which not everyone does. Our event manager would simply check in with the car club in the morning, then shake their hands when the event ended.

Motorcycle Training

A small two-person company reached out to me for a similar reason. They needed a clean and unobstructed parking lot to conduct beginner and intermediate motorcycle training classes. It was an important service that helped new riders gain confidence and understand how to safely avoid accidents and how to lay the motorcycle down when a crash was imminent. Like the car racing organization, this client was low-maintenance and added to our annual budget.

The parking lot programming paled in comparison to our youth field rental business operation, but it demonstrated to the executives that Alli and I were aligned from a creative perspective, and committed to generating non-traditional revenue, which is never a bad thing for a company.

Favorite Event

During my time managing the park, I saw every sporting event one could imagine, including soccer, lacrosse, rugby, kickball, hurling, Gaelic football, dodgeball, ultimate Frisbee, youth (tackle) football, and flag football. I have often been asked which event was my favorite. That's an easy answer: the National Veterans Wheelchair Games archery tournament.

According to its website at wheelchairgames.org, the National Veterans Wheelchair Games is "the world's largest annual wheelchair sports and rehabilitation event solely for military veterans." The 2022 edition of the Games included over 500 athletes, 22 events, and six days of competition. In 2010, the NVWG planning committee selected Dick's Sporting Goods

Park as the host venue for archery. It was an emotional experience to cheer and watch veterans of different ethnicities, age, and gender compete for the archery title. I was in awe of every athlete. One particular veteran caught my eye. The gentleman had lost both legs and one arm, and he used his mouth to draw back the bowstring and fire.

Each round began with a loud horn and a green traffic light signaling the start. After every competitor's arrow had been released, the traffic light turned red and the referee announced, "Please lay down your bows and arrows. Hold your fire." Safety was the top priority, and the tournament officials had multiple layers of safety rules in place. The "hold your fire" announcement was repeated twice, and a line judge determined when it was safe for volunteers to venture onto the course and collect the arrows. At the end of the competition, the organizer gave me two arrows as a thank-you gift. They remain one of the top two pieces of cherished memorabilia from my career.

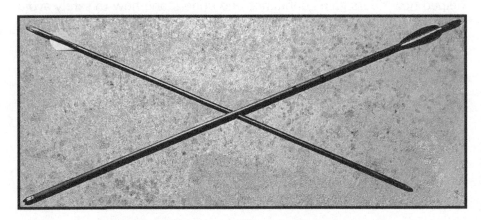

Two arrows I received as a gift from the archery event director of the National Veterans Wheelchair Games.

Wallace "Wassie" Bailey

As a child, one of my neighbors was a World War II veteran who taught me a great number of important life lessons. Wallace "Wassie" Bailey had been injured as a young paratrooper while fighting in the Battle of the Bulge. His nickname was Squeaky Wheels because he used a wheelchair.

He never let his injury prevent him from living an active life. He and his wife, Mary Rose, had a pool in their backyard with a specialized lift that safely lowered him into the water. In addition, his van had modifications that allowed him to drive.

Wassie was highly involved in our small town's community. He served on the City of Paintsville Water Works Board, and he was a supporter of the Special Olympics. His affable personality and positive attitude were contagious, and everyone respected him for a variety of reasons. Sports was one of his passions, and he supported Paintsville Tiger athletic teams, including football, basketball, baseball, and track and field. He helped with statistics and transported referees, coaches, and fans to and from away games. Furthermore, he worked as an Assistant Coach for the girls' basketball team, and was the only civilian allowed to drive his van on the field to watch Tiger high school football games. He also played wheelchair basketball for a period.

My high school has a Wall of Fame filled with painted "jerseys" honoring talented athletes and dedicated volunteers, and one of them says bailey #1 tiger fan in Wassie's honor.

As a young sports fan, Wassie and I often talked about University of Kentucky athletics. I watched games with my friends and parents, but the thought of attending a game in person was a dream. Thankfully, Wassie drove me two hours to Commonwealth Stadium in Lexington to watch my first UK Wildcat football game. We talked about life during the drive to and from the game. He was a great storyteller, and I often smile when I think of this trip.

One of life's passions Wassie and Mary Rose shared was the love of travel. They spent months planning an Alaskan cruise that would complete their goal of visiting all fifty states. A week prior to their departure date, Wassie received a clean bill of health at his annual checkup at the VA Hospital. Unfortunately, the trip never happened. During the night, Wassie suffered a heart attack and died at home. I had recently turned thirteen years old, and it wrecked my young soul. It was my first experience with death and losing someone close to me. I struggled in the days leading up to the funeral. I am an emotional person, and I wanted to pay my respects, but as a teen I did not possess the strength to attend his funeral and made the difficult decision to stay home. It is a decision I regret, but I also learned from it.

I was a member of the Boy Scouts, and Wassie helped me earn the Handicapped Awareness merit badge. I was the only Boy Scout in the region who earned the badge. Mary Rose took my merit badge to the funeral and placed it in his lapel pocket. One of their priceless gifts to me was the passion to see the world, because I love to travel. Years later, Mary Rose made the trip to Alaska to fulfill their dream and visit her fiftieth state.

The last conversation I had with Wassie was a discussion about UK Basketball and whether the program could rebound from NCAA sanctions that were handed down in the wake of a massive cheating scandal. We both were worried about our beloved Wildcats but hoped they would recover, and they did.

Mary Rose retired from teaching twenty years ago and still lives across the street from my parents. I learned important life lessons from her, too. She taught me how to do a cannonball, and she had the most creative names for their multiple cats. I attended a local Catholic school, so I never had her as a teacher. However, I think having her as a role model and a wonderful neighbor more than made up for that. When I am visiting my family back home, I walk across the street and visit her. The pool has been filled in, but we usually reminisce about summer memories of it, and Wassie, and of course a good travel story.

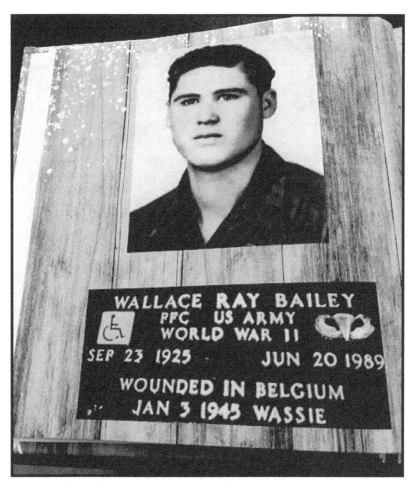

*Wassie Bailey's enlistment photo and tombstone
inscription in Mary Rose's scrapbook.*

Mary Rose and Wassie Bailey

Five Star Award

Most companies have some type of employee recognition program with awards such as Excellence in Teamwork or Employee of the Year. Kroenke Sports Entertainment celebrated with a red-carpet-style event called The Five Star Awards. A radio play-by-play commentator emceed the event, and it felt like a major production. All five awards were voted on by the employees. In 2006, when I had been with the company for less than a year, I had no expectation of winning anything. Prior to announcing each winner, the emcee told stories and provided hints about their background or their nickname. Each clue gave us a chance to guess which one of our teammates would get to walk down the aisle.

When it was time for the Visionary award, the emcee opened with the following lines:

> When we think of this word, we ask ourselves: Are they inspiring, imaginative, and confident? Who do we know that leads by example—someone with values and morals such as respect and integrity when dealing with people? A visionary exhibits a passion for the organization. A visionary is someone that gives guidance and helps others to be successful at their jobs. It takes vision to be a successful leader, and although this year's recipient of the Visionary 5 Star Award has only been with KSE this last year, they have proven to be a worthy recipient of the award.

> His peers had this to say about our winner:

> He comes up with great new ideas even when it comes to non-work-related things.

> If I can't figure something out, I know I can ask him, and he will find a solution.

> He has a great attitude, always positive and he is a team player who does not care about receiving credit.

> His work ethic is tremendous and he never watches the clock.

The next line was the giveaway: "Our winner grew up in Paintsville, Kentucky." This was followed by a sarcastic and predictable joke about small-town Kentucky. After that, I was not shocked when my name was called. However, there was one big surprise waiting for me. As I approached the stage to receive my award and shake our CEO's hand, my wife, Beth, walked out from behind the curtain to join me.

The award was just the beginning. Each Five Star winner received an impressive prize pack. The best item was a Gold Parking Pass, which allowed me to park in any Pepsi Center parking lot for free for any event at the venue. Running late to the Denver Nuggets game? No worries, just pull up to the closest lot and flash the gold parking pass and pull your vehicle in the space.

The second prize included a free hotel stay at an upscale mountain lodge in Vail, Colorado. The awards ceremony occurred in May, so I waited six months to redeem my free hotel room. In the meantime, the hotel partner decided not to renew their sponsorship. The company was nice enough to replace the hotel stay with a cash prize of the same value, which was close to $500. My wife and I took full advantage and booked a weekend getaway to San Francisco and spent the night in a swanky, boutique hotel on the waterfront. It was a fun trip and for one night we lived like royalty.

The final gift was a $500 Swiss-designed watch. I am a simple person; I know the major luxury watch brands, but I was not familiar with this one. The award meant more to me because it was my peers who thought highly of me and nominated me.

My Visionary 5 Star Award.

MLS Cup - Toronto, Canada—November 2010

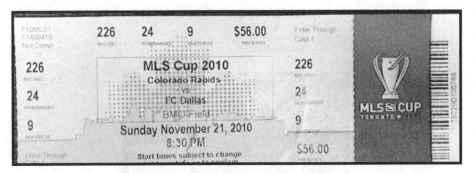

My MLS Cup ticket.

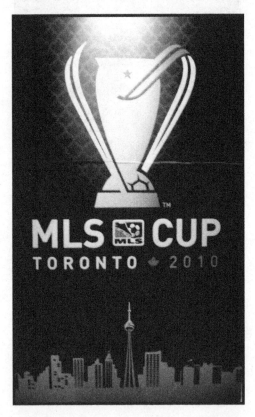

A welcome banner in one of the hotels.

In 2010, during my fifth season working for KSE, the Colorado Rapids advanced to the MLS Cup. The company generously offered all employees—everyone in the youth fields division as well as the pro soccer team division—the chance to fly to Toronto, Ontario, for the game. I was in disbelief. For some silly reason, I almost did not go, but thankfully my good friend Marisa told me there was no guarantee such an opportunity would happen again. Toronto is cold in late November, but our staff knew how to pack for a cold-weather game, and we took our ski gear, extra gloves, and pocket hand-warmers.

It was an unforgettable trip for a variety of reasons. The company chartered a flight for the entire front office and youth fields staff. I treated it as a five-day vacation because I had zero job responsibilities. We stayed out every night until 3:00 a.m. because of the downtime, and every night had a good story to accompany it.

The city of Toronto is magnificent and massive in size. It felt like New York City with a European flair. I remember seeing that the local newspaper was available in multiple languages.

One evening, we attended a Maple Leafs hockey game, which is a cultural event that every diehard sports fan needs to experience once in his or her life. When the puck was in play on the ice, no one moved from their seat. In between periods, it looked like a fire drill because everyone sprinted to the bathrooms.

We also visited the Hockey Hall of Fame, a popular tourist spot located in a historic bank building. The interactive exhibits were creative and well planned. Visitors could try their hand at calling some of the most famous play-by-play moments or put on the goalie pads and let a friend take slapshots at them. The crowning highlight was seeing the Stanley Cup, as you might imagine. We walked down a hallway, then entered a vast, open space where the Cup was the only thing on display. The presentation was fit for a king, and it matched the great respect players and coaches display toward the trophy.

After four fun-filled days of touring the hot spots and taking in the magnificent city, MLS Championship Night arrived, and it was bitter cold. We bundled up in layers because it was going to be a long night. The match was a close one, as you might expect from a game of this magnitude. FC Dallas scored first, then the Rapids answered with a goal to tie the game 1–1. It was a game of close calls and great defense by both goalies. Late in the second half, the Rapids drove the ball deep near the goal and fired a shot that ricocheted off a defender's knee, spun in the right direction, and fell into the goal. To be in the stands with my good friends, their eyes tear-drenched after having waited twelve years to experience this moment, was truly special. I wasn't usually a soccer fan, but I was one that night. The final score was 2–1, and we were MLS Champions!

Five days of partying and staying up way too late finally took its toll. I don't think anyone said a word once we boarded the plane to return home. I fell asleep before the pilot could inform us about the flight time and expected weather. Ten rows ahead of me, the MLS Cup was nestled in row 20, seat 2, with a seat belt fastened loosely around it for the long ride home.

Me and the MLS Cup in a Toronto sports bar, fresh off the big win.

Post-game recap: My time at KSE left me with great memories and lifelong friends. An important lesson I learned there was the value of getting involved with company committees. When you can engage with peers from multiple divisions, it makes a big organization (almost 500 employees, in this case) feel smaller. Plus, learning how other departments function can only make you better at your own job.

During my time at KSE, I learned an incredible amount about the sports industry and what it takes to execute game night entertainment promotions, ticketing campaigns, and community programs at a high level. It was an excellent place for younger employees to cut their teeth, with advancement opportunities, particularly in ticketing, if you worked hard and exceeded your goals. I was also grateful for the opportunity to open a world-class facility, but it was time for a change.

Chapter 10
Back on Campus
2005—2009, 2016, 2018-19

Pre-game: One of my initial career thoughts was to become a Physical Education (P.E.) teacher, along with coaching track and basketball. But it never surfaced as my true passion. I changed my major three times and needed to graduate after five years of undergraduate studies. As I got older, my mind kept returning to the what-if scenario and how I might have missed my calling to be a teacher. I kept thinking someday I would return to school and finish my teaching degree. The idea of teaching high school never came to fruition, but another opportunity presented itself, instead.

Johnson & Wales University (JWU) based in Providence, Rhode Island, started as a business school, then added programs in hospitality and culinary arts. As the school grew into other areas, including arts and sciences, engineering, nutrition, and wellness, someone wisely expanded the academic offerings to include sports, entertainment, and event management. JWU used to have a campus in Denver, although they no longer do.

During my time at KSE, I attended a local networking event and met someone from the Career Development department at JWU. She asked me if I would be willing to come and speak to a group of freshmen about career advice and the importance of networking. The Denver campus was located three miles from Dick's Sporting Goods Park, and I gladly obliged. I spoke for thirty minutes, sharing insight and stories. Not long after, I was invited back to speak to an upper-level Sports Marketing class. I enjoyed giving these talks, and the students seemed to appreciate them, as well.

Just like I told the students, the great thing about networking is that one interaction often leads to another. Two months later, I reached out to JWU to see if I could stop by and speak to a class about summer internship opportunities at KSE. They said yes, and the result was beneficial for both parties. We hired multiple students over time.

Talking to the students had reawakened my old interest in teaching, and I applied to teach a class at JWU as an adjunct professor. My friends provided advice ranging from effective answers to interview questions to what color tie to wear. Initially, I was passed over for someone with more connections and a better title, but that individual turned them down. I was next in line and was motivated to prove why I felt I was the right fit from the start.

Teaching college students was a second job I enjoyed very much. It gave me the chance to share career stories and advice with the students and provide insight on what it was like to work in the sports industry. It was important for me to spend time preparing my lecture material with a wide variety of current topics, combined with detailed examples of events, sponsorships, and promotions. I made sure to teach with passion and high energy. I was working in the industry, which provided instant credibility. It did not stop students from trying to take advantage of the rookie professor, but once they realized I truly cared about their career preparation, any animosity quickly faded. After the first two classes, I identified a student or two with whom I could joke and engage in jovial conversations. It seemed important to show my human side because my background was not that of a traditional professor.

With each course I taught, I started the first class by explaining some important reminders:

- I would bring my high energy to every class.

- I would encourage open dialogue and questions.

- I would call you out if you fell asleep, not in a bad way, but in a kind manner to let you know I was paying attention.

- I would push them to be creative and give 100 percent effort regarding their homework assignments.

I brought in a wide range of guest speakers from various sports companies, both male and female, to provide different viewpoints and stories. I did not do it because I didn't want to lecture, but rather because I knew how valuable it was for these students to not only hear from people currently working in the industry, but to also have a conversation with my friends who worked in various roles and ask questions.

I began every class with this line: "Someone is paying your tuition this quarter. It might be your parents, yourself, or a loan company, but I want to ensure that they get their money's worth."

I felt it was my duty to prepare my students for the realities of life as a sport management professional, yet also provide resources to fight through adverse situations and solve problems. I constantly explained real-life job tactics and scenarios the students would encounter in the workforce. I emphasized the importance of being creative and thinking differently. I also reiterated the importance of networking and why I believe it is the most important career skill. The fact that I brought in guest speakers meant that students had the chance to talk to professionals in a low-pressure situation. It broke down the wall of uncertainty and stress because the student could ask the speaker anything. The student could practice with no fear and preconceived notions and didn't need to worry about mistakes. I believe this gave them a confidence boost after graduation when it was time to interview for jobs. These contacts also led to opportunities for students to interview for summer internships.

I encouraged the students to be creative in their homework assignments and group projects. I knew most traditional professors stuck to a tried-and-true system and rightfully so, but I wanted to push boundaries and set their minds free. I felt like they appreciated this, based on their smiles and feedback received via my term evaluations. I also sensed it, based on their excitement when they talked about their group projects.

One of my favorite group projects involved a hypothetical expansion baseball team in Portland, Oregon. The students envisioned a stadium constructed from recycled wood. One of the creative ideas they came up with was a transportation system involving a canal system and a team-branded canoe. Fans could ride around the stadium concourse and bypass the typically crowded walkways.

A Group Project Goes Wrong

Sometimes a good idea leads to questionable results. As I mentioned, I encouraged my students to think creatively with group projects. One assignment focused on product endorsement and negotiating a hypothetical contract with a professional athlete to market a product. The winning concept was a customized golf cart for the colorful pro golfer John Daly.

The student had made his golf cart out of an appliance carton. It was covered with glitter and featured a loud clown-style horn and customized rims decorated in various colors using Sharpie markers. I vividly remember seeing the student in his car at the top of the classroom—there was a staircase with approximately twelve stairs leading down the middle aisle. I think the poor kid hit the second step, then tumbled head over heels the rest of the way. After I made sure he was ok— and hadn't hurt himself, I shared a hearty laugh with the entire class. Ironically, the student was Nate Stahlecker. In case you are wondering, yes, he earned an A for his project.

Another challenge I assigned to my students was to create a fundraising program for a charity close to their heart. It made them pause and think about what had impacted their lives to that point and how they would make a difference for their selected charity. Some of the stories were gut-wrenching, and others were inspirational. Unexpectedly, it allowed me the opportunity to see each student as a human being and gave them a chance to share an important part of their life. In the end, it opened my eyes because I realized how lucky I was, and it was a reminder of the blessings in my life.

> *Post-game recap: I enjoyed teaching at the college level. The age and maturity level of the students allowed for meaningful, and sometimes lighthearted and even hilarious, conversations. I was passionate about each class and made sure the students knew how much I cared about their career development and preparation to enter the workforce, not just the grade they earned in my class. Sometimes in life, we are redirected for a good reason, and that's how I felt about my days as an Adjunct Professor. I loved every minute and ended up teaching a Sports Media class at JWU and another Sport Marketing one at CU Denver years later.*

Part II

Write brief and honest responses to the following questions.

1. List specific things your instructor does that help you succeed in this course.

   Allows students to demonstrate knowledge through assignments & projects. He also brings in guest speakers and gives us opportunities

2. List any suggestions that you feel would help you to have a better understanding of this course.

3. Other Comments.

   One of the best professors I have ever had!

Part II

Write brief and honest responses to the following questions.

1. List specific things your instructor does that help you succeed in this course.

   He brings in many industry professionals and it broadens our networking horizons. He knows a lot about the subject matter and is willing to help in any way possible.

Part II

Write brief and honest responses to the following questions.

1. List specific things your instructor does that help you succeed in this course

He's Tosti what can I say?

Student evaluation comments—some serious, some comical.

Chapter 11

iHigh.com
A Wild Ride on Technology's Roller Coaster, Bluegrass Style, 2011-2012

Brandon M. Tosti
West Region General Manager

P.O. Box 102961
Denver, CO 80250

brandon.tosti@ihigh.com
www.ihigh.com

The
Global Youth
Network

Pre-game: Everyone should take a chance on a job out of your comfort zone at least once in your career. The learning opportunity is tremendous, if you are open to it. I had maxed out at my current job and I wanted to try something new. I could not pass up the chance to learn from a true legend in the industry—even though I was not sure how long he would remain with the company. How it unfolded is an inspiring story.

For the record, I despise working by myself. I thrive around people and working with a team. However, when a wonderful work-from-home opportunity with a massive upside came along, I knew I had to take a chance on it. This job was the second time in my career when I worked from home, and my first foray into sports technology. Although I was working from home, I was traveling around the metro Denver area multiple days a week, which made it tolerable. The company was growing at a rapid rate, which meant I also traveled out of state for events.

iHigh provided free live-streaming software for high schools, swim clubs, and other youth clubs across the country. The technology made it easy for each organization to broadcast events (such as school plays, PTA meetings, and sporting events) on its own internet TV channel. Plus, the organizations could sell advertising to generate revenue. Some schools created student-led newscasts, weekly sports shows, and other journalistic type programs. It was innovative and beneficial for students, teachers, and athletic teams.

My title was West Regional General Manager, and my territory included the western states spanning from Colorado to California to the west, and Washington and Arizona to the north and south, respectively. A majority of our business was conducted by phone and email, but it was still a significant territory to cover as one employee. It felt as if there were always more tasks to complete and another client to call, which provided a sense of job security. Most days I was overwhelmed because I was not sure where to focus my time and energy.

I was fortunate because I got to travel the entire state of Colorado on a weekly basis. For every swanky ski town like Vail or Steamboat Springs, I visited a small rural town where the locals immediately knew you were visiting from out of town. I appreciated the balance between the two, and being from a small town myself, I felt comfortable in either situation.

The fun part of this job was the people I met. I dealt with coaches 90 percent of the time. I enjoyed hearing their career stories and tall tales. If you've never sat with a longtime coach in his or her office and let them share their experiences, you are missing out on hearing from some of the best storytellers in life. One story leads to another, and the next thing you know, an hour has passed.

The athletic directors and coaches typically gave me a coffee mug or a T-shirt as a gift. School pride was evident on the eastern plains as well as in the metro area. The smaller the school, the more excited they were to share an item to represent their mascot and school colors. I am sure they were being visited most days by one traveling salesman or another, but iHigh's product had endless applications for education, promotion, and community building, and it was free, which made a difference.

One of my favorite sales trips was to La Junta, a small farming town in the southeastern corner of Colorado. I stopped in for lunch at a small corner cafe and ordered a standard ham and cheese sandwich with a snack-sized bag of Lay's potato chips. As I surveyed the room and saw that every customer was a farmer dressed in blue jeans, work boots, and a cowboy hat, I immediately knew I was the odd man out in my slacks, golf shirt, and shiny black dress shoes. It was not as if there would be any surprises; however, my waitress treated me like royalty. She checked on me at least three times. I left a generous tip, smiled, and waved to the locals as I left for the next stop.

That little town held a special meaning to me. It was not my first time visiting southeastern Colorado, let alone La Junta. When I was fourteen, I rode a charter bus from Lexington, Kentucky, to Philmont Scout Ranch in Cimarron, New Mexico, to backpack eighty-eight miles over twelve days. We stopped in La Junta for lunch one day and visited the Koshare Indian Museum. That trip was for fun, but this one was strictly business. La Junta is the home of Otero Junior College, and I had a meeting with its athletic director. Within minutes of my arrival, he handed me an Otero Rattlers T-shirt, and I could tell by the way he talked we would get along well.

After we finished our business discussion, the conversation shifted to life stories and career plans. It took longer than expected because student-athletes kept stopping by to either say hi, ask a question, or share a good grade from a class. It felt like a high school guidance counselor's office. I could tell the student-athletes viewed him as a father figure rather than some athletics department executive you never see or speak to one-on-one.

I shared with him that I had long dreamed of becoming an athletic director at a Division I university. He commented on the quality of the kids in Otero's athletics program, and not just the ones in the sport he had coached before being elevated to the athletic director position. Most junior colleges, or "jucos," as they are commonly called, are considered a steppingstone: the goal is to spend one or two seasons on campus, then hopefully transfer to a D-1 school. For student-athletes, junior college is a chance to improve their grades, bulk up, or take time to develop more skills. Others just want to start without the hoopla and pressure that comes with a well-known state university. Regardless of why they were at Otero, these kids had purpose, and their grades meant something to them, as did their athletic accomplishments.

The athletic director and I talked about his duties. He told me why he loved his job and had zero interest in leaving for a bigger job at a better-known school. Sure, he said, the money would be better, and the athletic facilities, too, but unrealistic expectations from fans and alumni are lurking in the corner, waiting to turn on you when things go downhill. He also mentioned how sports columnists love to have their moment in the sun by picking apart a coach, player, or program. I have often had a similar thought: Just because you can write a scathing article about a coach does not mean you have to. What does it accomplish? What purpose does it serve?

The other reason this athletic director loved his junior college job was that travel was minimal. Higher-level athletic directors travel often for fundraising, entertainment, and networking trips, but a junior college athletic director gets the chance to be home with his kids and family. This was the second time an athletic director had shared that sentiment with me. For the first time in my career, I wanted to change my long-term goal.

Front page newspaper article about iHigh's potential.

Jim Host

At the start of this chapter, I alluded to an industry legend who was a big reason I was excited to join iHigh. That man was Jim Host. Jim is a sports industry icon, an innovative pioneer, and one of the grittiest salespeople you will ever meet. Anyone who has worked in collegiate sports marketing or sponsorship sales should thank Jim Host for his creativity and perseverance, as his drive and his passion for the sports business has created jobs for hundreds, if not thousands, of people. After all, Jim is the individual responsible for developing the NCAA's Corporate Partner program.

I could try to explain what he means to me and the industry itself, but the best way to educate yourself about this man is to read his autobiography, *Changing the Game: My Career in Collegiate Sports Marketing* (The University of Kentucky Press, 2020).

Jim Host's autobiography, a must-read.

Host Communications was the company that acquired Summit Sports and Events back when I was working there. We all understood Dan and Cris's decision to sell the company, and we did not blame them, but it was the end of a road for our team of folks who had grown up in the event industry together. "Dead man walking" is an apt description of our office the final week or two. Before long, Jim and his executive team flew to Denver to meet with our team. They informed us that, in order to reduce capital expenditures and streamline operations, our Denver office would be closed. The events division would move to Dallas, where the country's 3-on-3 basketball tournament leader, Hoop It Up, was based. It made perfect sense, and we had known it was inevitable, but it was still an emotional time. We were grappling with a combination of frustration and disbelief, and muted happiness for Dan and Cris. Jim offered a number of us an opportunity to move within the company based on the large number of college sponsorship accounts they operated. If I remember correctly, I could have gone to Oklahoma State University or Florida State University, but I politely declined the offer. Adam Germek took the offer and headed to Tallahassee, Florida, and worked on the media sales portion of the business for the Seminoles. The rest of us politely declined the option to move to the company's Dallas office. Denver is a tough city to leave, and we were confident we could find new jobs in the city, even if it might take months rather than weeks. Denver was our home, and it felt right.

Jim slowly made his way down the hall, spending five minutes talking with each of us individually. I heard a door close nearby, and I knew I was the next man up. When Jim and two other executives walked into my office, it felt like he was the President of the United States with his bodyguards. The man walks with a purpose and has an imposing demeanor. I jumped to my feet, shook his hand, and acknowledged everyone.

I thanked him for the opportunity, and politely declined to move to another city. My reasons were genuine. One of them was that I had previously spent two years trying to find a sports job in Kentucky and the South, but it had never happened. Calmly, I walked him through my experience and frustration trying to break into the sports industry. Why would I want to move back there when I did not have any luck the first time?

The other reason, I told Jim, was that I had started to build my network in the West, and I wanted to stay and keep expanding it.

Jim gently laughed and said, "What's her name, son?"

I grinned and said, "Beth, sir." We were only dating, but somehow, he knew. The man's intuition and ability to read people were magical.

Before he left my office, he asked me if there was anything he could do for me.

I thought about it for a second. As far as important Kentuckians go, my parents looked up to the UK Wildcats head basketball coach and Jim Host, and not necessarily in that order. They respected him for two reasons: his unbridled passion for the state of Kentucky, and the enormous amount of business success he'd had in Lexington. I asked him, "Can you please call my parents and tell them I said hi?"

"No problem," he said. "Consider it done."

Some months later, I was emailing Jim with a question, and he told me he had tried multiple times to call my parents, but they never picked up. Jim Host is many things, and chief among them is an honest person. Later that week, I called my parents to tell them about it. Before I could explain the story, Mom mentioned that their answering machine had been out of commission for four months. I grinned and shook my head. Mom and Dad were disappointed they missed his call, and still ask about him today.

Fast-forward to 2012. I am a good networker and keep in touch with people. Jim is an individual of great stature with vast connections, so I purposely sent him an email and a Christmas card every year for close to a decade. I honestly thought little about ever needing his help until one day, when I sought some desperately needed career advice from him.

In the winter of 2012, after five years in my current position, I was at a crossroads where I knew I could not advance at KSE. I had invested more than three years of sweat equity in my charity, Sports for A Cause. I seriously contemplated leaving my steady job and trying to raise enough money to pay myself a decent salary as the charity's full-time manager. It would have been a giant leap of faith, so I reached out to my mentors to discuss the pros and cons. After some time, I was stuck, and I called Jim for career advice.

Our phone conversation started with a general check-in. Then he asked me how he could help me, and I presented my dilemma. Never one to waste time, he immediately asked me if I would be interested in moving back to Lexington, Kentucky, to be his Vice-President of Sales for iHigh. I kindly declined and informed him that Beth was six months pregnant with our second child. It would have been like a homecoming for Beth and me, but I fervently told Jim it was not a good time to uproot my family and move across the country. I thanked him for thinking of me, but my answer was a hard no. I was making $56,000 a year and he did not ask my current salary, nor did I mention it.

He paused, then said, "I will pay you $100,000 to be my VP of Sales."

I immediately backtracked and said, "You know what, uh, uh, yes, we can talk about it. I don't want to rule anything out. It would be silly not to listen to your offer."

The next step was to schedule a trip to Lexington to meet with Jim and his executive team to discuss the position in more detail. I immediately asked my boss, Jeff, for advice. He said, "It is a sales job, and you will be traveling every week anyway, so why not ask if you can stay in Denver? Denver International Airport is in the country's top five busiest airports. You can get to most cities within two or three hours with minimal connections."

At first, I thought my boss had lost his mind, but I took time to think about it and realized he was right. I decided to take a chance and make the ask. After all, wasn't that what I was always encouraging others to do? The worst thing that could happen is he would say no.

For the next few weeks, I nervously rehearsed my request to remain in Denver. I had a mental list of reasons why it would be beneficial for both parties, and I kept thinking about the potential objections to each one and what my next move or line would be. For that matter, what if he declined immediately and the matter was non-negotiable? He is a tough negotiator, and I knew if the debate got messy, I would not stand a chance.

I decided to seek advice from a senior-level sponsorship sales executive I respected at KSE. Mike took me to lunch. I appreciated the discussion and his time. We hadn't worked together much, but we were friendly. Mike's advice was to seize the opportunity to learn from one of the world's greatest sports marketers.

"What if he retires soon?" I fretted.

Mike countered, "Imagine what he could share and teach you in a year or two."

If I remained in my current job, I realized, it would be more of the same: rinse and repeat, as the saying goes. I would learn nothing new and would still be frustrated a year later.

A month later, Beth and I flew back to Kentucky and met with Jim Host, Rick Ford, and Tim Campbell, both longtime Host Communications executives and the cofounders of iHigh. It was a nice dinner, and the three sports industry veterans filled Beth and me in on the company and its projected growth pattern. I asked the standard business questions before we left for the evening, knowing we were going to resume our talk at breakfast the next morning. The three also asked questions about Beth's job and how they could help her network with their Lexington contacts. Beth and I both appreciated that kind offer, which honestly caught us off guard. Jim knew that moving was a big decision that would impact our family, not just myself, and Beth and I were both impressed he included Beth in the discussion. It was a kind gesture.

It turned out I need not have worried, because the first thing out of Jim's mouth the next morning was, "We've decided that you should remain in Denver and open the iHigh west region office, but we cannot pay you $100 thousand." It sounded fair, and I accepted the job offer on the spot. Both parties won the negotiation. Jim saved his company financial capital, and I still received a sizable raise and did not have to uproot my family.

iHigh grew at a rapid pace, and part of it could be attributed to the executives who had built Host Communications and knew how to scale efficiently, and how to sell a service or product. Approximately thirty years of experience as an innovative leader has its advantages.

Our sales representatives focused on large national organizations, not local or state chapters, outside of the state high school activities associations because those were valuable partners for us. The one characteristic all membership groups shared was passion. Whether it is BMX, skateboarding, or even horseback riding, the members have pride and disposable income to spend on their passion. No one else was offering a free product that enabled groups to broadcast their signature events, showcase their members' talents, and earn ad revenue while doing so.

The National High School Rodeo Association is a perfect example. I am guessing few people know about the organization. According to its official website, the National High School Rodeo Association consists of 10,500 students in the United States, Canada, and Australia. Their national finals event, the National High School Finals Rodeo, started with little fanfare but has become known as "The World's Largest Rodeo," regularly boasting over 1,500 students from over 120 participating organizations.

National High School Rodeo Championships – Gillette, Wyoming

Jim is known for his disgust regarding blue jeans. As a child, he only had one or two pairs and they had holes in them, which meant kids poked fun at him. He swore to himself that he would never wear blue jeans again. Fast forward to 2011. iHigh had secured yet another premier client, the National High School Rodeo Association (NHSRA). The national championship is their premiere six-day event and was held in Gillette, Wyoming.

The class A uniform for this event and all NHSRA staff were cowboy blue jeans, a western shirt, and an authentic cowboy hat. I did not own any of these articles of clothing, but the organization provided me with an allotment to purchase all these items. I spent close to $2,000 at the local western apparel store. The entire experience was eye-opening, and I could not believe some of the price tags. Even cheap cowboy boots are $250. It was not Nike Air technology, but the cushioned heel made a difference when you had to stand for eight hours. Normally, I would not put the words comfort and boot together, but they felt great right out of the box.

When the time came for iHigh to debut our live streaming software at the national championship, yours truly was selected as our company representative to manage the event. Gillette is a six-hour drive from Denver filled with dirt, cacti, and not much else. I envisioned every horror movie ever filmed as I sped across I-80 hoping to make it to my destination in one piece and not end up as a main character in a Stephen King novel. It did, however, give me an excuse to download ample songs and create an assortment of new iTunes playlists.

Jim had two of the three clothing items, and his wife, Pat, had to buy him a pair of blue jeans for the rodeo trip. She reached out to me while he was flying to the event and asked me to take a photo of him with his blue jeans on. I told her it would not be a problem at all.

Shortly after, we met in the hotel lobby and prepared to leave for the event. I asked Jim if he would mind taking a quick picture. I snapped the photo on the camera and left the lobby. Part of me wanted to ask him if he would take a picture with me, because NO ONE had seen Jim Host in a pair of blue jeans since he was sixteen years old. I wasn't sure what his response would be and I decided not to push my luck. Now that I look back, it is truly one of the only regrets in my life. I saw Jim Host in blue jeans. I do not know of anyone else who can the say same thing and believe me, this man knows hundreds of people around the world. When I called him to discuss this book, I told him the back story and we both enjoyed a good laugh. Damn it, I am still kicking myself!

Me in my rodeo uniform between events.

The event was nearly flawless in planning and execution. Instead of Air Jordans, flip flops, and backpacks, the event space was filled with Dodge Ram trucks, horse trailers, ropes, saddles, and other equine-related equipment. Something else I noticed was how polite and well-behaved the young participants were. Almost every time a student asked me a question, I was addressed as "Sir," and the kids picked up their trash before they left the arena. It was impressive, and I do not think I will ever see such a courteous crowd of students anywhere else.

My credential for the National High School Finals Rodeo event.

Brandy Medran

Brandy worked with me as part of our summer fields operation program at Dick's Sporting Goods Park and played soccer in high school and competitively in local adult leagues. Like most interns, she was eager to learn and was mature for her age. After graduation, she took a sales job, which was not an excellent fit for her skill set, but she still needed to support herself. Two months later, she reached out to me for career advice. By that time, I had changed companies. I had moved on to the West Region Manager position for iHigh and needed a production assistant. Brandy came on board and quickly adapted to the company's live streaming technology, even showing me some shortcuts and efficient methods for using the software.

During this time, Brandy's goal was to work for U.S. Soccer, but she hoped to someday work for an Olympic National Governing Body. She started working part-time for USA Judo. Each week, she drove over an hour each way to Colorado Springs to keep her Olympic career dream alive.

Through Doug Fulton's help and introduction, I met a Special Olympics Colorado executive and told them about our live streaming software. I thought it would be a great way for them to broadcast their Polar Plunge fundraising event and Winter Games. As my section of the business grew, I let Brandy manage the Special Olympics downhill skiing event. She did a fantastic job, and the client asked if she could be their liaison for their next large-scale event, based on her go-getter attitude and hard work.

The next major event for my region was an international soccer tournament in Las Vegas, Nevada. The Mayor's Cup is a brilliantly designed youth sporting event that features youth teams from multiple foreign countries. The tournament committee did a fantastic job with the event management piece. They also had the support of the local soccer community, including the University of Nevada Las Vegas coaches.

Due to the size of the event, there were multiple games to live stream at once, and I needed a second teammate to help me. Brandy and I left the airport and headed to the car rental area to pick up our car. We had reserved a compact car, but there were none left. The employee offered us a convertible, and before I could say anything, Brandy proudly exclaimed, "We'll take it!" After all, life is short, and it was a pleasant surprise to drive a convertible in the cool desert air of Las Vegas.

Three months later, one of the National Governing Bodies based in Colorado announced a job opening. It was a Youth Development Administrator position with USA Rugby. Brandy asked me for a recommendation letter. I told her that, although I would have been happy to write one for her, I didn't think she would need it to land the job. Brandy applied and joined the organization shortly after. A year later, she asked me to come to her office and share my networking speech with her young coworkers. I enjoy speaking to groups and helped one of the attendees with a career choice five months down the road.

Brandy returned the favor eight years ago when she spoke to our department's interns as part of our "Lunch and Learn" series. She came prepared with a creative and professional presentation titled "Career Sushi," full of helpful pointers and sound advice for the younger demographic. She was the group's favorite presenter of the summer.

Brandy excelled in her role at USA Rugby and was promoted to Youth Development Manager. She settled in with her new calling and proudly calls the rugby community home. Four promotions later, she is now General Manager, Commercial and Events. In 2022, she was a member of the bid team that successfully secured the 2031 Men's Rugby World Cup and the 2033 Women's Rugby World Cup to be played on US soil. I am proud of her and continue to celebrate her promotions and accomplishments.

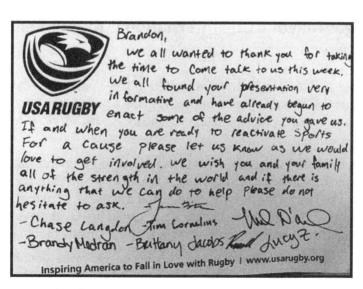

A nice thank-you card from Brandy and coworkers.

Brandy (middle) watches as the teams enter the field at the 2019 Women's Super Series (USA v Canada match). Photo courtesy of USA Rugby.

Las Vegas Mayor's Cup International Tournament & Showcase

The soccer event Brandy and I attended in Las Vegas, the Mayor's Cup International Tournament and Showcase was a major youth tournament and a great opportunity for iHigh to showcase its services to families across the globe.

Upon arriving in Las Vegas, we went to the soccer tournament headquarters. The first person we met was Roger Tabor, the Tournament Director. I remember he greeted us with a firm handshake and a sense of calm that surprised me, given what a huge event he was responsible for. Over time, I realized Roger loved the tournament and everything about it made him smile.

Roger, a Las Vegas native, began playing soccer at a young age. He remembers his first-grade team played one other team in the Catholic Youth Organization six weeks in a row, and that was the season. He fell in love with the sport and kept playing, eventually earning a scholarship to the University of Nevada Las Vegas. Athletically speaking, he was ready for the next level, but due to his ADHD, he was not ready for the rigors of college academics. The experience helped him mature quickly. He recognized the opportunity his scholarship represented and invested the necessary time and effort on the academic side to keep things moving in the right direction.

Roger established the Downtown Las Vegas Youth Soccer Club and got involved with a soccer tournament that had started as an initiative from the mayor's office. As Roger knew soccer well, he was asked to volunteer with the event. This tournament, called The Mayor's Cup, started small with sixty teams, fifty-seven of which were locally based.

In 2008, Roger became the director of the highly successful tournament. His next step was to invite a team from Mexico. Once he had secured this, he looked to Canada. He bought an ad in a Canadian magazine for $450 and offered one free tournament entry. The ad generated fourteen new teams from our neighbor to the north.

These initial successes made Roger think he might be onto something, and he set his eyes on elevating the tournament to a global scale. He intended on expanding the reach by inviting more countries. The next country to join his effort was Germany. The Borussia Mönchengladbach soccer club is one of the most storied clubs in the country. They sent a U17 team, which was a major boost to the tournament's legitimacy. One of the top goalkeepers in the world, Marc-André ter Stegen, was on the team.

Over time, participation in the Las Vegas Mayor's Cup International Tournament and Showcase surpassed 1,337 teams from 43 different countries, as well as hundreds of referees. Today, there are three tournaments: one boys' showcase, one girls' showcase, and one showcase for younger teams of both boys and girls. The traveling teams use between 50 and 60 hotels and approximately 26,000 room nights.

Warmth, Kindness, and Sierra Leone

One of the more memorable experiences centers around a team from Sierra Leone, which is located on the southwest coast of Africa. An international charity in Denmark heard about a soccer team in Sierra Leone that consisted of boys who had been orphaned by war. The charity raised money for the boys to travel to Las Vegas for the international tournament. Roger and a small group of volunteers were excited to welcome them at the airport. However, one important detail had been omitted from the communication between the two groups. The volunteers arrived at the airport and had not discussed how they would recognize each other. Roger and his volunteers were looking for boys in warmups, but when the team exited the plane, they were dressed in blue sport coats. The team, not knowing exactly who they were looking for, unknowingly walked past the host committee.

The team from Sierra Leone stayed in two mansions that were donated by a local businessman. The talented squad made it to the semifinals game, which was held in the evening. Las Vegas is known for its high temperatures during the day, but when the sun goes down, it can get chilly fast. The team had not packed any sweatshirts, pants, or jackets. Without prompting, local parents sprinted to the Sierra Leone sideline and covered the players one by one in blankets and jackets. The final outcome was irrelevant, because the local soccer community came through with a major assist even though it will never appear in the record books. Some things are bigger than winning a soccer match. Humanity was the ultimate winner on that frigid desert night.

*The portable stage used by the city of Las Vegas
for the Mayor's Cup trophy presentation.*

Official Las Vegas Mayor's Cup event banner.

Rick Ford

The list of successful men and women who worked for Jim Host and Host Communications is lengthy, and rightfully so. Rick Ford and Tim Campbell are two great examples. They accomplished a tremendous amount and created several successful programs.

In 1995, Host Communications was the publisher of all University of Kentucky game programs and the producer of the UK Radio Network. Rick and Tim recognized the potential for a website featuring all this content. Keep in mind, the internet was very young at that time, but they felt it was going to be life-changing in the near future. The final hurdle was to show Jim Host the massive potential for a website and convince him that

Host Communications should lead, not follow, the proverbial pack. They succeeded, and UK's first website was launched.

Then the Southeastern Conference (SEC) Commissioner, Roy Kramer, called Host Communications about the website and said, "We need one of those, too!" Rick told me how Host Communications did it. They sent four people to the SEC Basketball Tournament—two per team--to track the play-by-play on the website. Employee #1 watched the action and relayed the play-by-play details to employee #2, who typed them into the computer and hit Send to transmit the text to the office in Lexington, Kentucky, in near-real time. Employees #3 and #4 did the same for the other team. There was video, too, although live streaming was still years away. Each basket had a stationary camera placed above the hoop to capture the action and flow of the game. These cameras would automatically refresh every fifteen seconds. Sometimes the players were still on the other side of the court when a camera refreshed, meaning when the viewer at home refreshed their screen, all they got was a static view of the hardwood. But it was innovative and cool for the time.

A chance encounter sped things up. Rick and Tim flew to New York City to meet with a young tech entrepreneur and passionate Indiana University basketball fan who was living in Dallas, Texas. His name was Mark Cuban. Rick said Cuban was on top of what was happening in tech, and, more importantly, what was about to happen. Cuban was working on developing high-definition (HD) broadcasting and live-streaming over the internet. In that meeting, they agreed on a deal to stream the Final Four games through the NCAA Network and over Broadcast.com.

The next major project was the NCAA Final Four website launch in March of 1997. The site received 26 million hits on its first day, crashing the servers. It was the first website for the Final Four, with GTE (now Verizon) and Compaq as the first corporate partners, both sold by Rick and Tim. It was produced courtside before CBS or ESPN got involved, and served as the precursor to the March Madness website we all enjoy today.

Host Communications fervently believed high school sports was the next big frontier. The company had worked diligently to get the college space in a good spot, and they liked the revenue base, but they were looking to expand and felt the internet was the space to do it. The company asked Rick and Tim to develop a business plan for the new venture. While Rick was balancing his full-time job, he did not have free time to switch gears and focus on this new project. He kindly declined the opportunity to launch the website network, but he agreed to write the business plan. Three months later, Rick and Tim submitted a business plan for the High School Internet Network, then happily returned to their regular jobs within Host Communications. Two months passed and the Host Communications board of directors called the two of them in to present their plan. Their proposal was approved, including a $3 million investment and the question, "What else do you need?"

The High School Internet Network became iHigh.com. Its explosive growth was off the charts, according to Rick. Six months and $14 million later, iHigh had eighty-five employees: forty to publish content, ten to recruit and register new schools, and thirty-four to sell advertising. In less than a year and a half, the company had 10,000 out of the 23,000 high schools in the country actively using the iHigh.com network.

In December of 2000, the company was ready to expand and started working to secure the next $15 million of venture capital. Everything was perfect...until it was not. The dot-com bust began, and in less than a month, the company went from eighty-three to ten employees, and ultimately four. It was a turbulent time filled with uncertainty, confusion, and bewilderment.

The company stayed afloat as ihigh.com for three more years due to their commitment to their shareholders. To their credit, they recognized that ".com" now had a negative connotation, and they wisely changed the company's name from iHigh.com to iHigh, Inc. Rick Ford's team realized that to survive, they had to create, implement, and own their marketing programs. The first program created was called the Great American Rivalry Series, focused on high-school football rivalries. Rick's event staff traveled to small towns and large cities across the country to promote and support the nation's top rivalry games. The program is still running; as of 2023, it is in its twentieth year, and over 1,100 schools have participated since its inception. The company publicizes rivalry games on its national platform at greatamericanrivalry.com and engages with local media and sponsors to award trophies and stream live and archive game video, where available. Host schools receive a donation for their athletic program in exchange for participating along with the distinction of being named a Great American Rivalry Series CHAMPION.

Armed Forces Fitness Series

Rick's twenty years of experience in the U.S. Army helped him in his professional career. He was a paratrooper, attended Survival School, and attained the distinction of being an Airborne Ranger. Years later, based on Rick's extensive military background, the Navy Seals trusted his company to explore and create event programming opportunities. They developed and launched the Navy SEAL Fitness Challenge competitions in nine cities across America.

Future Lab

Another successful program created by iHigh was Future Lab, a traveling educational event focused on science and technology—a popular category for both investors and students. Future Lab: The Innovation Expo was a massive production; its interactive unit included forty computers, and the entire production filled a semi-trailer and deployed to occupy an entire basketball gym. It took almost two days to set up and break down in each market. In the span of ten years, the program reached over 400 schools in 42 states.

Rick had this advice for aspiring young entrepreneurs and professionals: "Some ideas will work, and some will not. Do not fret or give up. Keep thinking and working on the concept. Be curious and try to improve things. My advice to anyone is to take the chance."

Rick's tremendous knowledge and experience in marketing and event management led him to start Brainbox Immersive Marketing, which develops experiential marketing programs and digital strategies. Creative, innovative marketing is his passion.

Tim Campbell

Tim Campbell began his career as a collegiate disc jockey at Eastern Kentucky University. He worked closely with the University of Kentucky's sports radio partner, WVLK, and had ambitious dreams of moving to New

York City and rising to prominent fame as the next shock-jock sports talk personality.

His career plans changed after he had a chance to work with some of the radio broadcast employees at Host Communications. "The Host guys," as they were nicknamed, wore shirts, ties and sportscoats every day, which was unlike anyone else in the laid-back radio industry. Tim remembers how he revered all of them because of the way they carried themselves. There was an air about them, kind of like when a police officer or military personnel walks in a room. They looked and spoke like true professionals.

After graduation, Jim Host offered Tim an entry-level production job. Initially he was torn; he greatly admired the company, but still had his dream of trying to make it in a major metropolitan area. Tim decided he could learn from "the Host guys." The first thing he did was buy a bunch of neckties. He remembers Jim Host telling him that even if you just string cables, you need to look like a professional and be serious about your job responsibilities. The Host way was embedded early on. The company had eighty employees, but you would have thought it was in the Fortune 500 based on the demeanor of its people.

One of Tim's first tasks at Host Communications was producing sports radio and TV talk shows, including live broadcasts. He worked with the broadcast engineers and producers from top-name colleges, including Notre Dame and University of Texas. The next project was assembling the national broadcast team for the NCAA Final Four. He met basketball broadcast legends like Bill Raftery and Ron Franklin.

In 1992, a newspaper article about something called the "internet" caught Tim's attention. Critics called it "a quirk of the moment." Tim vividly remembers looking at a black computer screen with green letters appearing on it as someone from North Carolina sent him an email. He was astonished, but also curious how this might develop into something bigger over time.

Host Communications was the leader in collegiate sports marketing at the time, yet the high school audience was an untapped resource. Tim wondered what would happen if you combined a package of audio, video, and great service and marketed it to high schools across the country.

The primary hurdle was the fact that school administrators and teachers had to be willing to share content, whether it was a football game, a band performance, or a school play. Tim knew in his heart that if you could get students involved in producing their own event highlights, then the entire school would benefit and schools would want to come on board. What school would not want to share their events with the local community? The product was free and allowed schools of every size to broadcast any school event on the internet.

It was not easy to achieve the initial support. He just had to get schools on board; from there, Tim felt the program would rapidly expand across the country. He made the decision to hire sales representatives to visit schools and showcase the innovative program.

During a visit to one of the early clients, a school in Chicago, Tim realized the dream was trending in the right direction. He was touring the campus, and the principal showed him the iHigh classroom, where students were working on multiple school-related live streams and other creative programs. Tim remembers saying to himself, "We have the complete picture."

Another important milestone occurred during the Kentucky High School Basketball Tournament, or the Sweet 16, as fans and players refer to it. The tournament is held in Rupp Arena in Lexington, Kentucky. Tim walked across the street from his office to the arena to live-stream the game. He placed his laptop on a garbage can in the corner of the arena. Someone from the Kentucky High School Athletic Association walked by Tim's makeshift setup and said, with a bit of a sneer, "So, this is high-tech streaming?" Tim had dealt with it before. He smiled and calmly said, "Yes, but look at the number of viewers. We have more people watching this game on a computer than we have in the building."

I asked Tim to describe his feelings about his career in the sports industry. His comment might surprise you, but it provides an insightful look at the man himself. "It was great to be around big-time sports," he said, "and to make money for clients, partners, and investors. I thoroughly enjoyed the ride. However, I am most proud of the fact we created something that gave students impactful life skills and helped engage them in learning on a new platform. That was fulfilling and made it all worth it."

Tim mentioned the tight bond he and Rick Ford shared. They were more like brothers than coworkers or teammates. Yes, they fought and argued, sometimes more than normal, and Jim Host would step in when needed, but no one else came between them. Their personalities and backgrounds were wildly different, but mutual respect made their friendship unbreakable.

Tim worked for Jim Host for twenty years as a website developer. He is wired differently than I am; he has a vast understanding of coding and technology. I was amazed by his knowledge of the sector. Creativity comes in different forms, and Tim is near genius level when it comes to implementing a brand's sales strategy across various channels.

Tim has long been a pioneer in online and mobile digital video. He organized one of the first live college sports video streaming services in 2004 for the University of Texas Longhorns, the Kentucky Wildcats, the Southeastern Conference, and others. He capped his time in the collegiate sports market by working with the Southeastern Conference athletic directors to consolidate the entire conference onto one XM satellite radio channel. Tim led the negotiations and delivered millions to the SEC schools, as well as additional amounts to Texas and Oklahoma State, which were other collegiate clients of Host Communications. He told me it was impressive to see the powerhouse schools step up to ensure the smaller-budget schools earned an equal share.

Team iHigh

iHigh was a successful tech company in part because the executives spent time with employees. The sales reps would fly back to Lexington two to three times a year to receive strategic updates and new technology rollout plans, and to provide feedback on the technology and what our client schools were wanting next.

During these meetings, Tim would lead an open forum and listen to problems, complaints, concerns, and compliments with the goal of improving the product for our clients. From 1:00 p.m. to 5:00 p.m., we were entrenched in these lively discussions and brainstorming sessions while Tim frantically recorded our feedback on the nearest dry-erase board. He loved creativity and demonstrated positive energy and excitement for a new challenge. After dinner, we would split up to enjoy the evening and socialize with our teammates. Then Tim and the coding crew would work for hours into the night modifying the software to meet our ever-changing needs. At breakfast the next morning, Tim would unveil the software changes we had talked about the day before!

During these meetings with Tim, there was a feeling in the air of something special, as if Walt Disney's imagination was guiding us and the word *no* was never an acceptable response. I could not believe how fast Tim's mind worked, how he and the coders could change the software in one evening, or how they stayed up that late. Technology was his passion. He loved everything about it and was highly intelligent when it came to implementing new concepts.

After he left iHigh, Tim started his own media consulting company, which was no shock to anyone. Blue Million (bluemillion.com) is based in Lexington and helps clients navigate the constantly changing world of social media and digital branding. One of their first clients was Wrangler Jeans, for whom they built the Wrangler Network, a streaming platform that is now in its ninth year of operation. Other clients include Whataburger and the National Thoroughbred Racing Association. Blue Million celebrated its tenth anniversary in 2023 and shows no signs of slowing down.

I asked Tim what advice he would share with aspiring entrepreneurs. He replied: "Entrepreneurs are born with the passion to create things. It is in their blood, and it never goes away. You can be small and effective and control your destiny without investors, but to grow, everyone looks to investors at some point. Choose your investors carefully. The best ones are those who share your vision without corrupting the chosen path. When an investor forces you to change your vision, I have never seen it work better than the original idea."

Tim's storied career at Host Communications and iHigh provided him with a wealth of experience and knowledge. Like a successful jockey on the racetrack, Tim rode the inside rail when necessary but did not hesitate to break to the middle and chase greatness. Like most passionate entrepreneurs, he started his own business and bet on himself.

National Junior College Athletic Association

The National Junior College Athletic Association (NJCAA) is the governing body for the country's 500-plus junior colleges. The organization was based in Colorado Springs, Colorado, which meant the account fell under my jurisdiction. In fact, their office was an hour's drive from my house. The NJCAA became a client of iHigh, and we worked with their executive team to brand the technology as NJCAA TV. The first live-streamed game was a momentous occasion for players, parents, and coaches. Games at the junior college level were not televised, and a match that pitted Eastern Wyoming against Western Wyoming was not a fun drive to make in early January. Now, everyone could watch it on their laptop or smartphone.

NJCAA World Series

The NJCAA World Series, also known as the JUCO World Series, is held in Grand Junction, Colorado, and is the best-known championship hosted by the organization. True baseball fans know the history and importance of this tournament: many major league stars played in it before being drafted, including Kirby Puckett, Curt Schilling, and Bryce Harper. The pre-tournament banquet always features a nationally known speaker; in 2012, the year I attended, the speaker was legendary basketball coach Don Meyer. The short list of impressive Hall of Fame players who have spoken include Stan Musial, Willie Mays, Ernie Banks, Bob Gibson, George Brett, and Dale Murphy. Baseball fans will also recognize some of the game's best-known managers, including Billy Martin, Joe Torre, and Tommy Lasorda.

Grand Junction is located in the Western Slope region of Colorado. It is a breathtaking backdrop for America's pastime, with its red sandstone bluffs, wineries, peaches, and colored sand cliffs. The city loves the tournament, too, as evidenced by the sheer number of volunteers who comprise the tournament committee. It is a significant revenue generator for the city and for local businesses. The local newspaper, *The Daily Sentinel*, provided an overview of the economic impact. The Grand Junction Area Chamber of Commerce estimates that each week-long NJCAA tournament brings with it an economic impact of $2.4 million to the community. The tournament, which is managed locally by the Grand Junction Baseball Committee and run by the National Junior College Athletic Association, brought in $250,000 in ticket sales in 2018 and $280,000 in sponsorships. The ticket sales are split between Grand Junction Baseball and the

NJCAA. The goal is to bring in about $500,000 between tickets and sponsorships each year.

In 2012, iHigh live-streamed the tournament on behalf of the newly created NJCAA TV channel. During the event, I was focused on work and did not have time to meet anyone from the committee. Still, I wanted to talk to someone who was affiliated with the tournament about this book. I reached out to a sports reporter from the area, who was kind enough to forward my request to Jamie Hamilton, the chairman of the tournament committee.

Jamie Hamilton was born in Grand Junction and moved to Denver early in his childhood. He was a multi-sport athlete at Regis High School, then returned to Grand Junction to attend Colorado Mesa University. After graduation, he yearned to spend time in a different locale once he reached the minor leagues. He spent three years in the Anaheim Angels organization, primarily playing infield. When he and I were younger, the team's name was the California Angels. After spending hundreds of days and nights in small and midsize towns, he realized how nice of a town Grand Junction was to raise a family.

A local business owner jokingly told Jamie, who held a .190 batting average, "Well, you can't hit, maybe you can sell insurance?" Jamie hung up his cleats and never looked back. His passion for baseball never waned, though, and he was happy to help his hometown when the opportunity arose to volunteer with the Junior College World Series.

Generally speaking, a volunteer position is short-term and lasts maybe a year or two. Jamie, a baseball lifer, is now in his thirty-eighth year of involvement with the event. One of his first responsibilities was to chauffeur VIP guests and the banquet speakers from the airport to their hotel. It was only a twenty-minute drive, but the conversations were lively and filled with intrigue, personality, and outrageous stories that Jamie hopes to share in his own book someday.

His favorite story was when he picked up New York Yankees owner George Steinbrenner. The legend had flown in his private jet. Jamie recalls he was gregarious and had nothing but good things to say about Grand Junction and the tournament itself. On the return trip to the airport, Steinbrenner commented, "You guys have done great here. I am proud of you." Unbeknownst to Jamie, Steinbrenner had left a gift for the committee: a $25,000 check to support the event.

I spoke to Jamie by phone for thirty minutes. His passion for the event and city itself was electric. He emphasized the importance of the volunteers and how great people pull together to execute a first-class event—not only for the city of Grand Junction, but also for the teams, coaches, players, and fans. Why is the tournament held in such high regard? Jamie answered: "Everyone involved is empowered to make everyone feel welcome, from the players and coaches to the visiting members of the media. The committee is proud of their hard work, and they want to make it the best event in the world. No one cares about getting credit for their time or energy, which is humbling, but deeply impactful."

The tournament committee is a 501(c)(3) nonprofit and is supported by donors and corporate partnerships. Alpine Bank is the longtime title sponsor of the event. The committee also supports the local sports community with youth baseball scholarships and other area grantees.

As we shared our own sports stories as if we had been lifelong friends, Jamie offered one of his best ones. In 1978, the Salinas Angels were playing the Fresno Giants, and his manager used Jamie's versatile skill set to make a point. The term *utility player* is often used in the sport, and on this date, Jamie epitomized it. During a seven-inning game, Jamie played all nine positions for the Angels. In the first inning, for example, he gave up one run as the starting pitcher, then moved to catcher, then finished the inning at first base. It was a special memory for him to relive. To this day, he resents one small detail of the experience, and that is the fact that he took the loss as the starting pitcher despite having thrown only two pitches. I think he and the wonderful people of Grand Junction have delivered one big win after another since then.

My view of the JUCO World Series.

Olympic National Governing Bodies (NGBS)

Other organizations iHigh worked closely with included some of the US Olympic National Governing Bodies. The United States Olympic & Paralympic Committee is headquartered in Colorado Springs, Colorado. I spent two full days in the city with Jim Host, Tom, his friend from the NCAA, and another iHigh executive. I managed partnership accounts that were spurred by our whirlwind days of meetings. We met with executives from USA Wrestling, USA Figure Skating, and USA Hockey. It was fascinating to see how each entity operated and the passion each group demonstrated for its sport.

My favorite part of the Olympic Headquarters building was the conference rooms, which were named after different Olympic Games and their corresponding years, such as 1968 Mexico City and 1984 Los Angeles.

I am almost positive I would have had none of these meetings or experiences had it not been for Jim Host.

US Swimming Olympic Trials, 2012—Omaha, Nebraska

My event credential for the 2012 US
Swimming Olympic Trials.

The US Swimming Olympic Trials is a premier level event, and it required additional iHigh staff to provide the attention it deserved. Since I was only a one-hour flight away, I joined the event team at the last minute. It was more cost-effective for the company to send me rather than some-one from the Lexington corporate office.

It was my first time attending an Olympic Trial event. You could feel the energy in the air even though we were housed in the Convention Center, next door to the competition pool. I never made it inside the pool area because I was busy talking to coaches, parents, and athletes from across the country about their respective swim clubs and their favorite event.

The fan fest zone was impressive, both in size and creativity. The corporate partners had invested time and money to create inspirational branding and sponsorship activation areas for fans, coaches, and athletes of all ages. The displays featured high-res photos, bright colors, and gigantic structures. You could not help but feel motivated to chase your own dream. It was also gut-wrenching at times. At the Olympic level, mere milliseconds decide who qualifies to chase their lifelong dream and who returns home for three and a half more years of training. One minor mistake, one slip or twist, could mean the difference between a world record or finishing one place short.

Besides speaking with coaches and amateur athletes, I also interviewed Olympic swimmers from past and present, including a Paralympic athlete who held several World Records. These interviews typically happened with little to no warning. I am comfortable talking to anyone, but I had little time to be nervous or to practice my questions, because it was a live production. I spent five minutes rehearsing questions in my head, hoping they would make sense.

Me interviewing Olympic medalist Amanda Beard.

Sponsorship activation at the Sponsor Village in Omaha.

This banner is where the final 2012 Olympic
swimming team roster was announced.

Our daughter, Emily, joined me for a 3v3
soccer event in Vail, Colorado.

*A different traffic jam on the scenic route
from a sales trip to Steamboat Springs.*

The Steamboat Springs Winter Sports Club ski jump.

My live streaming setup for a youth ski racing at Vail Resort.

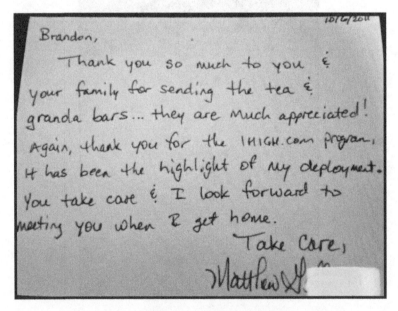

*A thank-you card from a fellow Coloradan who
was on deployment with the US Army.*

Marques Burnett

All iHigh's sales representatives were based in home offices across the country. We worked remotely before the coronavirus pandemic made working from home common. I struggled to establish friendships because the other five sales reps had been working together for years when I was hired. In baseball terms, I was the rookie who received the call up from the minors and had to fit in with the group.

The team encouraged me and helped when I had a question. Ultimately, they were focused on driving revenue and earning commission checks, which is understandable.

Marques Burnett based his office out of Atlanta and managed part of the Southeast Region. An Indiana native and yet another basketball fan, we formed a quick friendship over more than just our love for hoops. We shared an entrepreneurial mindset and a common bond of respecting people. He became a de facto coach for me, and we spoke on the phone often. I often referenced his penchant for style, because he would have won a best dressed contest amongst our team.

A year into my time with iHigh, the company encountered some financial difficulties. Six months later, the first round of layoffs began. This provided Marques with the red flag warning that he might be next. He took time to ponder his next career move and realized he enjoyed the live-streaming concept and high school sports clientele. The next challenge was to identify a way to differentiate himself from iHigh's business model.

Football is king in the South, but Marques knew basketball was popular in certain pockets. He felt basketball had room to grow but it just needed the right platform. His idea was to create his own premier basketball tournaments, stream them, and sell advertising. He realized that a tournament of his own was something he could control, rather than relying on schools to generate new website visitors.

When the day arrived and he was told his time at iHigh was done, Marques graciously thanked the executives for the opportunity. One month later, the Sports Utility Vehicle — SUV and SUVtv company was born. The company's primary goal is to develop a multi-faceted viewing platform featuring premier high school basketball tournaments with top-level talent.

Here are two of the top tournaments Marques works with as part of his company:

- **Flyin' to the Hoop Invitational** (www.flyintothehoop.com), is a high school basketball tournament that began in 2003 and is played in Dayton, Ohio. According to CBS Sports / MaxPreps, it is currently the #2 basketball showcase for high school basketball nationwide. Each year, over twenty thousand fans, college coaches, and media attend the event, pumping over $1.9 million into the local Dayton economy. Eighty-seven alumni of the event have been drafted into the NBA (or NFL).

- **Holiday Hoopsgiving** (holidayhoopsgiving.com) was originally a high school basketball event. In 2020, it expanded to also include elite NCAA men's basketball programs, hosting five games in State Farm Arena in downtown Atlanta. With top programs competing, the event was a tremendous success, even during the pandemic.

I am not surprised by Marques Burnett's success. I root for him from afar and am excited to see what he does next. If you find yourself at one of these events in the future, just look for the sharpest dressed executive with the million-dollar smile and the velvety voice, because that is my friend, Marques.

Marques during an interview at a basketball tournament.

Post-game recap: Technology is neither my favorite area nor my strongest, but I learned how to build and expand a business the right way. The team at Host Communications had creativity and energy that was incredible to watch. Jim Host, Rick Ford, and Tim Campbell each taught me something different about following your gut and taking a big swing. I appreciate the job and experiences I had with iHigh. None of it would have happened without Jim Host taking a chance on me—nor would I have talked with Jamie Hamilton or met the Olympics organizers and athletes, or my great business friend, Marques Burnett.

Rebuild. Rebound. Repeat. 2007-2018

Brandon Tosti
Founder and Executive Director
P.O. Box 102961
Denver, CO 80250
www sportsforacause org
Rebuild. Rebound. Repeat.

Pre-game: Sometimes in life, the next project finds you, especially when you are not searching for one. This was the case with my nonprofit, Sports for a Cause. I was a busy dad of two young kids; between family and my high-profile sports job, my plate was full, or so I thought. Then an article in Sports Illustrated changed my life. My next endeavor made zero sense on paper, but something in my heart told me to keep going and not worry about the critics or challenges in my path.

I have been reading *Sports Illustrated* magazine since I was in middle school. I saved multiple issues over the years, mostly historic ones, especially when Michael Jordan graced the cover. When my kids were small, the magazine was produced weekly. Each Thursday when it arrived, I would flip through the entire issue page by page to survey the articles and see which ones caught my eye. Then, I would eat dinner, put the kids to bed, and start reading at bedtime.

The August 27, 2007, issue was no different at first. College football graced the cover, and I figured I would thumb to that article first. But a feature article in the back pages of the magazine occupied the #1 spot in my brain.

It was a powerful and beautifully written retrospective article by long-time columnist Alexander Wolff. It focused on Hurricane Katrina and the New Orleans area, specifically the state of schools and playgrounds. This was two years after the historic storm made landfall, and the photos told a devastating and horrific story. Piles of rubble still lay where brick buildings had been. Shards of glass and overgrown grass remained on football fields. I struggled to comprehend why nothing had been done to help these schools. The reality was the media only showed certain sections of the storm damage. The amount of destruction was difficult to fathom until I saw it in person.

The following October, I emailed Alexander Wolff at his *Sports Illustrated* account to let him know his article had inspired me to start a nonprofit. I honestly did not expect him to respond. Instead, Alexander sent me a nice response shortly thereafter. He mentioned that even though one of the primary rules in journalism is to remain objective, this assignment and article had affected him. Even though we didn't meet in person, the fact that he took time to respond meant something to me. A successful sports journalist and author, he easily could have blown me off.

I named my charity Sports for a Cause. The concept was to solicit donations of money and/or sports equipment, then assemble small groups of volunteers to travel to New Orleans and repair or replace fields, courts, and playgrounds at schools and in neighborhoods. The concept seemed impractical for a variety of reasons. Who in the corporate Denver community would donate money to help another city five states away? Also, we would have to ship every major donation. The expense for that piece alone presented a formidable challenge. Still, I felt something in my heart. I tried to ignore the emotion, but I could not shake it.

Fundraising was the first challenge. I arranged meetings with potential corporate donors, explained the need to them, and asked for advice regarding fundraising techniques and effective promotional materials. To excel at fundraising, one must learn to be more than a *good* storyteller; you must be a *passionate* storyteller. I did my best to explain the level of destruction, which covered miles and miles of suburbs. It is difficult to comprehend how much damage water can do. I was not expecting a huge amount on the corporate fundraising front; I figured a small number of companies might donate $250 or $500. Luckily, my wonderful friends contributed in ways I could not have imagined. Individuals also stepped up. Sometimes a chance meeting with a stranger would lead to a donation. One time, I struck up a conversation with a passenger beside me on a flight to one of the volunteer trips. He was so moved by the story that he wrote me a check for $500. I hope to return the favor to someone else in the future.

Finding volunteer projects required calling friends and promoting the next volunteer trip on social media. Projects had to be doable from a skills perspective. Keep in mind, I never knew who would be joining me for each trip, nor their skill level. I, for one, am not handy at all. We also had to find projects we could complete in the time we had, typically two to three days. We tried our best to avoid leaving a project unfinished. Not only does an incomplete project leave the community unhappy, but it is also demoralizing for the people volunteering. My volunteers were spending their own money and vacation time to join me on a trip. I deeply cared that everyone should walk away with a good experience.

Everything about the actual trips was a challenge, but none of it fazed me. The months of March and October had the mildest weather, and they coincided with my slow times at work. I learned to be a savvy travel agent of sorts, because I oversaw hotels and rental cars for our group. We tried to minimize the number of cars to save money. The ride was cramped, but there is something to be said for traveling to a volunteer site with ten of your best friends. Discomfort is part of the experience, and we laughed a lot during those trips.

Upon arrival, we hosted a team meeting to discuss the city map, our projects, and what everyone should bring to the work site. Kind people opened their houses, hearts, hotels, and cars to me and my friends. When I flew for my first trip, I was picked up at the airport and transported around the city for four days. I offered gas money, to no avail. Instead, my guest treated me to a New Orleans Hornets basketball game on Saturday and a New Orleans Saints football game on Sunday. The energy and passion in the dome that day filled this sports fan's heart. Furthermore, a hotel executive insisted on providing complimentary rooms for me multiple times.

More than once we struggled with the communication piece; for example, the Volunteer Coordinator was busy overseeing rebuilding projects and the number of volunteer groups changed weekly. In February, we might have been assigned to a playground project at Smith School, but by the time we arrived in March, the project was completed, which meant we had to scramble at the last minute to find a new project. But we had incredibly generous support on the ground. I remember a local banker told us to stop by his house on the first day of our volunteer trip to gather tools. He opened his garage door and said, "Take what you need."

I mentioned wanting the experience to be a good one for volunteers as well as the local communities in New Orleans. On one of the plane rides, I thought about how to improve the approach to volunteer trips. I knew we were constantly brainstorming and researching potential sport retail companies to help us with our projects. Then it hit me. We could invite sporting goods companies to not only donate, but also send people to volunteer. Of course, our primary goal was helping the community, but each group of volunteers represented a networking opportunity for those involved. I imagined volunteers swinging a hammer beside a sports-industry executive. Talk about proving your work ethic! Opening doors and networking was not my initial goal or priority, but it evolved after I realized it just made sense.

After I got home from my first trip to New Orleans, I sent a heartfelt note to family and friends:

[Alexander Wolff's article] caught my eye because of the graphic photos and the fact that it focused on youth athletic facilities and schools that no longer have fields to play on for recess or sports. I told my wife that I was going to plan a trip to New Orleans and help clean one high school field or basketball court. I thought about it for a minute and realized that America's youth and the opportunity to play sports is a common theme shared by all of us who work in sports, regardless of whether it is a pro team, sporting goods retailer, university, or sports agency. I am somewhat of an idea guy, and my mind developed a template for a volunteer program.

Then, I realized the potential of this project, because each team or company has a different offseason or slow period, so the program could have an even bigger impact because people could volunteer steadily over twelve to eighteen months versus just one of our teams working for one weekend. Employees could raise money for their travel and expenses, similar to other cause related marathons and events.

The Plan

As some of you know, I just returned from my "scouting" trip to New Orleans. I have been working on creating a national volunteer initiative that uses the sports industry to help rebuild New Orleans schools and their athletic facilities. I have been working on this project since early September and appreciate everyone's help and support thus far. Below, I summarize my last few days, so I apologize if it is lengthy, but I wanted to provide a realistic account of my trip. The goal is to encourage other companies, agencies, and teams to get involved with the program by donating equipment, purchasing equipment, or volunteering for three to five days in New Orleans. I plan to launch a website in February that has all the details and provides a one-stop shop for planning a trip. The key is to have all the relevant people in New Orleans in place and ready to manage the day-to-day tasks of the project. I met with the Convention Visitors Bureau, Sports Commission, the Parks and Recreation Director, the top transportation company in the city, and the Recovery School District's Athletics Director, Superintendent and Volunteer Coordinator. They will oversee the day-to-day management and logistics since I am in Denver.

Resilience and Hope

I met some amazing people that lost everything they owned, including close family members. A large number of citizens could not swim and drowned in less than six feet of water, which is hard to imagine. The people are very resilient and grateful, and it was a blessing to work with them on Saturday as we built the nineteenth new playground in the area.

The entire experience was unforgettable and truly moved me. I repeatedly tried to offer them gas money or treat them to dinner. They said no and that the fact that I cared enough to come down to help was more than enough. I told them that the next time I come down that I will bring fifty friends with me. To put it in perspective, after they returned from the storm, they said that their houses looked like everything inside *had been placed in a washing machine fifty times, and everything from a picture frame to a couch was piled up in the center of the room.*

FEMA helped homeowners in the area, but only a few have purchased new homes in the past two years. You must understand the citizens lived in houses that had been in their families for decades. It was an emotional decision, and a financial one, to move.

Playground Build

The playground project was inspiring because over 100 volunteers of all ethnicities and various economic backgrounds worked for nine hours as just that, VOLUNTEERS. I worked side by side with a local, historic African American sorority, an AmeriCorps team of Chinese, Filipino, and Hispanic students, a handful of nine- to twelve-year-old students, and members of Tulane University's Marching Band, and no one cared what color your skin was, where you from, or how you were dressed.

One of the sorority sisters told me she saved one item from her house and that I would never guess what it was. She saved her top-of-the-line snow skis, laughed, and said, "You didn't think anyone from New Orleans skied, did you?" She is traveling to Breckenridge in March for a conference, ironically enough. We built a $65,000 playground in approximately eight hours. It was very inspirational. The school kids performed cheerleading and dance routines for us to show their gratitude and I do not think that there was a dry eye in the crowd.

School Tours

It was truly an unforgettable experience of my life. Another school that I visited resembled a prison because of the modular trailers and the wire fence with an electronic gate. Unfortunately, multiple schools are set up like this. I cannot imagine going to school in trailers with barbed wire fences all around and no playground, but that is the best solution for now so that the kids do not miss school.

I hope that we can create some kind of surface for these kids to have recess or just play a simple game of hopscotch or tag. The devastation is everywhere and overwhelming, but you must start with one school, and that is the plan.

A Funny Egg

Now, for a little lighter side of the trip. As my close friends know, I am an extremely picky and plain eater. The Athletics Director took us to a nice steakhouse for lunch and ordered an appetizer of deviled eggs, which I have never tried and do not particularly like the smell of at all. He ate three and asked me why I had not eaten one yet because this was the only restaurant in New Orleans where you could order deviled eggs as an appetizer. I told him I did not like deviled eggs and his response was in a slow, Creole/Cajun drawl: "Brandon, you eat eggs, don't you? It is an egg, how plain do you want it? You mean to tell me that you don't eat deviled eggs? What is wrong with you? Give me your cell phone so I can call your mama right now."

My friend, Tom, was in tears, and I cut my deviled egg in half and choked it down. I took hundreds of photos and videos of various schools and will try to send them to whoever is interested, but I will not have any videos until late January.

My good friend from college who is a film producer, Tom Williams, came down to shoot the video footage and I honestly did not know what he would think when he left, but he is officially engaged and hooked on the project now. I look forward to sharing this unbelievable experience with friends in 2008; I promise you it will change your life in ways you cannot imagine.

Accentuate the Positive—This photo always inspired me.

The life changing Kaboom! Playground build and the inspirational reason I moved forward with the project.

It is hard to fathom the power of water and its impact on a school building.

The finished product after two long days of work.

At the end of each trip, I made sure to connect with donors and show them where their hard-earned money had gone and how it had made a difference in someone else's life. I sent photos and handwritten thank-you notes. Where possible, I would ask the teacher or students to write notes, knowing their words would be more powerful than mine.

Like we've tried to play sports for our school in the past have not been able to succeed, this year has said a different story. Sports teaches us many things while playing. One thing it has tought us is using our team and that you can't win a game with just one person, but that you need the whole team. Also sports has tought us that communication is an important thing you need because teamwork is dependent on communication. Without communication you would not be able to win. On the other hand, we love playing sports because of many reasons. One reason is because our team gets to know new people and in your own team you get to know your teammates better. Also we get to represent our school and be able to learn how to play different types of sports. To sum it all up, you might say you don't like sports because you're too lazy and you don't know how to play, but trying new things and meeting new people can help you have a better life and help your represent your school.

A note from one of the students whose school basketball team received new basketball uniforms.

Fundraising Events

We were making a difference in small ways, which was part of the goal from day one. Then a chance encounter led me to think we could do more.

I was working at the University of Denver (DU) Lacrosse camp when the Head Coach at DU introduced me to a friend of his who was a longtime Head Coach at Notre Dame. We chatted about life, and I mentioned the charity to him. He told me to let him know if he could ever help me.

A month later, I met with DU's coaching staff to discuss another thought for a fundraising event. What if Notre Dame and DU played a scrimmage game in New Orleans with all ticket sales benefiting a New Orleans school? My idea also involved both teams volunteering for one day. The coaches had mentioned the teams would be in town for multiple days, so it struck me that there was time to do more for the kids in the community, such as a free lacrosse clinic.

On my next volunteer trip, I met with an executive from the Sugar Bowl to discuss the potential DU and Notre Dame lacrosse exhibition game. He was extremely helpful and offered to lean on his contacts for support where it made sense. I had to pinch myself, because ten years earlier I would not have imagined myself pitching a collegiate charity lacrosse game in New Orleans. The game did not come to fruition based on travel costs and other factors. I am glad we tried, though.

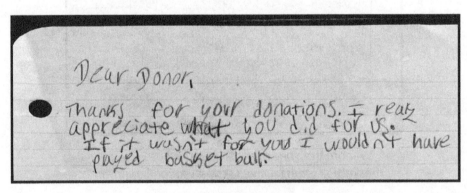

A thank-you note from a Denver school.

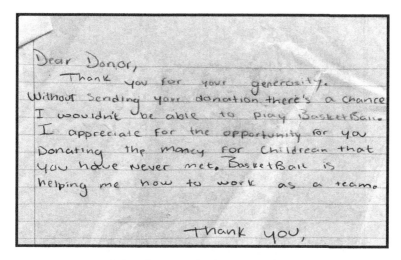

A thank-you note from a student.

Cajun Cornhole Classic Tournament

Every nonprofit needs its signature fundraising event. I knew we needed to create an event where people could have fun while participating with friends to support a good cause. The activity also needed to attract a wide demographic. The popular backyard game Cornhole was becoming more mainstream at the time. I thought a Cornhole tournament was the perfect choice because it is something everyone can do regardless of their athletic ability.

Next on the agenda was selecting a venue that would be affordable and have ample room to host multiple cornhole boards. The Board of Directors split up research calls and we discussed our options, but landed on one soccer field at Dick's Sporting Goods Park. In case you are wondering, I charged my nonprofit the current going rate for the field rental. Honesty is always the best policy when personal business intersects with work.

Once the Sports for a Cause board of directors approved the tournament, we had less than a month to pull everything together. The one-day event generated over $2,400. Most teams were from the metro Denver area, but one college student and her father drove two hours from Cheyenne, Wyoming, to play in the tournament. She had seen our event listed on Facebook, which was in its early days then.

*The scoreboard tent resembled the
old Summit Sports 3v3 ones.*

One of the custom board designs.

*It was time to have some fun and raise
money for a good cause.*

A local artist designed and manufactured customized cornhole boards for the tournament.

Denver North High School

The focus of my charity was primarily on New Orleans area schools, but we modified our state paperwork and performed work for Denver schools as well. A local high school football team, the Denver North Vikings, was dealt a bad hand in the way of a burglary. According to a newspaper article, their football storage room was broken into and thousands of dollars' worth of football equipment was stolen. If I recall correctly, the equipment was not insured. Local businesses were chipping in to help, and I figured we should do the same.

I reached out to the football coach and the Athletic Director. We met, and I proposed volunteering for a daylong city adventure race. This type of race had grown in popularity and is a scavenger hunt with various checkpoints across a city's landscape. Teams compete to finish the course by completing physical challenges and puzzle-type questions to advance to the next checkpoint. My charity would help with the event setup, and the players and others from the Denver North school community would assist with two of the checkpoints. The head football coach told me from day one that he wanted to help other coaches at the school as well, so the event became a benefit for other sports teams. The Vikings football players were hard-working and unselfish; they were responsible for most of the $10,000 the event netted.

After the race, we had a pep rally for the school. I wanted to treat these kids and teachers to a party they would never forget. I called in every favor I had. We had dancers and mascots from various Denver pro teams, and a professional DJ. Remember Shawn Martinez, a.k.a. Tribal Touch, who I worked with at Kroenke Sports Enterprises? He was my DJ for the afternoon, and he brought his A-game. A play-by-play commentator emceed the event. None of them charged me for their time or effort.

*Denver's professional teams played a huge
role in this high school pep rally.*

*Miles the Denver Broncos mascot and the
Denver North Vikings junior football team.*

After the Denver North project, we branched out to help other public schools in Denver. The zip code, mascot name, and school colors changed, but each school had a need. We donated golf clubs, tennis balls, soccer balls, and baseballs to George Washington, John F. Kennedy, Bruce Randolph, and Denver South.

We can all learn from the brave citizens of New Orleans. Their world was shaken and shattered, yet they still smiled and forged ahead. The strength and resolve they showed was simply amazing. What kept me coming back was the kindness and generosity of the locals. Rebuilding is never easy, but through the mud and muck, they made it happen with old-fashioned guts, determination, and courage. To witness their positive attitudes and work with them on projects provided a tremendous amount of perspective about life, and they inspired me to do more for Denver, as well. The trips were inspirational and made us grateful for our homes and simple possessions we often took for granted. I met some remarkable people in New Orleans. I have said this before, but I promise each one of them has a room to stay in the Tosti house, as long as I live.

> *Post-game recap: I started this nonprofit organization because I wanted to make a difference and help kids, teachers, and families in New Orleans. I was not sure what we could accomplish or how my friends and family would react to my outlandish brainstorm. With the help of friends, coworkers, bosses, and family, we defied rational logic and donated over $150,000 in new and used sports equipment over seven years. I do not say that to brag, but rather to encourage others. When a wild idea hits you, there will be critics, but do not let anyone tell you it cannot be done. Just smile and tell them you have a friend in Arvada, Colorado, who begs to differ.*

Chapter 13
Rookie Ball & Training Camp

Pre-game: During my career in sports, I estimate I have managed close to a hundred interns. It is a role I took seriously and performed with great pride. I have never understood why some people view interns merely as free labor; that is a selfish and irresponsible way to treat interns. The goal and emphasis should be on teaching, developing, and sharing your hard-earned knowledge. Take a moment to remember how your earliest bosses treated you and helped you prepare for your career. Remember how it felt to be respected and able to ask questions to learn? Be a positive source of inspiration and pass it on to your interns.

Below is an email I sent to interns who reported to me as part of their internships. I would send it prior to their first day. I tried to put myself in their shoes: Some of them were moving from another city, maybe having recently graduated college, and they were taking a chance on our company and our team. I imagined anxiety was relatively high. Anything I could do to make them feel welcome and put them at ease before they arrived was the right thing to do.

I managed interns in the past. I do not know everything, and I am not perfect. However, I possess a strong passion for ensuring that my students have a great experience with internships and will hopefully provide each one of them with opportunities to grow. Below, I summarize my philosophy:

You are here to learn. I want you to see as much as you can in your amount of time with us, whether it is one month or four.

Networking is the most important tool you can use to advance your career. I will emphasize the importance of networking and share with you how it has helped land jobs multiple times in my career.

I will not ask you to do anything I haven't done myself.

I will always make time to discuss your career plans and answer your questions that I can. I usually set up one-on-one appointments with everyone.

If you leave here the same person as when you arrived, then I have failed you as a manager and a coach.

I want everyone to be successful, but you have to put forth the effort and maintain a positive attitude, even when it's extremely windy and raining sideways.

I try to include you in meetings and other projects so you can truly have hands-on experience and gain insight into what a full-time job looks like.

You are part of our team, and I do not feel the title means something less. I will respect you from day one and will treat you like a coworker.

If you make a mistake, it ultimately falls on me. If you do a great job, it is also on me. I don't just pick your successes, but as in life, I claim the good and the bad. I will be here to support you as much as I can.

Work hard and have fun.

It is a common theme in life to step back from your current position and reflect on your past. What was the most important lesson you learned? What did you worry about that turned out to be minimal at the conclusion? Did you make the right decision? What other career path would you have chosen?

I did this often, and sometimes I would question my career choice. I knew how much I enjoyed teaching and coaching, whether it was a collegiate Sports Marketing class or a fourth-grade basketball team. At times I thought maybe I should have been a P.E. teacher after all. Is it too late to make the move? Probably yes, but this wish resurfaces more often than I would like to admit. I have always relished coaching and leadership opportunities. I also enjoyed the mental process of developing a team.

My passion for coaching was not shared by all my peers, as it pertained to college interns. Some thought that helping or coaching a new employee equates to lost time. This mindset baffled me. Did they forget they themselves were rookies once? I do not expect everyone in an organization to take on a time-intensive teaching role with interns, but everyone can share a story or a bit of advice every now and then.

I felt a duty to coach and develop the up-and-coming ticket sales executives, venue managers, and sponsorship salespeople. Some people prefer to place their success above everything else; for example, by keeping the plum assignments for themselves rather than involving interns in them. That is understandable on some level because you do have to take care of yourself first. But remember, early in your career, a manager invested time, effort, and energy when you were an intern and helped propel you forward on your path.

Interns frequently asked me for assistance with resumes and cover letters. One year, a student of mine who was an avid soccer fan mentioned he wanted to apply for a field operations summer intern position with the Colorado Rapids Soccer Club. He remembered I had opened the facility and spent close to six years of my career at Dick's Sporting Goods Park. I was happy to help proofread the letter and offer feedback and suggestions.

There was a red flag in the last line of the first paragraph of his cover letter. The student proudly announced his passion for soccer.

In other industries, the word *passion* simply means excitement. However, it is perceived differently in the sports industry. Organizations and teams, especially at the pro and college levels, do not want sports fans working for them—and nothing screams die-hard fan like the word *passion*. Fans may use questionable judgment because they do not want their favorite team or player to get in trouble, —and there is too much at stake for leagues to risk letting that happen. I cannot say for certain where I first learned this, but it was something I heard repeatedly when I was involved in the hiring process for both interns and full-time positions at every level.

I informed the student he would have to remove the sentence about his passion for soccer before I could make a call on his behalf. It was non-negotiable. I smiled and said, "If you repeat that line during an interview with any of my former teammates, they will shake their heads and say, 'There is no way Tosti sent you to me without telling you to delete that sentence.'"

Tips for Managing Interns

Give them plenty of your time the first day. Try to devote four to five hours to training on an intern's first day. You might sacrifice some of your productivity that day, but it will save you time in the long run. Talk to them about how your company conducts business and why. On a chaotic game day, you will not have time to stop and explain your decision-making process. Encourage questions the first day. Not only are you setting the stage for the intern's success, but you are also demonstrating to them you are in their corner. It will do wonders for their confidence.

Explain the big picture. The world of sports revolves around a season, and this is true at every level. Each segment of the calendar requires a different mindset and different operational decisions. Be sure to explain the logic behind these changes as the season unfolds. It is valuable information for sports industry interns.

Set a good example. Keep in mind, interns admire you as their coach and an influential person in the early stage of their career. How you talk to clients and coworkers matters because you are setting the example. They might not mention it, but they are watching you and are eager to learn from their supervisor.

Include interns in video calls. No one likes video calls, but they are an essential part of conducting business, and they are not going away anytime soon. Invite your interns to take part in these calls. Be sure to discuss and review the rules of conduct ahead of time, because things can go wrong on a group call.

When interns are present for a call, enunciate your words clearly and speak a tad slower than usual to ensure the group heard your answer or feedback. Encourage interns to take detailed notes. After the call, distribute a list of action items, highlighting any that are time-sensitive, and noting who is responsible for each task.

Include interns in meetings when and where appropriate. Prior to the meeting, you should discuss company culture and prepare them for the different personalities in the office. It is a terrific opportunity to see and learn how things work.

Spend a small amount of time talking to them about the company's methods and allow them to establish a base of knowledge for them to build upon. Urge them to keep a notebook handy and fill it with key points they learn from each meeting. After you return to your office, take a minute to let the interns express their opinions on how the meeting went, and encourage them to share at least one lesson they learned. Their opinions and observations are honest and interesting because they are observing everything from an outsider standpoint. You might hear a different point of view, which is never a bad thing.

Give interns a project. The students report to your office or the stadium on their first day excited, eager to expand their knowledge base and gain coveted real-world experience. Try to create a roadmap for success by allowing each student to lead a major task as part of a project. The purpose is to instill a sense of pride and confidence. Your job is to provide guidelines and important rules, explain timing and the expected result, and then get out of their way. Yes, they will make mistakes, but they will also impress you with their work ethic and different viewpoints. Be sure to follow up with a coaching session to explain any mistakes and use them as a learning opportunity.

Involve interns in event management. Students will benefit from understanding the time and effort required behind the scenes to put on an event. Event management also teaches valuable skills and lessons, from negotiating and conflict resolution to the importance of small details. Furthermore, they will learn to solve problems, work with difficult clients, and be prepared when expensive technology fails miserably, or inclement weather moves in. The ability to respond quickly to conflict while remaining calm during a windstorm in June is a vital skill earned by being in the moment; it cannot be taught with a line of text in a sports marketing book. Event management is not for everyone long term, but every student can benefit from some experience with it. There is an emotional rush and sense of satisfaction that accompanies it when fans, clients, and your teammates look to you for support, guidance, and answers.

Few things in my career made me smile more than a former intern calling me to notify me they landed their first sports job. It meant more to me than an award, especially when they thanked me for teaching them to do things the right way. It meant they had listened and adopted a good habit and would pass it on. Someday they will have the chance to coach a group of interns and understand the feeling.

Post-game recap: An internship can be a powerful experience filled with lifelong lessons when a manager invests time into the training program.

It is easy to forget we all start somewhere and even the most successful people made mistakes, endured setbacks, and eventually advanced in his or her career.

For whatever reason, managers tend to think one must be a superhero or a world-class coach. You just have to show that you care, and it is accomplished by teaching one item at a time.

Chapter 14
Lessons from the Game — A Look Back

Pre-game: When I set out on my journey, I had big dreams, energy to match, and determination to do whatever it took to stick around for as long as I could. I knew it would not be an easy path, but I focused on the experience and what I learned from each manager and teammate along the way. The memories and stories make me smile when I think about my teammates. I know how lucky I was to visit fun places and meet amazing people in different cities.

During the eighteen years, my career encountered dead ends, a couple meaningful accomplishments, tricky detours, and some unforgettable experiences. I thought about switching careers and taking a higher paying job. My gut told me I would not be happy in the end. In this final chapter, I reflect on the various roles and types of jobs I held during my career, including lessons learned from other teammates and departments. It was not always a smooth ride, but it was worth it.

As I look back on my career path, I think it is important to share some lessons I learned from the various jobs I held during this time. I am glad I was able to explore different areas within the industry. It provided me with a wealth of knowledge and the ability to understand what is important to other departments and my teammates, and why it matters. Plus, it prepared me for different personalities and how to manage or work with them.

Ticket Sales

This segment of the sports industry is fascinating to me based on two principles: commitment level and creativity. Account executives are constantly generating sales promotions and concepts to try and fill the stands for every home game of the season. It is not an easy task, and it requires months of determination and resolve. Here are three lessons I learned from my coworkers who were ticket sales account executives:

Appreciate other teammates' jobs.

True grit comes from dealing with rejection all day, months at a time.

This might be one of the toughest jobs in sports.

Sponsorship Sales

The unique part of sponsorship sales is that no two contracts or negotiations are the same. The budget, goals, and length of contract term all vary from partner to partner. The process also has a long sales cycle, and the brand's priorities can, and often do, change during the communication period leading up to a signed contract. It is a tedious process and one that sometimes requires multiple approvals from both the brand and their sponsorship or marketing agency.

The important lesson here is to listen to the partner's needs and what is important to the brand. Successful sponsorship salespeople are eager to learn what sets the brand apart. It could be why they include a special ingredient in their dough, or why they brew their coffee at a specific temperature. Whatever it is, you need to know it and design a sponsorship package that demonstrates you listened to their needs and understand the brand's objectives.

Building a customized package for a brand is not always easy, but for those who embrace the challenge, a commission check is not the only metric of success.

In sum:

Sponsorship sales is a long play, not a quick yes or no.

Listening to the partner is vital, whether you are prospecting or attempting to renew a contract.

Sponsorship Activation and Fulfillment

A sponsorship activation job requires patience, persistence, and a positive attitude. Another valuable trait is understanding what matters to the brand and their goals for investing in the sponsorship opportunity.

The activation experience prepares you to manage almost any situation. Mistakes will happen in sponsorship activation. It is how you react to them that really matters. Remember to focus on the solution and try to remain calm when everyone else appears to be upset.

An important takeaway is to remember to appreciate the person you work with on the brand side; do not just accept the check and assume the hard work is done. An astute activation rep values relationships and with little effort can transition from chatting about the company's stock price with an executive to dealing with an inexperienced intern who is working on the company's community fundraiser.

As in sponsorship sales, it is important in sponsorship activation to listen and learn what matters for the brand.

In this field, you will need to negotiate and deal with difficult people in high pressure situations.

Fundraising

Asking for money is an acquired skill, and you must approach it with unapologetic passion and zero fear. There is no shortage of nonprofits in the world for individuals and corporations to donate to. Hard work and hustle will help differentiate you from other groups, but you must find the right match when it comes to major donors.

Identify successful and established fundraisers in the market. Sometimes these are referred to as "movers and shakers."

Take time to understand, listen, and learn why people or companies give to charitable causes.

Design your fundraising goal as a pyramid with multiple ask levels. Start with the basic request, then move up and see if they are willing to invest at a higher level.

Technology

The technology sector is well-known for being a game changer. Whether it is broadcasting speed or tournament bracketing software, it improves the game for all parties. Technology is not just about efficiency; it can make a difference in client and patron communication, as well. It saves time and allows the event owner to provide updates to the client in a timely manner. You don't have to understand everything about the technology your business uses, but it helps to be able to navigate common trouble spots so you know what to do when clients ask for help.

Embrace technology.

Appreciate its power.

Always have a backup plan in case something breaks.

Venue Management

As a venue manager, one must maintain a process-oriented mindset. Managing a venue requires a tremendous amount of planning and preparation. Indoor and outdoor facilities have different challenges, but safety and the guest experience should always be at the forefront of every business decision. You must be able to react quickly to situations ranging from medical emergencies, to scuffles between two players, to safety issues and conditions of athletic fields. In addition, you are dealing with the public, and sometimes tourists who are not familiar with the area, especially with large-scale youth tournaments. Always remember to remain calm and help patrons stay safe while visiting your property.

Communication of goals, rules, and expectations is a vital skill for venue managers. You are dealing with multiple facets, including janitorial, food and beverage, parking, maintenance, police, fire, and paramedics. Be sure to listen for suggestions and ways to improve processes and policies, because the employees on the front line can often share powerful insights.

Understand that not everyone thinks the same way.

Get to know key personnel, such as building security and housekeeping. Thank them often.

Event Management

This will always be my favorite facet of the industry. I love the planning and brainstorming process of creating an event or activity for others to enjoy. It is fun to entertain people and help them forget about their stress for three hours.

Event management teaches a multitude of skills that transfer to everyday life. You experience a bit of everything, and you never know what situation you might deal with next.

Event managers have a tremendous amount of responsibility and decision-making control.

Expect the occasional medical emergency or tense situation that must be defused.

If you do not know much about budgeting and profit and loss (P&L) sheets, you will once you've tried event management.

High School

This is a sector that intrigues sponsors and companies but remains a quagmire filled with bureaucratic red tape, small-minded thinking, politics, and budget shortfalls. It seems every year, school districts face the difficult decision of which athletic programs to retain and which to cut. Most, if not all, school districts are apprehensive regarding the development of a corporate sponsorship program. Maybe it could save struggling programs and create new options for other teams, but someone needs to be the leader and make it happen on the local level.

I firmly believe sometime in the next decade there will be a high school homecoming week featuring a well-known corporate sponsor and not just a local pizza restaurant. I shared my opinion and reasons why it might work with some athletic directors and trusted friends in the Denver area. The group agreed it would be worth exploring the feasibility and developing an outline to share with school leaders.

If the concept comes to fruition, it needs to be comprehensive and well executed, similar to a traditional team sponsorship. Imagine students and teachers walking hallways decorated with colorful and inspirational floor decals. Halftime promotions could pay for scholarships. If someone builds and implements the concept the right way, local companies will find it difficult not to support local schools in some format. The standard homecoming dance and football game would never be the same. The program could be expanded to include other athletic teams, choirs, marching bands, and even academic clubs.

Maybe one day, I will launch a pilot program with a local school and see where it leads. All it takes is one company to step up with a small investment and support local students in this new format. I believe schools from across the country would soon adopt their own version of such a program.

Furthermore, high schools could create an educational curriculum for students interested in studying the basic principles of sport management. College athletic departments, minor league teams, and professional leagues often look for ways to engage with the community beyond just filling summer or fall internship openings. The best way to learn about event management is to plan and produce an event. The lessons the students would walk away with would be priceless. My guess is an Event Management class would be popular and would lead to additional classes in Sports Management and Sports Marketing.

One company that took action to help schools years ago is Dick's Sporting Goods. Kudos to the company for recognizing this issue and choosing to remedy it. Their Sports Matter program has donated thousands of dollars to high school programs and teams across the country. I hope to see other corporations follow their lead soon and find creative ways to support both boys' and girls' high school sports, because they need more than parents and friends in the bleachers cheering them on.

Charities, Nonprofits, and Economic Development Entities

I started a sports-related charity to help others and quickly learned how small the sports industry is when you ask for help with a special project. It is a powerful community of inspirational individuals, from major media markets to midsize towns tucked in obscure corners of a state.

Tips for Companies

The sports world is dynamic and unpredictable. Injuries, trades, and los-ing streaks play a major role in a team's popularity. These are factors that contribute to a surplus of water bottles, equipment, or T-shirts. At the end of a season, teams often clean out storage closets to make room for next season's inventory. Instead of throwing out outdated equipment, try to call a local high school or underprivileged youth program to see if they can use any of the equipment. Most water bottle labels can be removed if it is a player who has been traded.

Another popular item is practice jerseys. Some teams desperately need them but simply do not have the funds required to replenish old ones. The University of Denver's outgoing lacrosse coach donated 800 practice jer-seys, and we distributed them to multiple youth programs in the city. One beneficiary was a nonprofit after-school soccer program that needed 150 jerseys it could not afford. For the first time in years, every child received a jersey, and no one was upset that the text on the front said Reebok Lacrosse.

Anyone who works in sports should donate more than just a pair of tickets to local charity auctions. Equipment is not getting any cheaper. Schools and community-based youth programs will always need new or used gear. Any type of autographed memorabilia is popular at silent auctions, as are club seats and party suites. These items might seem simple and mundane because you deal with them daily, but for someone who does not have access to them, they equate to fundraising dollars.

I sincerely hope my friends and industry contacts will try to fill in the gaps whenever they can. You are in a position to help others and improve your community, one player and team at a time. I promise the smiles and heart-felt thank-you notes you receive from players will change how you feel about your job. Please follow all company procedures and secure proper approval (preferably in writing) from your supervisor before donating any old equipment from your organization.

Tips for Nonprofits

- Build a balanced board of directors including the following personality types:
  - Dreamer
  - Doer
  - Detail oriented
  - Event planner
  - Financial know-how
  - Legal
- Mentor access to a successful executive (Meeting or phone call two or three times a year)
- Tap into a donor's passion for the cause.
- Get donors involved and engaged on-site with beneficiaries whenever possible.
- Be a good storyteller and be able to share your passion.
- Honesty and transparency are crucial.
- Send project photos with personalized thank-you cards to donors.

When you are talking to someone about your organization and they ask how they can help, start by asking for advice, networking help, volunteers, and/or financial resources. Ask for money last. If you gain their emotional buy-in, the financial donation will eventually be made and will most likely be more than the amount you would have originally requested.

Collegiate Athletic Departments

As I previously mentioned, the collegiate space is where I hoped I would spend most of my career in sports. It never happened, but my affinity for the college atmosphere and spirit never faded. It is still my favorite level of sport to watch, whether it is basketball or football.

I am thrilled for my friends who were fortunate enough to break into this sector. If you decide to pursue a career in athletic administration, I highly recommend starting as early as possible because this path requires years to develop—and yes, you might have to move to another university to advance your career, so be prepared to switch your allegiance from the Gators to the Green Wave.

Grassroots Sports Tours

It felt like we were a traveling carnival. In some ways, we were a party planner and host in sixty-five different cities across America. We striped fields, repaired soccer nets, and set up and took down 10' × 10' tents hundreds of times, all while smiling and making memories of a lifetime.

Sundays had a different meaning to the event team. The weekend madness was finally over. We rested that evening, then quickly began working on the next weekend's tournament. The ultimate feeling of satisfaction came on Sunday afternoons, when parents pulled us aside, shook our hands, and expressed their gratitude for bringing our soccer circus to their city. A simple thank you provided a sense of pride for all of us. It made us appreciate the past seventy-two hours of stress, wind, humidity, and angry coaches.

I worked on the 3v3 tour for less than three years, but it was my favorite job of my career even though it paid the least amount of money. I often share that fact with students because it is an important life lesson.

The entire experience was invaluable, and it established a foundation for the rest of my career. I learned how to think like an entrepreneur and how to build a business with a focus on the grassroots approach.

The Pros

Revenue and growth opportunities typically rank at the top of the priority list for professional sports teams. The various sales teams endure constant pressure to increase the number of corporate partnerships, generate incremental revenue, and grow the season ticket base, not to mention retention rates for a lengthy list of club seats and suite clients.

The revenue is required to offset the expanding roster payroll, stadium operating costs, and other general operating expenses.

The pressure on coaches and players to perform is not visible in the front office, but its presence is felt. Regardless of your title or position in the company, winning takes priority, and the push to sell additional tickets never ceases. There is more financial risk at the major league level, which means job security is based on revenue and success. It is not suitable for every personality, and one realizes quickly if you want to pursue a job in sales or not.

Team owners are wise individuals who were initially successful in another field or industry. They do not reach the ranks of ownership by spending foolishly. Often, a savvy financial manager and an accounting team support them to closely monitor company expenditures, analyze risks, and weigh potential acquisitions. The owner has the final call, but everyone can benefit from advice and support from a wise team of advisors.

Walking Away

I no longer work in sports and haven't for ten years now. My drive to succeed did not diminish; rather, my focus and priorities changed. When it came time for me to leave the industry and pursue a different career, I went to a similar field, which is live music. The type of season and venue might have changed, but the experience has been similar. I still love entertaining fans and providing them with an opportunity to enjoy their favorite band at an iconic music venue.

I currently work on corporate partnerships (both sales and activation) for Denver Arts & Venues. My current job includes a handful of nights and weekends at Red Rocks Amphitheater. In addition, I manage one of our most popular fitness events, Yoga on the Rocks. It started as a single class experiment. Over time, it grew into a ten-week program that sells out every year. Our event team arrives at 4:00 a.m. to set up signage and assist with our Vendor Village. The event starts at 7:00 a.m. with 2,000 groggy yet smiling people in one of the most picturesque venues in the world.

In addition to Red Rocks Amphitheater, our agency owns and manages the Denver Coliseum and the Denver Arts Complex. However, my job is less late nights and long weekends than was required in my sports career. I am routinely home for dinner with my wife and children, which is important to me. I now have time to coach my kids in basketball and be actively involved with their lives.

My advice to young aspiring sports marketing students is to chase your dreams and buckle up for the ride. Yes, you will battle nasty curveballs and strike out more than once, but whatever you do, do not stop swinging. The sports industry has changed a tremendous amount since 2000, and new opportunities abound. Leagues have expanded, and the advent of Name, Image and Likeness for NCAA student-athletes means new opportunities in social media, sponsorship, and promotions.

The days in the sports business are long, but the nights are longer. One might say the grind of the job never stops, but it does not mean you cannot learn something new and enjoy the inspiring journey waiting for you on the field or the court. The life experiences, stories, and memories you share with your cohorts and friends will be worth the sacrifices.

In closing, here is my unofficial wish list for you. I hope:

- you feel the rush of working for a team on the verge of qualifying for the playoffs.
- you work for a rebuilding team, so you appreciate the effort required to win it all.
- you work for a perennial playoff contender.
- you get the chance to open a new stadium because there is nothing else like it.
- the team you work for wins a league championship.
- you get fired once, maybe even twice. It will toughen your heart and mind.
- you get promoted.
- you go for a job with everything you've got and get passed over for it.
- getting passed over for the job you want propels you to a better opportunity.

- you coach your interns the right way and treat them with the utmost respect.
- one of your former interns calls you when they land their first job, and you cherish the moment.
- you find great mentors.
- you take the time to mentor someone else who needs guidance.
- you call a mentor often to thank them, or for no reason at all.
- you get the chance to be a mascot, even if it is just for one day.
- you have a terrible boss, so you can appreciate a great one.
- you stick up for yourself even if it costs you a job in the end. It will be okay—trust me!
- you walk away on your own terms.
- you know how lucky you are to work in sports.
- you ask yourself the question, "Are the bright lights and long nights worth it?"

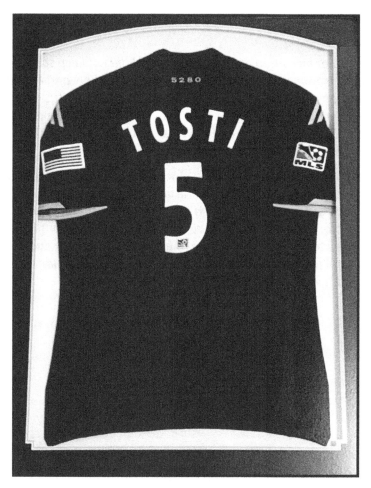

My five-year anniversary gift from the Colorado Rapids.

Post-game recap: As I reflect on the years I spent working in sports, I would not change much. Like an aging athlete, I knew when it was time to walk away. Our kids were getting older and became aware Dad had worked for long periods of time both nights and on weekends. When I turned forty, I realized the most important gift that we can give our children is our time. It is worth more than any plaque, commission check, or team golf shirt I received during my career. I was ready to leave the sports business, both emotionally and physically. I had chased my dream. I endured a couple of sucker punches, but I left with my integrity intact. I left on my own terms and knew I had given it my all.

Life is not measured on a stat sheet, and I did not keep score. My mentors taught me to help the next person in line, and I hope I did that and then some. I am proud my positive attitude never changed, nor did I change how I treated people. I respectfully chased my dream job and never stepped on someone else to advance my personal aspirations.

Like a favorite player's jersey, my memories are preserved for safekeeping, except most of mine are not framed behind a piece of glass but are forever etched in my heart and mind. There was no victory lap, farewell parade, or teary-eyed press conference. It was a tough decision, but the right one for this young dad. I am grateful for all the memories, earned game by game under those bright lights and long nights, one season at a time.

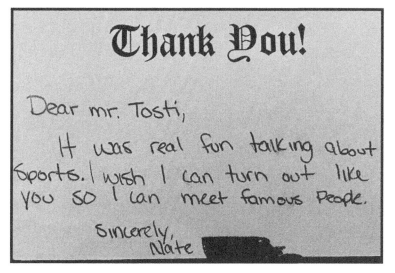

A thank-you card from a middle school student.

Acknowledgments

Mom and Dad: Thanks for believing in me and for the support while I continue chasing my dreams. I hope this book helps you understand why I could not walk away from my dream job for the longest time.

Brittany Tosti Pruitt: Thanks to my little sister for keeping me grounded and for making me laugh when I need it the most.

Jim Host: To one of the legends and founding fathers of the sports industry, thank you for taking a chance on this kid from Paintsville, Kentucky, when he needed it the most. People often talk about making a difference, while others do the work. I have met a number of successful people in my life, but your passion, drive, and innovative creativity will never be matched. I am grateful for the time I spent with you and your dear friend Tom Jernstedt in Colorado Springs. I had looked up to both of you from afar for years, and it was a special experience to listen to and learn from your stories. Rest in peace, Tom.

Cris Carrico: To one of my great bosses, I appreciate your advice, your unconditional support, and your reminders to own my passion and never shy away from being myself. You take my call every time. Every young employee needs someone like you who pushes them in a positive manner. You taught me never to run away from my passion, but rather to embrace it—and to never let an awful boss try to take it away. *Never.*

Dan Cramer: To the boss who taught me the value of a dollar and how to think through brainstorming sessions from multiple angles: Dan, thank you for the internship and for letting me make mistakes. I learned a tremendous amount about operating a company during my time with you. I did not have a law degree, but I am glad you trusted me to proofread contracts to identify discrepancies and errors. I appreciated the $5 Subway lunches more than you will ever know, and it is a simple and powerful tradition I continue with my interns.

Nate Baldwin: To one of my best business friends, thanks for the support, encouragement, and ear when I needed them the most. I am still hoping we start our consulting company someday, or if nothing else, a funny podcast to highlight the positive side of sports. We both know the world needs more feel-good stories.

Jon Andrews: To my college friend who continues to amaze me with his cover artwork. Thanks for your creative skills and talent. Everyone knows a book's cover plays a vital role in its success, and you always deliver.

Amy Clay: To my high school friend who manages my book summaries. She is a wizard with words and knows how to paint a powerful story. I cannot thank her enough.

Mike Williams: To my high school buddy who reminds me when I am doubting myself to focus on finding the little wins in life, especially when I am struggling to finish a manuscript.

Emily Melvin Mooring: To a childhood friend who supported this project early and often. I appreciate your time and commitment to proofreading the manuscript and for smoothing out the little details that mean a lot to a reader. The finished book is simply better because of you. I am grateful for you helping me secure two speaking engagements in Lexington, Kentucky.

Amy Bachelder Jeynes: To my editor, who continues to help me improve my writing and what I am trying to say with each project. Editing is a true art form and a specialized skill. I now know why other authors praise their editors so often.

Suanne Laqueur: To my project manager with Canoe Tree Press, thank you for your continued support and for understanding my ADD tendencies and general enthusiasm for writing.

Corey Stewart: To one of my proofreaders, thank you for your keen eye with the manuscript and for the friendly banter between your North Carolina Tar Heels and my Kentucky Wildcats. A book about sports without smack talk would surely disappoint any true sports fan.

Dr. Steve Parker: To my undergraduate advisor at UK who taught me what a good coach, teacher, and human being looks like every day, not just when things are easy. I will never forget the encouragement and support you provided me and other UK students.

Nate VanderWal: To a good friend, thanks for everything you have done behind the scenes to help me get to this point. You are one of the good guys and I am proud to call you a friend.

Rick Hatcher: To my first mentor, who taught me a great amount about the sports industry, but even more about life. I can never thank you enough for sticking with me through some rough patches. Like a good pitcher, you knew when to bring the heat and when a knuckleball was my best option.

Jeff Mathews: To one of my best work friends. Thanks for reminding me how important it is to laugh and enjoy life, in and out of the office. You are one of those friends who, when I hear your name, I immediately start laughing because of the good times we shared. I honestly do not know how we did not get into more trouble in Toronto, but man, we had fun! By the way, the next steak dinner is on me, pal.

Kieran Cain: To the most creative mind I've worked with, thanks for your friendship and support of Sports for a Cause from day one. I cannot wait to see what cool idea you think of next. Something tells me it will involve soccer or a food truck.

Mark Harrison: To one of the great CEOs in the marketing and sponsorship field, thank you for reminding me that some people stay grounded regardless of their level of success. I hope we can catch up again on a bus ride at a sponsorship conference. Thanks again for allowing this author to contribute to the Advance Praise section of your book.

Chris Austin: To my friend who is a talented photographer and videographer, thanks for always making me laugh. I appreciate your time and support, friend. I would love to include bloopers and outtakes on social media. Thanks for the creativity and professional eye you bring to every project.

Antionette Williams: To one of my favorite corporate partner accounts I managed, I appreciate your friendship inside and outside the scope of business. I am grateful for your encouragement and support to pursue my writing career. Not to mention, Miss Antionette will always be a #1 partner in the eyes and hearts of the Tosti kids.

Teammates: To all my teammates, especially the ones who shared their stories for the book, thank you for your support then and now. I am proud of your accomplishments and enjoy watching each of you succeed in your own way.

G.M.: To my good friend who has supported me from the first draft of my first book and constantly asks how the next project is coming along.

I appreciate your friendship and encouraging words, not to mention the time you invest in proofreading and editing each manuscript.

J.W.: To one of my beta readers and good friends, I am grateful for your support, honesty, and feedback which helps improve the flow of the book and the content itself. I hope you know how much I respect your approach to life and how well you treat others.

R.W.: To my friend who always has my back and is something of a second dad to me, I hope you realize what your encouragement means to me. Here is to another porch session or two.

Dr. Darin White: Samford University is lucky to have you. I am glad you responded to my note on LinkedIn even though we had never met. You took a chance on me, and I will forever be grateful.

Dr. Richard Lapchick: To the most inspiring person I've met in my life, you probably do not receive the attention you deserve for your unwavering commitment to fighting for all that is good in humanity. You continue to amaze me, and the world needs more courageous people like you.

Courtney Daniels Grossl: To an old friend who provided a significant financial gift in honor of her deceased mother, I owe you a Red Rocks concert with sunshine, clear skies, and no hailstorm.

To friends from various stages of my life who contributed financial resources to this book, including: Paraag Maddiwar, Keith Sayers, Matt Millar, Pam Duncan, Holly DeFranco, Missy Myers, and Michael Yu.

Marty Preston: To a dear friend of forty-five years and counting, thanks for believing in me and for the encouraging text messages, especially the ones with a hearty helping of motivation and a side of sarcasm.

To anyone who suffers from ADD, ADHD, dyslexia, or other learning disorder: This book is for each one of you. Never let your condition—or anyone, including yourself—hold you back. Writing might take extra effort, time, and medication, but I promise it is worth it. If I can write two books, then you can achieve your own lofty dreams and goals!

Chad Randall: To my college roommate who encouraged me to take a chance and write a book. He believed in me early on, and I appreciate the support. We always dreamed about starting a company together and I cannot imagine chasing this dream with anyone else. This book does not happen without you.

Beth, Kaden, and Emily: Thank you for putting up with me as I hustled to finish my second book. I know there were moments when a storyline appeared, and I ran to my laptop to type it before it left my mind. I hope you chase your own dreams someday. Remember, I will be one of your loudest cheerleaders.

About the Author

Brandon Tosti is the author of *Who We Meet Along the Way*, a 2022 Goody Business Book Award Winner in the Self-Help Memoir Category, and a proud native of Paintsville, Kentucky.

Twenty-eight years of working in the sports and entertainment industries has provided ample stories and material for this passionate storyteller. The past decade, he has managed corporate partnerships and fitness programs for Denver Arts & Venues and the historic Red Rocks Amphitheatre.

Tosti is entering his fifteenth year of coaching youth basketball and is an advocate for people with ADD and dyslexia. If you liked the book or if it made you smile, please consider leaving a review on Amazon.com or Goodreads. You can also contact Brandon and share your favorite story from the book or general feedback by using the email address listed below.

Tosti is a frequent speaker on college campuses and continues to teach the next generation of sports industry personnel the importance of building relationships and networking the right way. He is available for speaking engagements. Please send a message to btostiauthor@gmail.com or visit http://www.brandontostiauthor.com for booking information. Brandon lives in Arvada, Colorado, with his wife, Beth, and two children, Kaden and Emily.

Facebook: Brandon Tosti, Author

X: @AuthorTosti

Instagram: @brandontostiauthor

TikTok: @AuthorBrandonTosti

72546755R00236